Contemporary Classics of Child
Series Editor: Morag

Coming of Age in Children

C000024768

Contemporary Classics of Children's Literature

Series Editor: Morag Styles

This exciting new series provides critical discussion of a range of contemporary classics of children's literature. The contributors are distinguished educationalists and academics from Britain, North America, Australia and elsewhere, as well as some of the foremost booksellers, literary journalists and librarians in the field. The work of leading authors and other outstanding fictional texts for young people (popular as well as literary) are considered on a genre or thematic basis. The format for each book includes an in-depth introduction to the key characteristics of the genre, where major works and great precursors are examined, and significant issues and ideas raised by the genre are explored. The series will provide essential reading for those working on undergraduate and higher degrees on children's literature. It avoids jargon and is accessible to interested readers, from parents, teachers and other professionals, to students and specialists in the field. Contemporary Classics of Children's Literature is a pioneering series, the first of its kind in Britain to give serious attention to the excellent writing being produced for children in recent years.

Also available in the series:
Kate Agnew and Geoff Fox: *Children at War*
Julia Eccleshare: *A Guide to the Harry Potter novels*
Nick Tucker and Nikki Gamble: *Family Fictions*
Kim Reynolds, Kevin McCarron and Geraldine Brennan: *Frightening Fiction*

Contemporary Classics of Children's Literature

COMING OF AGE
IN CHILDREN'S
LITERATURE

Margaret Meek and Victor Watson

continuum
LONDON • NEW YORK

Continuum

The Tower Building	15 East 26th Street
11 York Road	New York
London SE1 7NX	NY 10010

www.continuumbooks.com

© 2002 Margaret Meek and Victor Watson 2003

All rights reserved. No part of this publication may be reproduced or transmitted in any form or by any means, electronic or mechanical, including photocopying, recording or any information storage or retrieval system, without prior permission from the publishers.

British Library Cataloguing-in-Publication Data
A catalogue record for this book is available from the British Library.

ISBN 0-8264-7757-7

Typeset by BookEns Ltd, Royston, Herts.
Printed and bound in Great Britain by The Cromwell Press, Trowbridge, Wilts.

Contents

CHAPTER 1

Introduction

Victor Watson

'Not yet mature, yet matchlesse'

Maturation is a theme, not a genre. It saturates children's stories and colours narratives of every kind.

When I was about nine or ten, there was a novel that I re-read several times, *The Ship That Flew* (1939) by Hilda Lewis, in which a boy buys a miniature Viking ship in an antique shop. It is a magical ship and he and his brother and sisters have a number of Nesbit-like adventures as it takes them all over the world and back into history. In the final chapter, however, the children stop believing in the magic and the older boy sadly returns the ship to the old man in the shop. Childhood is over, and the old man tells him that in time they will forget their magical adventures. *The Ship That Flew* is not what we usually think of as a maturation novel: that is to say, maturation is not a theme that the narrative seems especially or explicitly interested in. But it does tell – in the understated way that the best children's writers are so good at – how the children grow wiser, braver and more generous as time passes.

Most of the main characters in children's fiction are wiser at the end of their narratives than they were at the beginning. *Treasure Island* by Robert Louis Stevenson (1883) ends with these words:

> The bar silver and the arms still lie, for all that I know, where Flint buried them; and certainly they shall lie there for me. Oxen and wain-ropes would not bring me back again to that accursed island; and the worst dreams that ever I have are when I hear the surf booming about its coasts, or start upright in bed, with the sharp voice of Captain Flint still ringing in my ears: 'Pieces of eight! Pieces of eight!'[1]

Treasure Island is not usually thought of as a maturation novel. Yet there is a quality of mature hard-earned good sense in Jim Hawkins' closing words, validated by the integrity of his character, the adventures he has experienced, and his understanding of the moral ambiguities he has been caught up in. As a person who moves must change position, so a story in the telling must – however lightly – change its understanding.

Maturation in children's novels is often entirely implicit. Authors will indicate boundaries being unobtrusively crossed, private moments of inner growth, and quick volatile understandings – but they show these things (as Margaret Meek says of Philippa Pearce in Chapter 2) 'without seeming to mention them'. In this historical Introduction, I will give further examples of such writing; and I will also comment on those works of fiction in which the protagonists' physical growth and sexuality, and their capacity to shape or construct their own maturation,[2] are explicitly represented. In British and North American literature – from Daniel Defoe to Aidan Chambers, from L. M. Alcott to Cynthia Voigt – maturation has especially attracted writers who have been fascinated by narrative language and its relation to truth. Maturation fiction has been constantly fascinated by *itself*, by the practical business of using words to tell stories, and (in the late-nineteenth century) by its social limitations and (in the late-twentieth century) its metafictive possibilities.

By way of a prologue, I will start with an account of how the word *maturation* itself has changed, together with its family of related nouns, verbs and adjectives.

Meanings

I used to dislike the word *maturation*, believing it to be a graceless interloper of modern times. I was wrong about that: the word is of considerable antiquity and has had a wide variety of uses, among which are included medical (the ripening of an abscess or vesicle), alchemical (turning base metal into gold), and horticultural and viticultural (the ripening of plants, fruits or wine). Of men and women, the *Oxford English Dictionary* defines *maturation* as 'the action or process of coming to full growth or development'. Its first recorded uses in that sense occurred in 1616 and 1660. 'There happens to us Men ... Maturation, Decay, and Dissolution,' wrote J. Tyrrell in 1693.

That was my first surprise. The second was to discover that the adjective *mature* has a slightly different history. The contexts in which it usually appeared were particularly associated with reflection – 'of thought or deliberation: Duly prolonged and careful'. This usage goes back to the fifteenth century, as in 'mature deliberation' (1454), 'mature debating' (1543), and 'mature advise and deliberatioun' (1578).

The concept of *maturity* seems to have been emotionally neutral. Maturity was regarded as a stage human beings pass through on their way to 'decay and dissolution', with no intrinsic qualitative significance. However, Shakespeare's use of the word introduced a colouring of poignancy, a sense of coming loss:

> Nativity, once in the main of light,
> Crawls to maturity, wherewith being crown'd,
> Crooked eclipses 'gainst his glory fight,
> And Time that gave doth now his gift compound.
>
> [Sonnet LX]

These lines give voice to a particular personal bitterness within which maturity is perceived as a culmination, a time of glory and prowess, a moment of regal triumph briefly achieved just as decline sets in. In *Troilus and Cressida*, when Ulysses describes the young Troilus, there is a stronger and more measured appreciation of the promise of youth:

> The youngest son of Priam, a true knight;
> *Not yet mature, yet matchlesse*; firm of word,
> Speaking of deeds and deedless in his tongue;
> Not soon provok'd nor being provok'd soon calm'd:
> His heart and hand both open and both free ...
>
> [*Troilus and Cressida*, IV v. 97, emphasis added]

The phrase I have italicised, with its metrical balance and assonance, hints at the pleasure which the speaker finds in the contemplation of this young man. I think this is important – that maturation has a capacity to be of interest to observers and is mostly described retrospectively, by adults, either objectively or nostalgically.

No writer was more capable than Shakespeare of entering the heart and mind of the matchless young Troilus. But it was not possible for any writer to represent the slowly incremental and deeply private growth of maturity – through days and weeks and years – until the novel form appeared at the beginning of the eighteenth century, with its gossipy and inquisitive capacity to explore where it wishes and at great length, and to adopt whatever voices it chooses.

John Bunyan and Daniel Defoe

The first writer in English to find ways of representing biographical continuity in extended fictional prose was Daniel Defoe. The first novel in English[3] was Defoe's *Robinson Crusoe* (1719); this is also the first children's classic – a fact that reminds us that the history of children's fiction has never been entirely divorced from the history of adult fiction. Defoe did not write books for children; nor did he write for adults. He wrote for *readers* – anyone, in fact, who was sufficiently lucky and literate to have access to his work. Both children and adults in the 1720s and 1730s were reading – in addition to numerous cheap throwaway chapbooks – three great works: *Robinson Crusoe*, *Gulliver's Travels* (1726) and that greatly loved work, which for generations occupied a special place on family bookshelves next to the Bible and the Prayer Book, John Bunyan's *Pilgrim's Progress* (1678).

In the word *progress* is to be found the beginnings of maturation in fiction. To the dissenting middle classes, it meant both *movement* and *improvement*. It was a private word for the individual alone, a word of power, hope and responsibility, carrying within itself the idea that human experience was a journey from birth to death, where it was to be hoped the Christian would arrive safely with his or her soul intact.

The full title of Bunyan's great work was *Pilgrim's Progress from this world, to that which is to come*: simply stated but startling in its dramatic potency. Once you have the idea of life as a journey, you have the notion of biography as an adventure story – a thriller, in fact, for the path of the pilgrim is beset with dangers, distractions and all manner of temptations to thwart the traveller's longing to arrive safely at the desired destination.

Defoe, deeply indebted to Bunyan like all dissenters of his day, was concerned with the inner drama of the soul and with finding ways of describing the paradoxical ideas of permanence, continuity and change which constitute – through language, memory and narrative – the human sense of self. He was the first writer to incorporate in his work representations of childhood, rather perfunctory in *Robinson Crusoe* because it was not to his purpose, but extended, detailed and compelling in two other novels – *Moll Flanders* and *Colonel Jack* (both 1722). He was the first author to find ways of writing persuasively about the complex connections between the child and the adult that the child matures into.

However, it comes as a shock to modern readers to find that, for the young eponymous heroine of *Moll Flanders* (1722), maturation brings with it a kind of psychological mutilation. There is a division of continuity between the child and the adult and Defoe emphasises this breach by giving them different names: the child is Betty and the woman she becomes is Moll. Defoe openly builds into his narrative what he must already have seen as problematic – the autobiographical distinction between the subject and the objective account.

This is challenging: readers of the account of Betty's early years are obliged to sustain an appreciation of a child's innocence seen from the narrator's ironic perspective. This difficulty becomes acute when the narrative reaches Betty's adolescent years and she has her first experience of sexual passion. Because we are being told this story by an adult woman who is a reformed whore, the account of Betty's youth and developing sexuality is seriously skewed. Old Moll, the narrator, encourages us to misread her younger self by talking repeatedly of her vanity, 'that unhappy Snare to all Women'.[4] There is no third-person narrator to point out that Old Moll no longer understands her younger passionate self and the novel becomes an account of a diminishing sympathy, a divorce between the older narrator and the young subject. How that beautiful, wilful and clever girl matures into such a cynical and uncomprehending old narrator is both the subject and the misfortune of this novel.[5]

Here is an example of this narratorial mismatch. It occurs when Betty is seduced by the elder brother. The older woman who is recounting the story can see only the ruin of an empty-headed and vain girl. She got what she asked for, Moll implies, and blames herself as much for not making more money out of the situation as for giving herself up to ruin.

> In short, if he had known me, and how easy the Trifle he aim'd at, was to be had, he would have troubled his Head no farther, but have given me four or five Guineas, and have lain with me the next time he had come at me.[6]

But what is no more than a sexual *trifle* to the older narrator was no such thing for the young girl; the writing makes it clear that she is passionately aroused by the elder brother's attentions and is critically in love with him. The reader must learn to steer a difficult course between the young girl's romantic view of herself as a passionate innocent, the repentant narrator's view of her as a sinner, and the cynical older woman's view of her as a naive fool.

In Defoe's novels lie the origins of children's fiction. Readers of all ages in the 1720s were participating in a different kind of reading – new extended fictions in which credible and flawed men and women wrote intimately in the first person, their silent voices speaking quietly into the mind of the reader. These early novels confirmed the fact that human stories begin with childhood; and that all childhood stories are mediated through an adult understanding which may be faulty. But *Moll Flanders* – the first account of a girl's maturation in the English novel – seems to concede the near impossibility of an adult narrator being able to understand the volatile passionate idealisms and sheer reckless excitement of the young. The older narrator and the maturing young woman are uncomprehending strangers to one another.

Colonel Jack, however, is different. Here, there is no mismatch between the perceptions of the wiser adult and those of the naive child. He is an engaging boy, and the adult narrator is comfortably interested in his childhood self with no loss of sympathy and understanding. It is of great interest that the first two accounts of maturation in English prose fiction – both by Defoe – should be so markedly different on the basis of gender. Jack manages to preserve, through his early London life of petty crime, a sense that he is destined for better things and, unlike Moll, maturation for him is a steadily successful discovery of his true nature. It is impossible to know if this difference exemplifies the dangers of an older male author[7] writing about a maturing girl; or whether it exposes an intrinsic problem with regard to gender and narrative; or whether it is a cultural issue peculiar to Defoe's own class and time.

There are in Defoe's fiction three characteristics which are also to be found in most subsequent maturation novels – reflection, epiphany and the symbolism of place.

From the prevailing Lockeian thinking of his time, Defoe took the notion that what distinguishes men and women from beasts is their ability to reflect upon their experience. His narrative manner is constructed to demonstrate this, with paragraphs of action invariably followed by paragraphs of reflection. But, from his Puritan cultural ancestry, Defoe took a rather different belief in the possibility of individual revelation, the conviction that any person might at any time experience an unexpected moment of transforming insight. Two-and-a-half centuries later, these two features – reflection and illumination – were to be central to a good deal of maturation fiction, for example Cynthia Voigt's *Tillerman* series (see Chapter 3).

Furthermore, the lives of Defoe's fictional autobiographers are shaped by the symbolic power of spaces and places, of barriers and boundaries, of doorways and thresholds. The most famous is Crusoe's island, which is liberty and empire to him, but also an enclosure and prison from which he cannot escape. The early section of *Moll Flanders* plays out its drama of secret adolescent sex in an intensely claustrophobic atmosphere of staircases, passages and upper rooms. Defoe's use of setting as psychology links him with the many writers who later employed the psychological possibilities of islands, flowing rivers, secret gardens, gaps in hedges and concealed entrances; and, in one case, a window seat where a fictional child would seek refuge with her book.

But that was much later.

Catherine Morland, Fanny Price and Jane Eyre

Authors came increasingly to take it for granted that childhood was the appropriate way of beginning a fictional biography. Fielding represented the life of the young Tom Jones; Sterne saw Tristram Shandy's childhood as a rich source of his distinctive humour; Fanny Burney and Jane Austen shared with Samuel Richardson a concern with older children and the ways in which they might grow up into silliness or wickedness.

These authors were writing fictions mostly concerned with conduct or comedy. They did not enter deeply into the central privacy of their child characters – until, that is, the young Fanny Price appeared in the second chapter of *Mansfield Park*. Fanny is ten years old when she arrives at her new home and, by the following chapter, she is fifteen. This apparently perfunctory interest in her young heroine exemplifies Jane Austen's extraordinary dramatic economy and her ability to tell the inner story and the outer story simultaneously. Despite its brevity, in the account of Fanny's first few weeks at Mansfield Park – her intelligence, modesty and thoughtfulness, her treatment by the rest of the family, her love for her brother, and especially Edmund's kindness to her – lie the origins of everything that is to follow. Fanny is the first of countless fictional children humiliated by the people around them because of their poverty, ignorance, clothes or shyness. This story refuses to be silenced and *Cinderella* lies at the back of it.

Jane Austen had already shown the importance of education and upbringing in *Northanger Abbey* (1818). Critical approaches to this work have been complicated by its parodic elements, which seem to excuse the commentator from taking seriously the character of the young Catherine Morland. However, Jane Austen makes clear from the first chapter that, despite her fondness for Gothic novels, her seventeen-year-old heroine is a sensible and unassuming young woman, with a personal integrity strong enough to survive the affectations and hypocrisies she encounters at Bath and the insensitive avarice she finds at Northanger Abbey.

So, by the beginning of the Victorian period, the adult novel had established that an appropriate way to begin a fictional life story is to start with childhood and youth. However, it came to be increasingly accepted that childhood and maturation were more than just stages in the human life story. Maturation became the critical stage, charged with a dangerous and fascinating dramatic significance. The reasons for this are complex and have to do with changing assumptions about childhood. These were not brought about by the Romantic poets alone; but their poetry did provide a voice for some significant changes in perception. Blake's was the most passionate and dramatic, but his influence was minimal; the poetry of William Wordsworth and Coleridge was more persuasive and more widely read. This is not the place for an account of Romantic assumptions about childhood: all there is space to say is that, once it becomes accepted that children are *essentially and absolutely different* from adults, maturation becomes a more interesting process. It leads the individual from a lost magical state of innocence and perception into the prosaic state of regretful adulthood. Maturation then becomes critical, not incidental; and writing about it becomes a process of retrieval and recovery, retelling the story of how a paradise came to be lost, endlessly absorbing to adults who look back on it. There are a million motives for writing about fictional children growing up; but a powerful factor is the fascinated focus of the adult gaze on a stage in life which it sees as fraught with uncertainty, loss, danger, promise and, above all, dramatic interest.

It might not have developed in that way at all if it had not been for *Jane Eyre* (1847). Readers found, in the first chapter of that novel, that a new reading experience was being offered, involving a child hiding away with her book in the insecure refuge of a window seat, 'shrined in double retirement', with the clear panes of glass 'protecting but not separating her from the drear November day'[8] on one side and the unsympathetic Reed family threatening her on the other side of the curtains. Contemporary readers were accustomed to children having significant roles to play in fiction; they would have read *Oliver Twist* (1837–9), *Nicholas Nickleby* (1838–9) or *The Old Curiosity Shop* (1840–1). But the opening of *Jane Eyre* is unlike anything which had preceded it; more passionate and more arresting. This little girl is not described objectively or ironically; the 'I' of the narrative is simultaneously the child Jane once was and the intelligent adult she has grown into, so that the reader is both inside and alongside her. Charlotte Brontë solved the autobiographical difficulty which Defoe had encountered: maturation for Jane Eyre involves none of the fracturing that Moll Flanders endured; quite the reverse, in fact. Maturation in this novel means preserving and strengthening an integrity already there in childhood. And this integrity is no straightforward state of innocence; nor is the child's world a lost paradise.

I have argued elsewhere[9] that *Jane Eyre* constitutes the imaginative antecedent of what came to be called children's literature, telling us as it does in the passionate but measured words of an intelligent narrator about privacy and loneliness – about a book, a child-reader and a hiding-place. And *Jane Eyre* – like the fictions of Defoe – also tells us about confinement and escape, wide open landscapes and dark enclosed houses, along with visions and periods of serious reflection. However, although the great Victorian novelists would certainly have read *Robinson Crusoe*, Defoe's explorations of the narrative dynamics of fictional biography in *Moll Flanders* and *Colonel Jack* were as good as lost to Victorian writers. They were regarded as inflammatory and dissolute, and they fell into neglect and obscurity. It is therefore impossible to see Defoe as a direct shaping influence on the great Victorian novelists. He was, though, the first great writer to find fictional ways of expressing the modern self – predominantly Protestant and middle-class, dramatic and insecure, private and social, but above all with a dynamic sense of its continuity and capacity to change and develop. This persistent vision reappeared dramatically in the mid-nineteenth century novel and found an audience ready with its own understandings on both sides of the Atlantic.

Little pilgrims

The Puritan perception of life as spiritual drama endured into the nineteenth century – with its worst austerities softened but its sense of constant inner crisis intact – and shaped one of the most famous and influential series of novels ever written for young readers.

Little Women (1868) is a novel which one might reasonably expect to be a novel of maturation: its very title contains within it a pivotal contradiction, suggesting an ambivalent state combining the characteristics of little girls and grown-up women. And in many ways it does fulfil those expectations. The main characters are authentic, convincing and extremely engaging people and the narrative takes us through the years from their early teens to their marriages (except for Beth). The social comedy is excellent, and the dialogue is sharp, intelligent and often amusing. There is also a strong sense of growing older and growing up. Near the end of *Good Wives*

(1869, known in the USA as the second part of *Little Women*), Jo says to Laurie:

> ... but, Teddy, we never can be boy and girl again: the happy old times can't come back, and we mustn't expect it. We are man and woman now, with sober work to do, for playtime is over, and we must give up frolicking. ... We can't be little playmates any longer, but we will be brother and sister, to love and help one another all our lives, won't we, Laurie?[10]

It is clear, in the story of the March family, that adult life involves the putting away of childish pleasure and a growing awareness of the seriousness and sadness of human experience.

But, in spite of the skill with which Alcott suggests this sober progression, the novels do not engage seriously with the changes and challenges of maturation. Only the comedy saves the narrative from being almost overwhelmed by pieties, usually deriving either from the narrator or from Mrs March. The trouble with such pieties is not that they are sentimental but that they are formulated as certainties – and certainties are the enemy of exploration, of dramatic tentativeness and of doubtful ironies. They allow conflict and doubt, and insight and remorse, but only in terms laid down by a set of convictions about right and wrong, personal and social conduct. The convictions are never challenged, never doubted; maturation in such a setting is always a matter primarily of responsiveness to instruction.

The narrative of *Little Women* is constructed upon a basis suggested by *Pilgrim's Progress* and, while it is true that Bunyan's notion of a personal progress towards heaven is a powerfully dramatic one, it is equally true that it has no interest in maturation as a distinctively critical line to be crossed. The only line that interests the Puritan reader is the line between sin and virtue – and this line threads the whole of human existence from infancy to death, a single and enduring knife-edge of personal drama. The conflicts between temptation and righteousness are as important for an eight-year-old child as they are for an adult. The romantically charged change from child to adult has no special significance – except insofar as it leads to greater temptations.

The drama of the March sisters, compelling though it is, is the action of piety in the face of temptation. The piety is backed by the weight of accepted authority which is never found to be wanting. The dark places of the March sisters' souls are not explored (how interesting it might have been to have known why Jo is so angry when Meg falls in love; or why fathers are more significant by their absence); the social world they are born into is not seriously questioned; for them, (even for Jo, the rebel) maturation in the end can only mean a joyful and thankful acquiescence.

Family reading and family fiction

Jane Eyre proved to be a popular work with young adult readers and it also had an inspirational effect on other novelists. Almost all the great Victorian novels which take their readers through processes of maturation, were published in the fifteen years that followed – including *David Copperfield* (1849–50), *Hard Times* (1854), *Great Expectations* (1860–1), *The Mill on the Floss* (1860), *Silas Marner* (1861) and *Wives and Daughters* (1866). The nature of this fiction is inseparable from the means of distribution and contemporary reading habits. Many mainstream novels were published first in the great periodicals of their time, and thousands of literate families seeking entertainment and self-improvement received these periodicals weekly or monthly. They determined the ways in which children – either as readers or as family listeners – took possession of the great fiction of their day. I believe we need to know more about the experience of reading a serialized fictional life story which might take up to two years to complete. It would have sharpened the significance of important episodes, enabled a sense of incremental intimacy with the main characters, and intensified through the slow release of linear narrative the crucial sense of change and development over an extended period of time.

The popularity of reading in the mid-nineteenth century led to two developments in children's books. One was that, for the next hundred years, there were dozens of fictional children (mostly girls) passionately seeking in books an escape from the vicissitudes of maturation; and another was that family reading practices became associated with the development of family fiction.

The great writers of adult novels in the Victorian period lost interest in childhood in the 1860s, and it was left to a new generation of writers and new publishing practices to provide a different kind of literature – especially in North America, where, largely under the influence of romantic and transcendentalist thinking, Louisa May Alcott, Susan Coolidge, Kate Douglas Wiggin and L. M. Montgomery developed with extraordinary success the practice of the family series in which it was possible to explore maturation in an extended sequence of novels.

It is usually misleading to trace a literary influence straightforwardly through a succession of writers. However, there is an exception here: as Susan Ang has suggested,[11] *Little Women* is the prototype for the *Green Gables* series and many others that followed. The list of dates and titles is revealing:

1868	Louisa May Alcott	*Little Women*
1869	Louisa May Alcott	*Good Wives* (in North America *Little Women II*)
1872	Susan Coolidge	*What Katy Did*
1873	Susan Coolidge	*What Katy Did at School*
1875	Louisa May Alcott	*Eight Cousins*
1876	Louisa May Alcott	*Rose in Bloom*
1886	Susan Coolidge	*What Katy Did Next*
1903	Kate Douglas Wiggin	*Rebecca of Sunnybrook Farm*
1907	Kate Douglas Wiggin	*New Chronicles of Rebecca*
1908–21	L. M. Montgomery	*Anne of Green Gables* and its sequels
1913	Eleanor H. Porter	*Pollyanna*

These writers faced considerable difficulties in writing about maturation. One was how to show a continuous and gradual development from child to adult when the pervasive influence of Wordsworth posited a disruption. The romantic conviction that there was an absolute difference between a child and an adult – a difference of understanding, of vision, of power, even of *being* – presented novelists with an almost insuperable barrier which only Charlotte Brontë, Charles Dickens and George Eliot had addressed. It is impossible not to feel that implicit in the novels of Alcott, Wiggin and Coolidge there is a feeling of loss and regret that the heroically reckless and imaginative child must renounce the person she once was in order to accept a diminished adult role. The author who most successfully overcame this – by directly addressing it – was Montgomery in the *Anne of Green Gables* series. The problem for authors was to represent that loss as a welcome and positive advance, to find a way of representing maturation as more than a sorry transformation of brilliant gold into base metal. Another difficulty was polemical: how to demonstrate convincingly that the liberal and comparatively unrestrained education which Alcott and her successors championed would lead to a responsible and self-disciplined adulthood.

But the main protagonists – Rose Campbell,[12] Rebecca Randall, Anne Shirley and Katy Carr – do achieve an impressive level of social and moral maturity. The authors' solution to these intrinsic problems was a kind of narrative gradualism representing maturation as a series of encroaching intuitions and developing understandings, while making frequent references to changes in physical growth, at the same time lending weightiness and point to the narrative with frequent references to romantic poetry. But it cannot have been easy, and their authorial embarrassment is revealed by their two most frequently used – and somewhat contradictory – figures of speech: one saw maturity as a coming into flower, the other as the realization that playtime was over.

The first work to show the influence of Alcott was *What Katy Did*. In this work and in its sequels some central assumptions are made: that children are by nature unruly, reckless, unable to foresee consequences and incapable of reflection; and that the effects of this are sometimes amusing, always interesting, and occasionally cata-strophic. Katy has too much energy; she is 'all legs and elbows, and angles and joints';[13] and her vitality explodes in every direction. She and her friends play in a wilderness ironically called 'Paradise',[14] where they indulge in absurd and romantic ideas about what they will do and be in adult life.

But the central assumption of *What Katy Did* is a belief in the value of suffering. Cousin Helen is a sanctified character, not unlike Marmee, and a great influence on Katy during her affliction. And the suffering is not minimized or sentimentalized: Katy becomes 'selfishly miserable'[15] and it is only the love of the family and the help of Helen that enable her to see this period as the School of Pain, where there are lessons in patience, hopefulness, cheerfulness, neatness and making the best of things.[16]

Katy emerges more considerate, wiser, more responsible, better able to see silliness and insincerity in others, and able to manage the household when Aunt Izzie dies. When Helen visits, she sees that to all the other children Katy has become 'the centre and the sun':[17]

> [Helen] saw Katy meet them all *pleasantly and sweetly*, without a bit of the dictatorial elder-sister in her manner, and with none of her old, impetuous tone. And best of all, she saw the change in Katy's own face: the *gentle* expression of her eyes, the *womanly* look, the *pleasant* voice, the *politeness*, the *tact* in advising the others, without seeming to advise.[18] (emphasis added)

The words I have italicized indicate a strongly held (later much condemned) ideology concerning the rôle of the mature woman. The sentence is constructed to ensure that the changes in the maturing Kate are seen from outside, by a specially sanctioned observer – and since the reader is placed alongside this observer, we too are invited to see and accept these signs of a maturing womanliness. This was to become a feature of almost all these great family stories: as the child matures, her inner life becomes increasingly secret until she can finally be viewed only from outside.

The sequel, *What Katy Did at School*, is one of the first boarding-school stories for girls. It is fast moving, gossipy, and extremely engaging. Its central point is that Katy, because of her development in the preceding story, is more mature than any of the other children. Indeed, she is sent to school because she has become *too* mature and shows signs of growing middle-aged before she is twenty.[19] At school, she forms friendships, recognizes silliness and snobbery, and stands up for herself when wrongly accused. Maturity in the *Katy* books is seen in terms of character forming, a good education completed so that the grown girl can take up her adult womanly responsibilities. The framing at the beginning of *What Katy Did* and at the end of *What Katy Did at School* suggests that the two novels were planned as a pair, ending when Katy ceases to be a child. However, there is also an early defining of children's literature here, indicating perhaps some uncertainty of purpose:

> [When Katy] took her place once more as manager of the household, her grown-up life may be said to have begun. So it is time that I should cease to write about her. *Grown-up lives may be very interesting, but they have no rightful place in a child's book.* If little girls will forget to be little, and take it upon them to become young ladies, they must bear the consequences, one of which is, that we can follow their fortunes no longer.[20]

However, the author did return to Katy in other novels, but not until an interval of fourteen years had passed. *What Katy Did Next* is not interested in maturation at all; it is a travel story and a romance. Katy's character remains consistent – the kindness, the ability to be a sick-nurse, the special sympathy with young children, and the sharp perception of vanity and silliness. But it is also a love story, very low-key, and hardly explicit at all. The heady nature of Katy's first experience of love is subtly transposed into her excitement at being in Venice: 'They seemed to float on pleasures for the next ten days.'[21] For her, being in love is – literally – travelling in a foreign country. The embarrassment facing an author of that time writing about love for a readership mostly comprising adolescent girls was acute, indicated by the way this short idyllic account of their stay in Venice ends by shifting into an arch manner and the language of fairy tales:

> . . . it was just a fairy tale, and she was in the middle of it as she had longed to be in her childhood. She was the Princess, encircled by delights, as when she and Clover and Elsie played in 'Paradise' – only, this was better; and, dear me! who was this Prince who seemed to belong to the story and to grow more important to it every day?[22]

Something similar happens in Kate Douglas Wiggin's *Rebecca of Sunnybrook Farm*: here too the reader's final view of the heroine is from the outside, in this case that of an older male friend, Mr Ladd, who has quite clearly been falling in love with Rebecca since she was about twelve years old. He is content to wait for her to grow up; but, just as the narrative seems precisely poised for Rebecca to realize that she has loved him all along, it unexpectedly draws back and Mr Ladd sadly acknowledges to himself that there is in Rebecca 'no experience of men or women, no passion nor comprehension of it'.[23] It is a curious development, an emphatic closing down of imminent narrative romance. Rebecca's future remains 'close-folded still – folded and hidden in beautiful mists'.[24] *More About Rebecca* (first issued as *The New Chronicles of Rebecca*, 1907) is not a sequel; it is a retrospective filling-in of some of the gaps in the first story, but it confirms the earlier closure and leaves Rebecca sadly aware of her vanishing childhood and as yet unfulfilled womanhood.

> It was as if childhood, like a thing real and visible, were slipping down the grassy river-banks . . . and disappearing like them into the moon-lit shadows of the summer night.
>   'I am all alone in the little harbour,' she repeated; 'and oh, I wonder, I wonder, shall I be afraid to leave it, if anybody comes to carry me out to sea!'[25]

Roses in bloom

So, for the North American novelists, the limit of their exploration of maturation was sex. Over and over again, they approached and withdrew. They took their heroines to courtship and marriage; then they either left them there, or turned their attention to the next generation of children. Readers were left in the lurch: having been absorbed by character, they had to settle for appearance and conduct. There was no sustained account of maturation from childhood to full social and sexual maturity until D. H. Lawrence wrote *Sons and Lovers* (1913) and *The Rainbow* (1915) and James Joyce published *A Portrait of the Artist as a Young Man* (1914–15) almost half a century later.

The reluctance to address this had nothing to do with limiting notions of the role of children's literature. Indeed, throughout this period children's fiction had not yet fully detached itself from adult fiction. The overriding factor was that strict social proprieties made it impossible for any writer to address sexuality in any but the most tentative or disguised manner. Furthermore, the concept of unconscious sexual drives was unacknowledged. By the time a later generation of adult writers – Virginia Woolf, James Joyce, D. H. Lawrence – sought ways of using narrative language which would enable them to explore deeper than surface motivation, children's fiction had defined itself more clearly – and set off in a different direction.

At the end of *What Katy Did Next*, the fact that love might have uncontrollable physical and intensely private manifestations is briefly but vividly hinted in a description of a massive blush:

> ... At [her sister's] words a sudden deep flush had mounted in Katy's cheeks. Deeper and deeper it burned as she became conscious of Clover's astonished gaze, till even the back of her neck was pink.[26]

Blushing in these novels is both sign and symptom, always described as seen, never as felt, and in Alcott's *Rose in Bloom* notions of redness, blossoming and fulfilment are implicit even in the title. The interpretation of Rose's progress towards maturity is managed largely through the metaphorical possibilities of her name. Mac wonders, for example, 'how many more leaves must unfold, before the golden heart of this human flower would lie open to the sun';[27] and the narrator tells us:

> ... Yet, with all her human imperfections, the upright nature of the child kept her desires climbing toward the just and pure and true, as flowers struggle to the light; and the woman's soul was budding beautifully under the green leaves behind the little thorns.[28]

But Alcott seems dissatisfied with the limitations of this horticultural figure of speech. I felt when reading this novel that Alcott was bursting to break free of the sexual restraints imposed upon her fiction. It is an adult love – full blown and sexual – that she wants to indicate in both the female characters, and she does this with symbol and descriptions of physicality. Mac gives Rose a statue of Cupid to go with her Psyche, 'not the chubby child with a face of naughty merriment, but a slender, winged youth'.[29] And Rose is continually blushing: 'She turned as red as a poppy';[30] Mac's presence 'shed a sudden sunshine over her, making her eyes fall involuntarily, her color rise, and her heart beat quicker for a moment'.[31] Alcott's descriptions of Rose's friend Phebe are startlingly sexual: she is emphatically a mature young woman in love, 'no longer the image of a handsome girl, but a blooming woman'.[32] The authorial eye seems fascinated by Phebe's physicality, her 'reserved power and passion'[33] and her 'large and wholesome growth'.[34] There is a heavily sexual description of her viewed through her lover's eyes, with her 'glossy black braids', her 'damask cheek curving down into the firm white throat' and 'the little brooch which rose and fell with her quiet breath'.[35]

However, as in all these North American novels, the main theme is education and the domestic role of women. The author faces head-on the issue of maturity raised in the preceding novel, *Eight Cousins*: will Rose's eccentric liberal education enable her to find her way safely through the confusions of passion and courtship? Later, Uncle Alec convinces the doubting Rose of the value and importance of the numerous caring roles she fulfils, and maturity for Rose finally comes in the acceptance of these domestic and public responsibilities, ennobling them and welcoming them.

> The lesson came to Rose when she was ready for it, and showed her what a noble profession philanthropy is, made her glad of her choice, and helped fit her for a long life full of the loving labor, and sweet satisfaction unostentatious charity brings to those who ask no reward, and are content if 'only God knows.'[36]

A concise symbolism of place comes into play as this story of duty and love closes. Rose wanders through the big house: her uncle, newly recovered after a serious illness, is in one room surrounded by affectionate relatives; Steve and Kitty are 'making love' in another; Phebe and Archie in a third; and finally she comes into her own floral chamber, where she finds Mac waiting for her. He has added to her garlands and ferns by placing a 'purple passion-flower' at Cupid's feet.[37] Rose's maturation is complete in an embracing context of affection. The novel closes with these words, which sum up Alcott's view of the role of a mature woman at a time when socially and culturally little else was possible, a role which – transfigured by language – is seen as sacred. And, again, the mature woman is finally observed from outside, as if conceding that her subjective life has – with the arrival of maturity – moved beyond authorial reach:

... looking at her as she stood there in the spring sunshine, glowing with the tender happiness, high hopes, and earnest purposes that make life beautiful and sacred, Mac felt that now the last leaf had folded back, the golden heart lay open to the light, and his Rose had bloomed.[38]

This shift to an objective outside view of the mature woman is decisive. These fictional girls are open, comprehensible and endlessly fascinating; as they become mature women, however, they withdraw into an impenetrable and unwritable privacy.

'A tall serious-eyed girl of fifteen'

What distinguishes Anne Shirley – apart from the colour of her hair – is her dependence on her imagination. Although this gets her into innumerable scrapes, it is not just childish silliness. She has had a tough life, and imagination has enabled her to believe doggedly in alternative possibilities. There is a question lying within *Anne of Green Gables*: what will Anne do with this imagination as she grows up? Will L. M. Montgomery represent maturation as a dimming of Anne's young radiance? Or will this growing child, like all the others, vanish into the unspoken mysteries of womanhood?

In many ways, Anne resembles Rebecca, Katy and the March sisters. She matures through her own mistakes and reflection upon them; through her experience of the inevitable realities of ageing (Marilla) and death (Matthew); through education; through glad self-sacrifice; and through friendship. And like the others, there comes a point when she is viewed objectively – but not, this time, from a male perspective:

... Marilla felt a queer regret over Anne's inches. The child she had learned to love had vanished somehow and here was this tall, serious-eyed girl of fifteen, with the thoughtful brows and the proudly poised little head, in her place. Marilla loved the girl as much as she had loved the child, but she was conscious of a queer, sorrowful sense of loss.[39]

Marilla's observation allows the reader to take fresh bearings: it comes as something of a shock to realize that out of so much schoolgirl comedy should emerge this tall serious-eyed girl of fifteen, literally looking down on the older woman. This is what happens in real families – the sudden sharp realization of *loss*, which is exclusively an adult perspective upon growing children.

Unlike her predecessors, Montgomery challenges in her narratives the authorial difficulties besetting her: if the end of childhood inevitably involves a loss of radiance and vision, how can adults bear to go on living? And how can a writer avoid a loss of readerly interest? And because Anne herself is fully aware of the difficulty and frequently articulates it, this apparently intractable authorial predicament openly becomes the theme of the novels. After one of Anne's many disappointments, we are told that:

> ... the bloom had been brushed from one little maiden dream. Would the painful process go on until everything became prosaic and hum-drum?[40]

It seems for a while as if that is exactly what is going to happen, for when her love for Roy proves a disappointment, she thinks:

> True, it was not just what she had imagined love to be. But was anything in life, Anne asked herself wearily, like one's imagination of it?[41]

However, imagination is not the mischief-maker. It was stubbornness and pride that betrayed Anne into denying her love for Gilbert. Imagination brings her back to him and, as she matures, she is not obliged to renounce the imagination of her childhood; quite the reverse, for it nourishes her adult capacity for love. Her passionate appreciation of the landscape of her beloved Prince Edward Island and her ability to embrace the many people in her life are the consequence and validation of imagination.

Despite the psychological reticence of the period, the intensities of a maturing young woman are there for the attentive reader: in *Anne of the Island* Anne feels 'suddenly left out and inexperienced'[42] when Diana gets engaged; in *Anne's House of Dreams*, the sight of Diana holding her baby sends through Anne's heart 'a thrill that was half pure pleasure and half a strange, ethereal pain';[43] on their wedding night, she tells Gilbert how much she loves the house where they are to keep their 'bridal tryst'.[44] And Montgomery allows herself one engaging moment of sexual humour: in *Anne of Windy Willows* one of Anne's acquaintances strongly disapproves of a local man who was 'always kissing his wife in the most unsuitable places!'. Anne, writing to Gilbert, asks 'Are you sure you kiss me in suitable places, Gilbert?' – and speculates about the nape of her neck.[45]

Anne's fictional existence extends through a series of eight novels covering her adult life, her marriage and motherhood, and the death of two children. Her maturation is represented within the wider processes of history. The series is full of old people, each with a story to tell; it is also full of children who, like their mother, get into scrapes and have friends and grow older. I doubt if many readers today read the entire series, including the two *Rilla* books; this is a pity because this extended series of narratives is a remarkable achievement, providing a loving and sometimes rhapsodic picture of humanity renewing itself as it grows older, an often transcendental account in which ageing, illness and death have their place, and in which human beings are represented as frail, crusty, proud and unkind – but always susceptible to the influence of love and understanding. And there is no sentimentalizing of tragedy: when Anne's first baby dies a few hours after her birth, we are given an uncompromising account of her anger and grief. It concludes:

> Anne found that she could go on living; the day came when she even smiled again over one of Miss Cornelia's speeches. But there was something in the smile that had never been in Anne's smile before and would never be absent from it again.[46]

Magical changelings

Despite their apparent realism, the heroines of these great family sagas are changelings, children with a touch of magic about them, growing up in the wrong families. They are disrupters of orderliness and 'scapegraces' with active imaginations; they are outspoken and courageous; they have a keen sense of justice; they challenge and expose the foolishness and hypocrisies of their communities; and they have the ability to rescue dried-up adults from loneliness and bitterness. Their maturation involves experience of suffering, caring for the sick, bereavement, distinguishing and valuing true friendship, and understanding and facing the financial realities that govern their lives.

But they are also 'special' – Rebecca with her mysterious eyes, Anne with her hair, Katy 'the *longest* girl that ever was seen'.[47] Clearly, an unusual child makes a more interesting story, and if the child is also orphaned or displaced there are additional narrative opportunities. But it is important also to remember that where the fictional child is, there the reader is too – private and privileged. Reading itself becomes an act of solidarity with a vibrant alternative childhood, gleefully secret and magical, rebellious and confirming, subversively eyeing the adult world.

The heroines themselves are all impassioned readers, and often writers as well. No doubt this reflected the priorities of their authors, but it is also true that literature seems to have shaped this entire body of fiction. Bunyan was a powerful influence; so was George Eliot's Tom and Maggie Tulliver passing 'the golden gates of childhood' and entering the 'thorny wilderness'.[48] Another was the poetry of Wordsworth, especially the 'Ode on Intimations of Immortality from Recollections of Early Childhood', with its totally convincing sense of loss that the visionary gleam of childhood has fled, and its rather less convincing hope that the clouds that gather round the setting sun will have their own sober colouring. This great poem is quoted repeatedly in the novels, sometimes as chapter heads, sometimes uttered by the characters, or appearing as phrasing slipped into the authors' own prose. It is a rich source for a novelist, for it sees growing up as an irretrievable loss, and maturation as an intensely dramatic process of acceptance and love.

Alcott, Wiggin, Coolidge and Montgomery defined in their work the precise limits of fictional accounts of maturing girlhood in the late nineteenth and early twentieth centuries. But, when all is said and done, their appeal to readers probably lies elsewhere. All four writers are supreme comic realists, brilliant at dialogue, with a gossipy interest in the goings-on of the small communities they describe in such authentic detail, interested in babies, clothes, and what the neighbours are doing. After Aunt Miranda dies in *Rebecca of Sunnybrook Farm*, the narrator comments:

> ... [Death] can stalk through dwelling after dwelling, leaving despair and desolation behind him, but the table must be laid, the dishes washed, the beds made, by somebody.[49]

That is characteristic of the authorial voices of these novels – sharp, direct, realistic, and with more irony in them than those folded flower buds and blooming roses might suggest.

Narratives of healing and wholeness
Frances Hodgson Burnett's *A Little Princess* (1905) is not a maturation novel in the same way that the *Avonlea* novels are: Sara Crewe learns some painful lessons about greed, social poverty and injustice, and her own capacity for endurance and kindness; but at the end of the novel she is re-established as a surrogate daughter. Sara has certainly become a wiser girl but it is not part of Frances Hodgson Burnett's purpose to represent her as a developing young woman. Like many of the works of the Edwardian period which subsequently came to be regarded as classics, *A Little Princess* was a novel of understanding, of growing towards an achieved wholeness. These novels recounted small, barely acknowledged moments of emotional growth, often at

odds with rational understanding. Their child characters found their developing selves through an abrasive contact with uncompromising real life, not ceasing to be children but learning tough lessons about their lives and their capacity to grow into their integrity.

A Little Princess – like many other children's novels of the period – combines two modes. On the one hand, it can be regarded as the first section of an unwritten adult novel, a truncated *bildungsroman*; it is not stretching the imagination too much to concede that a different writer might have continued this novel into something resembling *Middlemarch* and shown Sara Crewe's development into a mature Dorothea Brooke. It is also an extended but straightforward moral fable, cleverly presented with all the trappings of realism and held together by the teller's strong authorial voice. The ending of *A Little Princess* confirms this duality: 'You see,' says Sara to her new guardian, 'I know what it is to be hungry, and it is very hard when one cannot even *pretend* it away.'[50] A lesson is certainly being presented here; but it has also been proved upon the pulses of the reader by the muscularity of the narrative, and this speech is followed by Sara's first act of *charity* – not *kindness*, for she has been kind many times before, but charity – the responsible use of her wealth. Maturity here is both understanding and action.

Most of the great children's novels of the first half of the twentieth century achieved classical status because they managed this combination: they were on the one hand moral fables; but at the same time they were written in the manner of the great adult novels of their day. It is fanciful, I know, to have suggested that Sara Crewe might have become Dorothea Brooke; but it is not fanciful to point out that readers of *A Little Princess* were learning how to read *Middlemarch*.

The Secret Garden (1911) is more complex. Here Hodgson Burnett does what novelists from Defoe to the Brontës had done: she uses setting as psychology. The realism of the house and garden is imbued with a rich symbolism uniting themes of education, play, space and confinement, and, above all, growth. What is at stake for the children in *The Secret Garden* is healing. Commentators have objected because Mary is in the end excluded from this, almost completely absent from the closing pages.[51] But this shift of focus from Mary to father-and-son was deliberate: in *The Secret Garden* Frances Hodgson Burnett re-worked many characteristics taken directly from *Jane Eyre* – but she could not allow even a hint of a developing love between Mary and Colin because, in 1906, marriage between cousins had only recently been legalized and was still repugnant to many churches and individuals, as Thomas Hardy had found only eleven years earlier.[52] The end of *The Secret Garden* indicates not a shift from the feminine to the masculine but a fullstop to any notion that maturation for Mary might mean romance.[53]

The same decade saw the publication of *The Railway Children* (1906), a novel which has many of the features of the North American family sagas – poverty, an absent father, childhood scrapes, a strong sense of family loyalty and a sharp but benevolent authorial voice. In the *Bastables* series and the *Psammead* series, E. Nesbit had learned how to re-tell childhood as moral comedy whilst never losing sight of the fundamental seriousness of children's lives. There is a deeper story being told in *The Railway Children*: like *The Secret Garden*, it tells of the female recovery of an injured or lost male. And it hints at Bobbie's maturation in terms of strange and essentially feminine intuitive knowledge. Just before the famous climax at the railway station, Bobbie drops her classroom slate. 'It cracked just across the little green mark that is so useful for drawing patterns round, and it was never the same slate again.'[54] This diminutive symbol of the end of childhood is characteristic: Nesbit somehow manages to suggest that, for Bobbie, important secret boundaries are being crossed and an identity is incrementally growing. But not explicitly – for the outer story is a narrative of recovered family wholeness, and, as the novel's closing words indicate, once it is reunited there is nothing else to tell.

Although the best of these children's books were written in the manner of adult realistic fiction, they had one distinctive feature: magic. It might be disguised as coincidence (*A Little Princess*), or represented as the transforming power of human good nature (*The Railway Children*), or tied in with natural forces (*The Secret Garden*). Increasingly, as the century progressed, magic was also openly employed as a device of plot. Fantasy became increasingly popular, and its predominant themes continued to be growth and wholeness, an understanding of time and its processes. The authorial tone often had a touch of melancholy, as in Mary Norton's *Borrowers* series (from 1952), Lucy Boston's *Green Knowe* series (from 1954), and *Charlotte's Web* (1952) by E. B. White. Two American writers inventively extended the Nesbit manner and celebrated the secure world of family life in the US: Edward Eager with *Half Magic* (1954) and its sequels, and Elizabeth Enright, with *The Saturdays* (1941) series, and the two *Gone-Away Lake* books (1957 and 1961).

The impact of the Great War

The Great War had an almost devastating effect upon books for children. Of course it led to the growth of new kinds of adventure stories, but for many British and Commonwealth authors, the deaths of thousands of young men raised bitter questions about childhood and adulthood: why celebrate maturation at all – why even think about it? – if its consummation was to come in such a terrible form?

The extent of this abrupt and cataclysmic change can be seen if we return to the *Anne* novels and consider the last of them:[55] the difference between it and the early books of the series is a precise measure of the effect of the war upon authors who wrote for young readers. *Rilla of Ingleside* (1921) is a dark work, an impressively convincing 'home front' novel set between 1914 and 1918. Montgomery does not penetrate the darkest areas of wartime psychology; she accepts the orthodoxies of the time – that if men are to be courageous in battle women must be courageous at home. But she represents with a persuasive authenticity the anguishes of that acceptance. *Rilla of Ingleside* is an elegy for a vanished way of life, the old life of Avonlea. To Montgomery, everything the early *Anne* books believed in was challenged and undermined by the War. Those Green Gables days, Anne comments, 'belonged to another world altogether. Life has been cut in two by the chasm of the war. What is ahead I don't know – but it can't be a bit like the past.'[56]

Repeatedly this novel emphasises that something has ended and Canadian life can never be the same again. Even the omnipresent Wordsworth has come to seem 'as ancient as the Iliad' with 'little to do with the present world-welter'.[57] It is hard not to feel that the creative impulse has been almost stunned – but not silenced, for this novel courageously questions the assumptions implicit in the earlier novels of the series, especially the value placed upon the centrality of joyous imagination. For the young Anne, imagination could create new worlds, and, more importantly, transform the beauty of the real one, making it more transcendentally true. But what place is there for imagination in a world transformed by war into hideousness? Anne herself – a background figure in *Rilla of Ingleside* – admits that all she can imagine now are the trenches and battlegrounds of Europe and her sons in the midst of this horror.

Rilla of Ingleside is truly a novel of maturation – and a bold one, for Montgomery has created a heroine who has nothing remarkable about her. Rilla – the youngest of Anne's children – is no changeling; she is an ordinary girl caught up in world events and experiencing the profound shock that the Great War brought to Canada. A new authorial and cultural maturation is being recorded here, in this novel about an unremarkable teenage girl whose soul 'comes to its full stature in an hour'.[58]

One consequence of the Great War was that for more than half a century writers of children's books set their hearts against maturation. The War did not initiate this: there was already – particularly in Britain – a cult which saw childhood as sacred, magical and doomed. Its great texts were Richard Jefferies' *Bevis* (1882), Kenneth Grahame's *The Golden Age* (1895) and *Dream Days* (1898), and the manifold versions of J. M. Barrie's *Peter Pan*; its institutional triumph was the founding of the Boy Scouts movement (and later, with a little less enthusiasm from Lord Baden Powell, the Girl Guides); and Christopher Robin was to become its icon. Critics have pointed out that the writers who most passionately subscribed to this view of childhood were mostly male; and there is no doubt that this literature had an essentially bachelor quality about it.

The cult might have been shortlived if it had not been for the Great War. But the period following the War saw an intensification of the social and cultural need to enshrine children, to convince the adult world that childhood remained a safe sanctuary. This was an entirely understandable reaction to a War that had seen the deaths of the young on a scale never before experienced. There seems to have been an overwhelming national need to believe that the dead remained close by, a yearning for spiritualisms that went beyond traditional religious faiths, extending even to a belief in the literal existence of fairies.

Children – and children's books – were caught up in this great national yearning, the connection between them betrayed in the extraordinary story of Sir Arthur Conan Doyle who, while grieving for his dead son, was persuaded by two schoolgirls into believing they had access to fairies.[59] This episode is precisely symbolic, uniting three factors: adult need, a belief in the visionary power of imagination, and children. The addition of contemporary photographic technology added spice and authenticity. If only we could know what Wordsworth or Blake would have made of this!

Children's books did not go in for spiritualism;[60] but they did, until around 1960, focus their plots and characterization almost exclusively upon childhood adventures. The innumerable series of school stories, camping-and-tramping stories, career stories, one-off adventure stories and fantasies that were produced with such amazing abundance had little to say about maturation. The original cult qualities disappeared, but the orthodoxies which the cult had nourished lapsed into unquestioned habit: it was taken for granted throughout the 1920s, 1930s and until some time after World War II that children's books should be predominantly about play.

That is not to say that this fiction was irresponsible. It is true that it mostly eschewed any exploration of adolescence as conflict, doubt or loss, it rarely considered the ways in which maturation might be shaped by social environment, and it entirely avoided sexuality. However, the middle-class protagonists of these novels were mostly concerned with honourable and responsible conduct, how to maintain fairness, honesty, truthfulness and courage, and the acquisition of skills and understanding. Characteristic of the best of this kind of writing was Arthur Ransome's *We Didn't Mean to Go to Sea* (1937), a classic rite-of-passage novel, in which the children survive a convincingly terrifying boat-trip across the North Sea. Yet there is nothing in the *Swallows and Amazons* series as a whole to suggest that maturation was a main interest to the author; it becomes a matter of urgency in this novel because Ransome is seriously committed to his characters and to representing their dangers authentically. Maturation is a by-product of Ransome's authorial integrity.

Apprentice authors

Around the middle of the twentieth century, a number of writers became interested in older children and the realities of growing up in the post-war world. The four most important of these have occupied an ambivalent position in Britain – not exactly adult writers and not exactly children's writers either. Jane Gardam's status has long been acknowledged, but Rumer Godden's fiction for older readers has not received the recognition it deserves, and Dodie Smith – though well-known for *A Hundred and One Dalmatians* – is given scant critical credit for her other outstanding novel, though it has remained faithfully in print and has recently been re-issued. Antonia Forest's work is hardly known at all.

We have already seen that writing up their daily experience of life was important to both Anne Shirley and Jo March. In the *Emily of New Moon* trilogy (1923–7) L. M. Montgomery focused entirely on the childhood and adolescence of a girl setting out to be an author. Cassandra, the narrator of Dodie Smith's *I Capture the Castle* (1949), is another determined young writer, seeking to 'capture' in words her life in the castle which she and her unusual family live in. For Cassandra, words are of paramount importance, and imagination is an exciting but dangerous vehicle. Writing her journal is a private process of reflection and self-judgement during which Cassandra records the real and imaginary risks she has taken and subjects them to analysis.

Cassandra's journal is written in speed-writing which no-one else can read; and she keeps it hidden. Her father, too, is a writer, but one experiencing a writer's block of several years' duration. Dodie Smith's account of maturation is in terms of writing, failing to write, struggling to find meaning and clarity, as well as the more practical matter of finding a place and time to write. The writing of the novel becomes the subject of the novel, while the journal itself is a focus for the privacy and intensity of adolescence.

Why is becoming a writer such a consistent theme in so many novels, from Louisa May Alcott to Dodie Smith? An obvious answer is that their authors see maturation in terms of their own lives, in which writing was important. But there is more to it than that, especially if a journal[61] or notebook is involved: a private journal is a precise metaphor for reflective adolescence. Like their fictional owners, these journals are private, self-obsessed, intelligent, the place where meaning is grappled with, where flights of imagination can be indulged, where self-honesty can define itself. A journal is a potent way of exploring maturation because it enables its writer to see her life in time and context. The current of the narrative can flow freely in any direction the author is interested in; the structure of the writing – its chapters or entries – gives episodic shape and dramatic or moral emphasis to the author's experiences; and it sees the inner and outer changes in the protagonist's life almost entirely as a struggle for meaning.

Although the story Cassandra's journal tells is a love story, it resists the clichés of romance at every point. Cassandra is an honest and impassioned writer, generous in her judgements of other people and ruefully aware of her own shortcomings in dealing with the complexities of first love. Her first kiss, her experience of being kissed by the wrong man, guilt and embarrassment, learning about the excitement and confusion of arousal – these are all the staple ingredients of the hormonal maturation romance. But the real enterprise for this author seriously recording her maturation is the struggle for meaning and symbol, the search for integrity of language and narrative. Towards the end, Cassandra decides to give up writing the journal because 'there are thousands of people to write about who aren't me ...'.[62] It is clear that the journal has been her apprenticeship in authorship; and, at the same, time the story of her first love.

The narrator of Rumer Godden's *The Greengage Summer* (1958) is another determined young writer. She is the second of a family of four girls and one boy who find themselves more-or-less unsupervised in a hotel in rural post-war France, where they are caught up, unknowingly, in a robbery and a murder. The oldest sister is sixteen and very beautiful and determined; the narrator, Cecil, is thirteen – and she is the one interested in the precision of words and the task of achieving accurate vividness in description.

The opening sentences are precise in connecting the children's feelings of guilt with their sense of growth, fullness and ripening:

> On and off, all that hot French August, we made ourselves ill from eating the greengages. Joss and I felt guilty; we were still at the age when we thought being greedy was a childish fault, and this gave our guilt a tinge of hopelessness because, up to then, we had believed that as we grew older our faults would disappear, and none of them did.[63]

This novel represents maturation as a growth, not from innocence to experience, but from one kind of complicity to a greater one; the mature complicity is more knowing, more sexually manipulative than the immature, but neither is entirely innocent. 'You expect yourselves to be comfortably riddled with faults . . .' Eliot says to the children. 'We are,' they cheerfully reply.[64]

The sexual metaphor of ripening fruit is present throughout. Cecil, the narrator, thinks of her small breasts as 'deux petits citrons'.[65] She tells us –

> The greengages had a pale-blue bloom, especially in the shade, but in the sun the flesh showed amber through the clear-green skin; if it were cracked the juice was doubly warm and sweet.[66]

The children's sexual knowledge is obtained through scraps of observed adult behaviour, and through gossip with the disreputable and unscrupulous hotel boy, Paul. They see and overhear the life of the hotel, only partly understanding. Maturation in this novel is a process of learning about the wider arenas in which bigger wickedness can take place, and in which new kinds of compromises and more complex rule-breaking loyalties can form. They learn that their presence – and their so-called innocence – can be exploited. They discover the capacity of youth (the lovely sixteen-year-old Joss) to provoke wickedness in adults, knowing they are doing it but not quite knowing the consequences. And they find a good deal of adult life is ugly and confused; they *need* to manipulate it in order to survive its injustices.

The children in *The Greengage Summer* are not simply corrupted by wicked adults; they actively conspire to be corrupted, not because they too are wicked but because they are ripening into the same condition themselves. In this novel, there is an inevitability about becoming mature; like the seasons, it cannot be stopped. When Cecil has her first period, she comments: 'no matter how reluctant, one was pushed into the full tide'.[67]

> ... I had to manage for myself with those strange first necessities of being a woman, and it was inexpressibly lonely. When I was comfortable I began to cry with excitement and self-pity.[68]

When she tells Eliot what has happened ('I have turned into a woman'), he tells her that she is ready now for love. His kindness and his gently positive view of growing up cheers her enormously – yet this message comes to her from the most wicked man in the novel, a jewel-thief and a murderer. In the closing pages, it is made clear that in Rumer Godden's fictional world there is no straightforward innocence/experience division: the children are collaborators in Eliot's wickedness, and he is complicit in their cunning innocence.

In *A Long Way from Verona* (1971) by Jane Gardam, maturation is seen as social comedy. Jessica, too, is going to be a writer. She is an extraordinarily impulsive girl, following her hunches and coming up repeatedly against a reality she had not anticipated. As in *The Greengage Summer*, it is the nature of children to be everywhere, go where they are not supposed to, hear what they are not expected to, see things that are meant to be private. They are by nature spies and eavesdroppers, snapping up all manner of unconsidered adult trifles as material for their own understandings. For example, through the floorboards of her bedroom, Jessica hears this conversation:

> ... Father said, '... We really *know* our children now. They don't have secrets from us. I suppose that's good.'
>
> 'My parents didn't want to know me,' said Ma. 'They weren't the least bit interested in me.'
>
> 'I wasn't the least bit interested in my parents,' said Father. 'I didn't want to know them.'
>
> 'I expect you did really. They were so nice.'
>
> 'I wasn't,' said Father, 'I was a swine.'
>
> They droned on. They amaze me all the time. They are like children.[69]

Early in the novel, Jessica is told by a visiting speaker at her school: 'JESSICA VYE YOU ARE A WRITER BEYOND ALL POSSIBLE DOUBT!'[70] She is fired by this conviction but finds that writing does not come easily. She has plenty of experiences because the novel is set in the north-east of England during wartime. She is briefly molested by a deranged prisoner-of-war and narrowly misses being killed in a bombing raid. She also gets into a good deal of trouble at school – not mischievous scapes and japes, but muddles caused by a wilful and demanding girl at a time when adults were preoccupied in keeping things going.

Jessica's life becomes a resolute trying out of other people's opinions (including writers') – and finding them not quite sufficient. Other ways of life are subjected to her judgement: an example is her satirical mockery of the upper-middle class: 'And the way they talk – awfun for often, and atome for at home and Red Crawss, and all that laughing when they're not really amused.'[71] Poetry is present everywhere too, sometimes parodied to make a bitter comment on reality: 'If I should die think only this of me, I look as dreary as a cup of tea' – said of a loathed dress.[72]

Jessica's maturation comes about through a crisis of thought and perception, an agony of doubt about her being a writer. This novel tells the story of how a single poem comes, finally, to be written to Jessica's satisfaction ('There was nothing in it I wanted to change.'[73]) and gets published in *The Times*. But even this triumph has its comedy, for Jessica discovers that the ghastly boring book she has been given to read about the Lake District was written by the very man who first told her she was definitely a writer.[74]

The most sustained and substantial account of a girl maturing in Britain is the *Marlow* series by Antonia Forest, a sequence of ten novels published between 1948 and 1982. Four are school stories, some are holiday stories, three are thrillers, but in all but one of them the central interest is the character of Nicola Marlow. I have written more fully about this neglected series elsewhere;[75] here, it must suffice to say that this extended account is the fullest and sharpest representation in English children's literature of a child's development, her growth in self-understanding and autonomy, her maturing sense of integrity and ability to judge others. No other children's writer has so richly shown the complex intermeshing of family and culture, of private values and social assumptions, and of physical, emotional and aesthetic pleasures. Furthermore, these novels do not set Nicola Marlow against a static backcloth: the other members of the family and the other children at school are also represented as complex and changing; and circumstances constantly change, too, the grown-up world beset with illness, death and real-life problems. The *Marlow* series subtly and unobtrusively champions the maturing mind, providing a fictional enactment of the growth of reflective thought – a growth which never leads towards isolation or élitism but always towards life, people, and the great cultural expressions of humanity – religion, art, music, drama and literature.[76]

Wisecracks and wise guys

These British representations of maturation were written from a socially privileged position – middle-class, highly educated and literary. In the US, however, there were some significant develop-ments of a different kind in the 1950s, one of which was the publication of *Fifteen*, by Beverly Cleary, in 1956. This novel makes no attempt to suggest that its teenage heroine has a rich life of the mind; she is a triumph of fictional minimalism. Every extraneous possibility is pared away from this story: a nice girl, with a nice family, living in a nice part of town, meets a nice boy, and they have a nice relationship. Yet, for all that, it is an engaging story, convin-cingly conveying the surface realities of everyday adolescent life with a good deal of comedy. It was immensely popular and subsequently inspired numerous young adult novels about 'the pangs and miseries of growing up'.[77]

Fifteen is about the etiquette of dating. There is no reference to desire, arousal or anatomy. The critical points in a boy–girl relationship – meeting, holding hands, kissing – are represented as social, not sexual. Nor does the writing show any sign of being interested in ethical or philosophical issues, or in a future seen in terms of possible adulthood.

It is not, therefore, a novel about maturation. Neither were its many imitators. Through the second half of the twentieth century, the range of possible explicit description widened and the first kiss gave way to the first sex. When Judy Blume explicitly described sexual intercourse in *Forever*, she famously extended the range of reference – but she extended nothing else. There is no *literary* advance between Jane's admission in *Fifteen* that she 'had not known a boy's lips could be so soft'[78] and Katherine's discovery in *Forever* of what an erect penis looks and feels like.[79] These novels are 'how to' books, and their role is reassurance and education. Their relationship to maturing readers is that of a guidebook to tourists.

However guidebooks are useful and may be well written. The difficulty with teen-romance is that its perspective allows an

essentially innocent and nostalgic view which assumes that maturation takes place in the immediate context of family and community –
and that both of these are safe places. But during the 1960s it became
clearer that families were helplessly caught up in world events, or
might themselves be the *loci* for neglect or abuse. Furthermore, most
fiction had represented children maturing into adult communities
governed by political and religious certainties; the hypocrisies they
espied in the adults around them were mostly small and provincial.
But that subsequently became more difficult as young people
matured into a pluralist world with no unanimity, little certainty, and
an infinite range of perspectives on ethical, political, sexual and
religious issues. More and more writers came to see maturation in
terms of identity and to show the fracturing of self in deprived or
immigrant, often silenced, communities. Maturation was coming to
be seen as a progression not from innocence to experience but from
innocence to anger, or confusion, and sometimes breakdown.

The first – and many would say the greatest – of such novels was
The Catcher in the Rye (1951) by J. D. Salinger. Here, in Holden
Caulfield, was a new voice, pretending to be disengaged yet obsessed
with the world and its hypocrisies, recounting the crazy things that
happen to him when, having been kicked out of yet another school,
he drifts for a few days and nights around the city. He smokes, he
gets drunk, he goes to clubs, he has an encounter (unsuccessful) with
a prostitute, he gets beaten up. He calls or visits various people who
come into his mind – fellow students from his past, old teachers, girls
he once dated – but they all turn out to be 'phonies'.

But nothing silences Holden Caulfield. His voice is what
determines the character of the book. He is wittily and extravagantly
articulate, with a gift for wisecracks, dismissive one-liners and
outrageous hyperbole, often rounded off with an engagingly self-
deprecatory remark. This voice is honest, outspoken and above all
energetically funny about subjects that were silenced by the taboos of
their time, especially sex and death.

But *The Catcher in the Rye*, though, contains within itself the kind
of fiction it has outgrown, for between the lines there is another story
to be read. Holden is – or might have been – precisely the kind of
straightforwardly nice boy who belonged in the world of Beverly
Cleary's *Fifteen*. He adores his little sister; he admires his older
brother; he loves reading; and the only girl he really likes is the girl
next door. His language changes when he writes about these. But his
life is *not* straightforward: another brother has died; Holden has
witnessed one of his friends leap to a horrible death from a window

because he was being bullied; and, if he is to be believed, he has many times been the victim of – or narrowly escaped – sexual abuse.[80]

The screwed-up Holden Caulfield is not the first fictional American boy to think he is a failure precisely because he is loyal, loving and honest in a cruel and crazy world. *The Adventures of Huckleberry Finn* had, in 1885, provided a literary precedent of maturation as disillusionment. Mark Twain had demonstrated the unique kind of irony that arises when an 'innocent' boy observer witnesses adult corruption and folly, modestly disowning his perceptions as muddle-headed or just plain bad. Huck Finn and Holden Caulfield speak a similar language – the satirical demotic; the difference is that Huck has a purpose and a true friend, and, although the Mississippi may be unpredictable and dangerous, at least Huck has a route to follow and a destination to reach. Holden, on the other hand, wanders aimlessly around New York, appalled to find the words 'Fuck you' scrawled on the wall of his little sister's elementary school and then again at the museum – either a precise expression of the relationship between urban America and its maturing young people or a symptom of Holden's imminent breakdown.[81]

Salinger's great novel has had many imitators, but no author has more successfully developed the practice of the narrative-as-cure than Paul Zindel. In a string of popular young adult novels, Zindel has represented adolescents as both the truth-tellers and the victims of urban American life. From *The Pigman*, his first real success, Zindel has constantly represented maturation as a process in which the accommodation of horror is a requisite for survival. The similarities between his work and *The Catcher in the Rye* have often been commented on: the first-person demotic, the zany wisecracking manner, the barely disguised sense of hurt, the outrage at the incompetence or cruelty of parents. But there are differences: death is more closely and directly present in the lives of Zindel's young characters, and they more frequently form close and often problematic relationships with old people. The consequence of this is that Zindel's young characters mature not only within adult society but also within a grasped awareness of time, change and decay. The most significant difference, however, is that all Zindel's novels either assume or explore friendship. His characters are not totally alone. They are intelligent, sensitive and articulate, but their survival in the urban gothic of adult New York depends upon friendship. This is one of the oldest features of satirical romance – the discovery of a like-minded companion with whom to form an alliance against a crazy and corrupt world.

One of the best of Zindel's novels is *A Begonia for Miss Applebaum*, which is prefaced by an address 'To Any Kid Who Reads This', promising that 'there are no lies in this book and nothing phoney'.[82] It reads like a script for a Woody Allen film: its teenage protagonists – Henry and Zelda – have similar insecurities, similar humour, the same manic preoccupation with their appearances, and the same zany interest in amazing cosmic facts. Zelda and Henry take turns at a word processor to tell their story, and we learn about Henry's parents who are so weird that – according to him – they mate by appointment.[83]

A Begonia for Miss Applebaum differs from Zindel's earlier novels in that its adult world is mostly humane and sensible; it is an understanding of death, not society, that these two characters have to mature into. Henry and Zelda share a fear of dying, but they are brought into direct contact with death when they discover that their favourite teacher has terminal cancer. Miss Applebaum is no ordinary teacher; she is an inspirer of the young, a worshipper of human creativity, a purveyor of weird and unverifiable information ('On the average, each human being contains two molecules of Julius Caesar's last breath'[84]) – in short, a joyous pedagogical eccentric. She takes them on a triumphant introductory tour of Central Park, feeding the down-and-outs, telling them about the statues, and finally rolling with them down a grassy hillside. But at about this point the humour stops. An exhilarating visit to the Metropolitan Museum turns into a grim lesson on how the Egyptians prepared for death, and it dawns on Henry and Zelda that they have been 'chosen' by Miss Applebaum to arrange everything. They are trapped in the death-taboo, unable to tell anyone; even Miss Applebaum herself will not discuss it. They are to make the decisions, and she entrusts herself to them. So these two young hopefuls do their best, organizing a second medical opinion and an investigative stay in hospital.

However nothing stops Miss Applebaum's decline, and the children are never allowed the luxury of knowing that they acted for the best. Finally the old lady asks them to wheel her from the hospital to her flat, through her beloved Central Park. It is winter now, and with the imagery of dying around them, she tells the two youngsters not to be sad for 'winter has a purpose too'.[85] She dies that night and, with a tender touch of gothic, the story ends with an account of how they bury her in the Park.

A Begonia for Miss Applebaum is an uncompromising novel which resists the attractive consolations of more facile maturation narratives. Readers are not told that the protagonists have come to terms with dying; they are not allowed to believe that Miss Applebaum died happy; the narrative does not cut hopefully to the friendship of Henry and Zelda, for the narrators have been reticent about themselves. Readers are left with a sad sense of two idealistic youngsters muddling through their growing up, and intelligent enough to know that their efforts are always inadequate – but still have to be made. But the old lady, whose death they have to deal with, is the same person who earlier showed them a join-the-dot trick and explained that 'the secret of the nine dots is like the secret of life itself. The true answers are always beyond our expectations.'[86] So this novel, too, has something of the fable: it is the fate of maturing young people that they must learn from a dying generation.

Post-modernism

Paul Zindel's novel required patience, perseverance and maturity in its young readers. In England, a number of new writers offered their readers challenges of a different kind – challenges of language and form. Two writers in particular were engaged in seeking new ways of representing the effects on maturing young people of the fragmented complexities and conflicts of the post-modern world. Alan Garner's *Red Shift* (1975) was a work about the violent emotions of young men and women, and the apparent impossibility of their being accommodated or resolved in the late twentieth century.

In his preceding work, *The Owl Service* (1965), Garner had made no concessions for young readers. He seemed to be working towards a narrative manner which – in William Blake's phrase – 'rouzes the faculties to act',[87] providing no authorial explanations and frustrating the traditional expectation that the narrator's voice should provide constant reassurance. The only explanations are those the puzzled characters work out for themselves. *Red Shift* is concerned with contemporary teenage lovers, Jan and Tom; the reader has at first no way of understanding why alongside this narrative two others are also being told – one set at the end of the Roman occupation of Britain, the other at the time of the English Civil War.

The drama in each narrative is determined by historical and cultural context. But the basic mythic pattern is constant in all three, the interest focusing on sexual loyalty and the three-way dynamics that occur when a young woman is torn between two men. In each of the three narratives, one of the males is a dreamer – wayward, passionate and desperate – while the other is a pragmatic realist who knows how to deal with life as he finds it, casually or brutally. The imaginative focus is on the young woman who is drawn towards both kinds of maleness. In the two stories from the past, the young woman can, somehow, contrive to make the world safe for her vulnerable lover by colluding with the other man. These mythic conflicts are openly sexual and – in two of the three narratives – take place in a historical context of rape and butchery. But in the third narrative – set in contemporary England – no kind of resolution is possible. An obsessive madness has taken possession of Tom, which he and Jan are incapable of dealing with. Tom is highly educated, full of quotations, a lover of significant punning; Jan is lovingly supportive, a believer in psychological therapy. Both of them are full of sex – she passionate and full of affection, but he cerebral and full of words. But they are unable to meet in a state of achieved passion and understanding.

Red Shift demands to be re-read: there are clues in the narratives which cannot be understood by a first-time reader. Another challenge is that Garner employs long episodes of unattributed dialogue composed of utterances which follow psychologically rather than logically; this has the effect of removing the sense of an author's shaping control and of miming the uncertainty of actual speech. Here, for example, a significant action is 'hidden' in the dialogue, where Tom is distressed because Jan has arrived wearing a bikini under her clothes:

> 'Bikini!'
> 'I love you.'
> 'Bikini!'
> 'It's hurting you too much,' said Jan. 'I'll get rid of it.'
> 'Have you caught up?' said Jan.
> 'Don't.'
> 'I only want to know.'[88]

Between 'I'll get rid of it' and 'Have you caught up?', Tom and Jan have made love for the first time. But readers can understand this only if they have attentively remembered that earlier – when Tom learned that Jan was not a virgin – he said (perhaps with a bitter pun on 'lap') that he felt as if he were 'a lap behind'.[89] This textual silence is appropriate for Tom, for whom sex is literally unspeakable, and for an age and culture which still required sexual reticence in novels for young readers. It clearly demonstrates Garner's approach, which sees both narrative and maturation as riddling or code-making processes, often baffling, in which meaning has to be made out of mystification or silence, or accepted as almost beyond comprehension. The novel's title is symptomatic: a reader has to grasp the astronomical significance of 'red shift' and work out how that contributes to a reading of a complex book about passion and history.

Garner's relationship to his reader is as Tom's to Jan. On the end-papers of *Red Shift* there is a letter from Tom to Jan composed in a complex code with a shifting key, derived from Lewis Carroll. 'If you can read this, you must care,' it says. It is typical of Tom that his farewell letter to his girlfriend should be in code – but it also exemplifies Garner's attitude to narrative and meaning. Maturing young people, it seems to suggest, are required to break all manner of adult codes; but they are equally capable of putting codes to their own uses.

Breaktime, by Aidan Chambers, was published in 1978, the first of a group of five novels, each focusing primarily on one aspect of adolescence in contemporary Britain.[90] It was a controversial novel, breaking new ground both in its explicit treatment of young male sexuality and also in the playfully post-modernist ways in which it involved the reader in narratorial puzzles and games. These five metafictive novels provide shifting perspectives upon young adult anxiety and obsession. *Dance on My Grave* (1982) is about a brief gay relationship between two boys; but the deeper story is about how the narrator of the novel, sixteen-year-old Hal, is obsessed with death – and then has to confront it, intimately and closely. In *Now I Know* (1987) the storyteller is seeking to understand religious faith and the existential reality of the crucifixion. *The Toll Bridge* (1992) provides an appropriate metaphor for the crossing-over from childhood to adulthood.

Such an account might suggest that the novels are schematic, but nothing could be further from the truth. These mercurial texts shift freely in manner, authorial perspective, page-design and font. There are sometimes several narrators, but the dominant voice is always that of the first-person young narrator – angry and rueful, articulate and witty, full of quotations and word-play, self-conscious, self-obsessed, sex-obsessed, explicit and vivid, full of the facetiousness and stylistic fireworks of intelligent adolescence. Here, for example, Nik word-plays upon the biblical story of the loaves and fishes:

> If it happened at all, of course. The whole thing might be just
> a fiction. I.e.: all cod.
> Is God a cod?
> Were the loaves fishy?
> Have we used our loaves about the five thousand?
> Were the five thousand only bait on a hook in a crook's book?

> If so, who was shooting the line? Jesus of Nazareth?
> Didn't he have better fish to fry than a few thousand poverty-
> stricken peasants from an outback area of one of the third-
> world outposts of the Roman Empire?
> In brief: Was Jesus a con-man?[91]

The young-adult world which Chambers' young protagonists inhabit is a dramatic, highly-coloured place of uncertain friendships, violence and cynicism. They are thinkers, exhibitionists, passionate enquirers and symbol-seekers, pitiless scoffers and vulnerable egotists. And in these five novels there is – more than in any other young adult fiction – a powerful sense of adolescent physicality – an inquisitive fascination with bodies and a fastidious and narcissistic interest in the details of violence and sex. Furthermore, the writing is preoccupied with meaning, with words, with the difficulty of accurately communicating truth. One of the young narrators, Hal, writes in his journal:

> ... The words are not right. They just ARE NOT RIGHT.
> They won't say what I want them to say. They tell lies. They
> hide the truth. I read the words and I can feel – FEEL – what
> they should be saying and they aren't. The meaning is hidden
> behind them. They are like bricks. They make a wall. A wall
> hiding from view what's happening behind. You can hear
> muffled noises coming through but you can't quite, never *quite*,
> make sense of them. They might be coming from someone
> being murdered, or from a child playing, or from a couple
> making love, or from someone playing a game trying to trick
> you into believing something is happening that isn't really.[92]

Writing of this kind suggests an author articulating his struggle with the materials of his craft; but it challenges readers too, teasingly inviting them into an authorial conversation about fiction and truth. This is precisely the debate which Ditto and his friend Morgan have in *Breaktime* – except that the issue is not just discussed but exemplified in the narrative the reader has just completed. 'Are you playing games?' Morgan finally asks Ditto, when he has read his account of his half-term adventures:

> 'Do you mean, have I written fiction?'
> 'Declare!'
> 'Could be. How do you know I didn't sit in my room at
> home all week making the stuff up?'
> 'I don't believe you.'

'Thank you. That's the best compliment you could pay me.'[93]

Is anything resolved in these novels? Perhaps a more appropriate question would be: can anything ever be resolved in a narrative devoted to adolescence? If it is the nature of maturation that it is always in process and never complete, maturation narratives must accordingly be fluid, uncertain and open-ended. Maturation involves crossing the bridge – and a toll of some kind must be paid. When the bridge has been crossed, different kinds of fiction might become appropriate: closure may be possible in romance or tragedy, and resolutions are always possible in comedy. But Chambers' maturation narratives are inevitably always unfinished, not just a series of events still unfolding but a conversation between an impassioned writer and an engaged reader about the existential dilemma of adolescence – what it is like to know everything and to have experienced nothing.[94] But something is, if not resolved, at least formulated in these five fictions – some conviction or clarity about the nature of guilt, or heroism, or death, or love. An example is the account of religious faith which Julie writes for Nik in *Now I Know*:

> Anyway, I do think it is true that if God is to be found by belief, she is to be found by living gladly and with attentive love in the world where we are. Because God is here and now and is all of us and everything.[95]

These moments of achieved understanding are usually made possible with the help of a newly-discovered (girl)friend, for in all of these novels the ability of the young to reach out and find a trusting, affectionate and – above all – articulate friend is the central aspect of their maturation. The fifth novel, *Postcards from No Man's Land* (1999), is conceived on an altogether wider scale and brings a group of contemporary young adults into an intimate understanding of the details of World War II in Arnhem. Here, the young find themselves learning *from* the old and *about* the old, while the old learn about themselves and the meaning of their own adolescence. The process of adolescence is brought into direct communication with the process of dying.

Jacob, though less intensely anguished than Chambers' other young protagonists, has a moment of fear in a backstreet café in Amsterdam when it occurs to him that the adult state he has always longed to achieve might mean nothing more than being alone. 'Is that what being grown up, being adult, *means*? Solitude?'[96] he wonders. But

Chambers' characters are never content to remain enclosed in solitude. People in this novel come close to one another through courage, love and curiosity, but above everything is the need to *tell*. They are all either talkers or writers. This novel is a celebration of people's capacity to make words bring them together in understanding and love – an activity which in Chambers' fiction is central to maturation. In the first four of these novels, the focus was on the maturing young people, but the wider canvas of *Postcards from No Man's Land* embraces the middle-aged, the old and the dying too, all with their own processes of understanding or acceptance to go through.

Philippa Pearce, Cynthia Voigt and Jan Mark

Children's writers cannot avoid maturation. Its small eddies of progress and clarity are likely to emerge in the narrative languages authors employ even when they are not self-consciously tracing their characters' currents of growth and development.[97] Here is an example of the kind of writing celebrated in this book: there is a key moment in Emma Smith's novel *No Way of Telling* (1972), in which the heroine, Amy, has been caught up in a potentially deadly hostage crisis. This story is a thriller, but at another level it is concerned with the difficulties of *trusting* – in particular the problem faced by an intelligent child in deciding which adults can be trusted when her life might depend upon it. Here, faced by yet another stranger showing all the signs of honesty and truth, she must decide if she can trust him with a vital letter on which everything depends:

> But still she kept hold of the envelope, merely going a step or two nearer without relaxing her grip on it, to gaze up searchingly into the man's face.
>
> 'For what are you looking, my child?' he asked her, smiling a little.

Others have smiled and spoken gently to Amy before – and then proved false. But this time, after a long scrutiny:

> 'You can tell by the eyes,' said Amy briefly; and then she gave him the letter.
>
> He received it from her with a curiously formal bow, as though he were paying homage to more than either a letter or the person giving it: to a moment in history.[98]

That is what the three writers featured in this book repeatedly and unpretentiously do: *they pay homage to significant moments* in personal history, which is quite different from representing the passing of time. In the remaining three chapters, we have looked closely at the narrative language of three distinguished authors: with Philippa Pearce and Jan Mark, attention is given to a selection from their novels and shorter fiction, with Cynthia Voigt the focus is exclusively on the *Tillerman* series. All three are reflective and word-perfect writers, as meticulous with the details of vocabulary, syntax and tone as they are with the outer and inner lives of their protagonists. Indeed, the two kinds of meticulousness are indivisible, for it is in that writerly attention to words – that understanding of homely phrasing – that readers are likely to find they have developed an attention to the privacy and seriousness of maturation.

Endnotes

1. Robert Louis Stevenson (1944), *Treasure Island*, Oxford University Press, p. 238.
2. See Peter Hollindale (1997), *Signs of Childness in Children's Books*, Thimble Press, p. 14.
3. Some critics would dispute this: it has been argued that Richardson's *Pamela* (1740, 1741) was the first real novel, and F. R. Leavis at one time refused to take seriously any fiction before Jane Austen. Others might point to Aphra Behn (1640–89), who also wrote prose fiction. The general view, however, is that Defoe was the first to represent fictional biographical continuity.
4. Daniel Defoe (1971), *Moll Flanders*, Oxford University Press, p. 19.
5. It is impossible to know whether the author was aware of this; most commentators have found Defoe's writerly self-consciousness problematic.
6. *Op. cit.*, p. 25.
7. Both these novels were published in 1722, when Defoe was 62.
8. Charlotte Brontë (undated), *Jane Eyre*, Nelson, p. 2.
9. See Morag Styles, Eve Bearne and Victor Watson (1994), *The Prose and the Passion*, Cassell, pp. 169–71.
10. Louisa May Alcott (1953), *Good Wives*, Dent Dutton, p. 243.
11. Susan Ang (2001), *The Cambridge Guide to Children's Books in English*, ed. Victor Watson, Cambridge University Press, pp. 38–9.
12. Rose Campbell is the main protagonist in Louisa May Alcott's *Eight Cousins* and its sequel, *Rose in Bloom*.
13. Susan Coolidge (undated), *What Katy Did*, Blackie, p. 15.
14. Ibid., pp. 16–25.
15. Ibid., p. 119.
16. Ibid., p. 123 *ff.*
17. Ibid., p. 190.
18. Ibid., p. 190.
19. Susan Coolidge (undated), *What Katy Did at School*, Blackie, p. 31.

20. Ibid., p. 191.
21. Susan Coolidge (undated), *What Katy Did Next*, Juvenile Productions, p. 173.
22. Ibid., p. 174.
23. Kate Douglas Wiggin (1903), *Rebecca of Sunnybrook Farm*, A. & C. Black, p. 270.
24. Ibid., p. 276.
25. Kate Douglas Wiggin (1907), *More About Rebecca*, A. & C. Black, p. 276.
26. *What Katy Did Next*, p. 182.
27. Louisa May Alcott (1990), *Rose in Bloom*, Virago, p. 279.
28. Ibid., p. 47.
29. Ibid., p. 290.
30. Ibid., p. 305.
31. Ibid., p. 297.
32. Ibid., p. 21.
33. Ibid., p. 116.
34. Ibid., p. 118.
35. Ibid., p. 117.
36. Ibid., p. 331.
37. Ibid., p. 341.
38. Ibid., p. 344.
39. L. M. Montgomery (1925), *Anne of Green Gables*, Harrap, p. 212.
40. L. M. Montgomery (1925), *Anne of the Island*, Harrap, p. 79.
41. Ibid., p. 265.
42. Ibid., p. 12.
43. L. M. Montgomery (1926), *Anne's House of Dreams*, Harrap, p. 9.
44. Ibid., p. 44.
45. L. M. Montgomery (1936), *Anne of Windy Willows*, Harrap, p. 100.
46. *Anne's House of Dreams*, p. 120.
47. *What Katy Did*, p. 15.
48. '[Tom and Maggie] had gone forth together into their new life of sorrow, and they would never more see the sunshine undimmed by remembered cares. They had entered the thorny wilderness, and the golden gates of their childhood had for ever closed behind them.' George Eliot (1979), *The Mill on the Floss*, Penguin Classics, p. 270; quoted in Kate Douglas Wiggin (1929), *Rebecca of Sunnybrook Farm*, A. & C. Black, p. 243.
49. *Rebecca of Sunnybrook Farm*, p. 275.
50. Frances Hodgson Burnett (1961), *A Little Princess*, Puffin, p. 222.
51. See Lissa Paul, 'Enigma Variations: what feminist criticism knows about Children's Literature', *Signal 54* (1987), pp. 198–9.
52. See Thomas Hardy (1896), *Jude the Obscure*.
53. The parallels between the two novels are startling; but, if they are to be strictly carried through, Mary would have to fall in love with Colin's father, her uncle. This would have been unthinkable.

54. E. Nesbit (1906), *The Railway Children*, Wells Gardner, Darton & Co., p. 181.

55. *Rainbow Valley* and *Rilla of Ingleside* are usually listed as separate from the *Avonlea* series; but they are nevertheless a continuation of Anne's story.

56. L. M. Montgomery (1928), *Rilla of Ingleside*, Harrap, p. 181.

57. Ibid., p. 181.

58. Ibid., p. 142.

59. In the summer of 1917, Elsie Wright, aged sixteen, and her ten-year-old cousin, Frances Griffiths, claimed to have seen and photographed fairies in the woods at Cottingley, near Bradford. Nothing much happened until 1919, when Sir Arthur Conan Doyle and various theosophists, spiritualists and clairvoyants became interested. Conan Doyle's article on the Cottingley fairies was published in the *Strand* in December, 1920.

60. They did, however, go in for fairies, especially in books for younger readers.

61. Anne Shirley does not, in fact, keep a journal; Rilla, however, does.

62. Dodie Smith (1949), *I Capture the Castle*, William Heinemann, p. 337.

63. Rumer Godden (1993), *The Greengage Summer*, Pan Books, pp. 5–6.

64. Ibid., p. 100.

65. Ibid., pp. 51–2.

66. Ibid., pp. 5–6.

67. Ibid., p. 144.

68. Ibid., p. 145.

69. Jane Gardam (1982), *A Long Way From Verona*, Abacus, p. 94.

70. Ibid., p. 14.

71. Ibid., pp. 101–2.

72. Ibid., p. 104.

73. Ibid., p. 143.

74. Ibid., pp. 171–2.

75. See Victor Watson (2000), 'Jane Austen Has Gone Missing', *Reading Series Fiction*, RoutledgeFalmer, pp. 173–89.

76. See also Susan Ang (2000), *The Widening World of Children's Literature*, Macmillan, pp. 143–53. It was Dr Ang who introduced me to the work of Antonia Forest.

77. Beverly Cleary (1962), *Fifteen*, Peacock Books, back cover.

78. Ibid., p. 174.

79. Judy Blume (1975), *Forever*, Bradbury Press, pp. 73–4.

80. J. D. Salinger (1994), *The Catcher in the Rye*, Penguin Books, p. 174.

81. Ibid., pp. 180, 181, 183.

82. Paul Zindel (1989), *A Begonia for Miss Applebaum*, The Bodley Head, address to the reader.

83. Ibid., p. 64.

84. Ibid., p. 159.

85. Ibid., p. 168.

86. Ibid., pp. 33–4.

87. William Blake, letter to Dr Trussler (23 August 1799) (1966), *Blake: Complete Writings*, Oxford University Press, p. 793.

88. Alan Garner (1985), *Red Shift*, Flamingo edition, William Collins Sons & Co. Ltd. p. 130.

89. Ibid., p. 129.

90. At the time of writing, a sixth novel is promised.

91. Aidan Chambers (2000), *Now I Know*, Red Fox, p. 82.

92. Aidan Chambers (2000), *Dance on My Grave*, Red Fox, pp. 163–4

93. Aidan Chambers (2000), *Breaktime*, Red Fox, p. 138.

94. Ibid., p. 7.

95. *Now I Know*, p. 231.

96. Aidan Chambers (2001), *Postcards from No Man's Land*, Red Fox, p. 133.

97. The exception is the kind of comic writing which sees childhood as slapstick.

98. Emma Smith (1974), *No Way of Telling*, The Children's Book Club, p. 214.

CHAPTER 2

Philippa Pearce

Margaret Meek

Preface and protocols

Philippa Pearce should need no introduction to adult readers of children's literature. The distinction conferred by important awards (the Carnegie Medal and the Whitbread Award), reviews, expressions of high regard, all demonstrably deserved, are the outward and visible signs of her success. For half a century her books, stories, talks and a range of other encounters have played an important part in the growing to maturity of her readers and listeners. Most of them are pre-adolescent, the period when intellectual growth still includes play, learning to read and learning about reading. Their world is expanding. The part that books play in this process is now generally acknowledged.

Children's growing independence, their interest in things and people outside the family, involve them in new experiences and different emotional tangles and contradictions. School, the society of children, influences their desire to conform to prevalent conventions and enthusiasms (shoes, TV personalities), and, at the same time, to challenge the rules. As a consequence of television, children now enter the actual world of their elders before they leave primary school. The evidence for the influence of these outside and inside 'realities' is less tangible, less dramatic than the events and upsets of adolescence, but the intellectual and emotional aspects of children's experience of them have been shown to derive coherence and a depth of understanding from the reading of fictive narratives.

Before the publication of *Minnow on the Say* in 1955, Philippa Pearce had been a scriptwriter and producer for BBC Radio, and an editor in two prestigious publishing houses. This work involved the close reading of texts and their presentation to listeners and readers. The consequent experience and skill are evident in the directness of her style; it has a clear, distinctive quality of 'voice'. The punctuation and paragraphing are as transformative as the tone and pace markings on a musical score. Simple as some of the texts for young readers appear on the surface, these are crafted, 'poetic' in the sense of being made. They usually mean more than they say. This is one of the important reading lessons of middle childhood. Not all children learn it.

When Philippa Pearce talks with children about writing stories, she wins their respect by showing them the 'constructedness' of texts; how every detail counts in the creation of a scene for the inner eye, and how the end of a story changes the beginning. Her listeners are being trusted with inside, expert information about how a story works. They are then more confident in trying new kinds of narrative. From the linguistic subtleties embedded in the direct telling, young readers discover that their imagination makes it possible to hold together two different worlds in their head at the same time, the everyday one and the world in the story. (If this seems unlikely, ask children where they are when they read.)

This bifocal awareness that comes with reading stories makes readers feel 'a head taller';[1] more aware, more daring, more sympathetic; that is, 'more themselves'.[2] Adolescents experienced in reading novels discover 'how the author does it'. Before then, primary school children extend and confirm their knowledge of themselves and the existence of others as they practise different kinds of reading, or re-read what they find interesting. This is the challenge to the writer.

In her short stories, Philippa Pearce gives children a chance to discover some of these things. Here then, as prologue to looking at the famous novels, is a glimpse of the writer at work.

The Rope

The story,[3] retold, seems simple enough. When Mike, his mother and sister are staying with his paternal grandmother, an enthusiast for children's exploits as signs of growth, he wakes from a dream about a rope, a hangman's rope. He is anticipating what he fears – a challenge from the local children who can do it – to swing across the nearby river on a rope that will just reach the other side and swing back again. The river isn't deep and he can swim. The feat demands a certain amount of skill in running, jumping, and controlling the rope itself; it would be Mike's first attempt, but that will not serve as an excuse if he fails. He knows how the adults will react: Gran will praise the effort, his sister knows that he is afraid, while she is confident; his mother, sympathetic, would rather avoid the scene altogether. The local children, who have had lots of practise, have forgotten their first attempts and their early failures.

Mike does everything he can to put off the moment when it is his turn. His sister has already been successful. He tries hard, but makes the mistake that means an inevitable drop into the water. Here is Mike holding the rope, trying to make his hand let go and 'feeling as if his shoulders would split open'.

> He hung there on the rope, twirling slowly round over the middle of the river. Now he could see the people on the far bank: there were quite a lot of them, Ginger's friends and acquaintances, and they were all looking at him and giggling among themselves. Oh, yes! They were laughing all right! Now he couldn't see them any more, because he had rotated further, so that now he was facing the near bank, from which Ginger and Shirley were watching him. They watched in silence. And beyond them, coming across the meadow towards the rope, he saw two more people: his mother and his grandmother. They had finished the washing up and were coming to see how Mike and Shirley were enjoying themselves.[4]

See how many things the reader is invited to notice almost at once. The scene is described in such a way that reading it takes about the same time as the event as Mike endures it. Behind his glimpse of his mother and grandmother are all his fears of failure. There is no solution to Mike's predicament except to let go of the rope, but this now depends on his willpower to let go; to will his jump into the water before being compelled by pain and exhaustion: 'he also achieved the shout he willed himself to make. It came out partly as a scream, but it was also quite distinctly a word: "Whoops!"'[5]

The family behaves as he expected. Ginger, a friendly, local lad who tries to encourage Mike out of his misery, comes home with the family for tea. Reconstructing the scene, he praises Mike for his forethought in calling out 'Whoops' before he fell. The word had conveyed that this was a mistake, carelessness rather than the result of the fear that the reader has already experienced with him. When Mike later confesses his reluctance to swing on the rope, Ginger then tells him what he had never told anyone else: he had fainted at the sight of blood when his father nearly cut off his thumb with a chainsaw. In the telling, laughing at *himself*, he begins to cry.

'You won't tell,' said Ginger.

'No' said Mike. He pondered. 'Blood – that's funny. Shirley fell out of a tree once and cut her head. She howled a lot, but she didn't mind the blood; nor did I.'

'Much blood'?

'Quite a bit. But I didn't mind.'

Ginger patted the surface of the bathwater with his hand. 'Funny . . .' he said.

Mike fished around in his mind for something his mother often remarked – nothing very witty or original, but just true: 'People are different,' he said.[6]

The mode of the telling transforms the actuality of the events into an experience of deeper understanding of what, for both boys, was at stake. Mike had to face what he feared. Ginger was afraid that the others would consider him a baby.

In this short tale we see the family as individuals. There are glimpses of all the relationships that occur in other stories: between the generations, between contemporaries, between a sister and a brother. Ginger tells Mike his secret because Mike's family are going home the next day so he can't tell the others about his faint. Mike promises he won't ever tell when he comes back to see his Gran. Children learn early that a promise is a hold on the future.

Throughout her working life Philippa Pearce has been an inspiration to young writers and critics. She has moved with the times, not simply in the obvious way of ensuring that her stories reflect surface cultural changes, but in recognizing that the complications of being a child are no less in each successive generation than they were in the immediate post-war period when she contributed so out-standingly to the new flourishing of books for children.

Short stories

The notable feature of Philippa Pearce's short stories is that they are perfect for reading aloud. This activity is not so common as it was once in homes and schools, but there are opportunities, certainly in the latter, for its revival. The benefits for less experienced readers are well known. To be successful, short stories have to convey the essence, the intrinsic distillation of storytelling in both its ancient and modern forms. The listener–reader gets the experience as an artistic whole, a distinctively memorable satisfaction.

There are short stories to match the children's growing awareness of the people around them and the recurrent features of the everyday.

Here Comes Tod (1992, 1999) is at the height of the pre-school hero. Tod opens the front door. 'At first, all he saw was a pair of trousers. Then the man outside stooped down to look at Tod looking at him. They recognized each other.'[7] The postman has brought Tod a parcel, which he hopes contains a helicopter. Instead it's a fine knitted sweater. A subsequent parcel has another sweater to wear when the first is in the wash. Later, two very small sweaters arrive. Tod is furious and protests he is no longer a baby until he discovers they are matching ones for his teddy bears. In proper telephone style Tod helps his teddy with the message of thanks. His other activities include making friends with Susie, planting an orange pip, exploring the garden as unknown territory. When Tod's mother has a birthday, he thinks she should have a helicopter. All very tame? Think then of the expertise needed to convey with lucidity the firstness of these events in words for beginning readers.

Mrs Cockle's Cat began as a fine picture book illustrated by Antony Maitland in 1961. Now in Young Puffin, it qualifies as a text for 'first solo reading'. During a wet and windy summer, Peter, the favoured cat, leaves his London home with Mrs Cockle in search of fresh fish, (supplies have failed) and doesn't come back. Mrs Cockle becomes less than her robust self in his absence, so much so that when a strong gust of wind catches her at the corner of the street where she sells balloons, she is carried up aloft and blown right down the Thames and out to sea. Hear how reasonable this is:

> In the ordinary way, for someone to walk along the River Thames from London down to the river's mouth would be very long and dull and tiring. For Mrs Cockle, tripping lightly overhead, it was none of these things. Only towards the end did she even begin to wish there were a cup of tea to be had.[8]

The satisfactory ending sees Mrs Cockle and Peter settled in a young fisherman's house by the sea. Here, again, is the coupling of extra-realism and the fanciful-possible that is part of children's thinking at this stage.

One more step up in the publisher's grading system is the collection *Lion at School*, 'for those who have developed reading fluency'. It is interesting to see if the increased number of sentence units can be made to march in step with children's actual experience. Philippa Pearce works outside this framework. She recognizes just how *huge* are children's emotions; fear, pleasure, pain and worry can take them over, completely, and not just at the level of their size or reading competence.

The title story and four of the others in this collection were part of the BBC's successful radio series, *Listening and Reading* (1971). The little girl who meets a lion on her way to school allows him to come with her on condition that he doesn't eat anyone and lets her ride there on his back. The lion is a compliant pupil during the morning. Lunch is less to his liking. In the playground he frightens the school bully with his roaring, then, deciding he has had enough, he goes away. The little girl is no longer afraid of the bully. He knows her lion friend may return.

In the same vein is *The Great Sharp Scissors*. It conveys, without comment, the intensity of a child's anger. Tim wants to go with his mother to see his Granny, but she is ill and he is 'often naughty', so he has to stay at home on his own and not let anyone into the house (a narrative convention not now much in use). A strange man with a suitcase solicits entrance. He sells knives, scissors and battleaxes. Tim would buy a battleaxe, but none is available, so he settles for scissors that will cut anything. That is what they do to buttons, a carpet, chair, sofa and table legs, the clock and the goldfish bowl. 'They would cut his whole home into a heap of rubble; and they had begun to do so.' Then a kind lady appears. She is prepared to exchange her best spray-on glue for the scissors. When Tim's mother arrives home, everything is spick and span, except for the water spilled from the goldfish bowl. This little psychological thriller has a number of antecedents in older tales. It is not one that is easily forgotten.

When the stories of *The Elm Street Lot* were first broadcast in a slightly different form on *Jackanory* and published by the BBC in 1969, there were fewer tales of 'ordinary' (i.e. working class) children than a decade later when the collection was produced by Kestrel Books (1979) and then Puffin. Part of the readers' pleasure in the gang's activities is in their energetic freedom to roam – now part of fantasy wish-fulfilment of the next generation.

The maturation element – children reading ahead of themselves – is clearer in *What the Neighbours Did*, a collection also derived from BBC sources and published by Longman in 1972. The virtue for children in hearing more complex stories read aloud is that, if they then encounter the written text, they already know 'how it goes'. They also know the tune on the page. In terms of building the children's confidence that they will become experienced readers worthy of books without age demarcation, familiarity with a favourite author is one of the best guarantees of success. Philippa Pearce's stories find their own level with young readers if they have a range of collections to choose from.

Still Jim and Silent Jim (1959) is a restrained tale of a young man's determination to keep his elderly grandfather in touch with life outside the house where he lives with his daughter's family. Young Jim takes old Jim to the Over Sixties' Club. Later, his grandfather suggests a visit to his birthplace (Little Barley, as in *Minnow on the Say*) to see the tombstone of his great-grandfather, who was nearly eight feet tall. Listeners to stories about this giant are sceptical. The visit is intended by the old man to settle the matter. It does. The grandson pushed the wheelchair all the way. The journey is easier for both on return.

Not all of the stories here are as idyllic as those for younger readers. Their growing children, as in *The Great Blackberry Pick*, make parents uneasy. Here the father is trying to recapture the recollected rural pleasures of his own childhood, with tiresome results for the young. The engagement in *Return to Air* anticipates the suspense in *The Rope*.

Apprehensions, those night sounds, unexplained silences, and unexpected events that provoke recurrent unease are good topics for short stories, providing the timing is right. Children who are still prone to nightmares don't need the prophylaxis of having scary stories read to them in the hope that their fears will be dispelled. But there is some excitement in *daring* to read when you feel fully safe. *The Ghost in Annie's Room* (2001) shows how children associate untraced sounds with haunting: squeaking, creaking, mouse and fly noises, and unfamiliar footsteps. There are explanations for most of these when Annie sleeps away from home in an attic bedroom, but not for all.

The Shadow Cage, the title story of a collection of ten eerie tales that combine local superstitions with ordinary happenings are as gripping as any classic tales for adults, except that the protagonists are mostly the sensible young. The prose keeps an even, light tone of menace, enhancing the extraordinary in the ordinary. To return to the novels after reading some of these crafted narratives is to interpret more than you first thought of in both.

Behind most of the short stories, in even the most realistic, lies a tradition that John Goldthwaite calls *The Natural History of Make-Believe*.[9] We see Philippa Pearce's attachment to this word-hoard of storytelling in her own fairy tale, *The Squirrel Wife*, and in her retelling of *The Pedlar of Swaffham* for the Scholastic series, where famous authors retell a folk or fairy tale for today's children. Her gift to her readers is a wide choice of reading kinds and a confident belief in their positive responses.

Real children: *The Children of Charlecote*

The *locus classicus* for discussions about the 'reality' of children and childhood and books for the young is Jacqueline Rose's *The Case of Peter Pan: or the Impossibility of Children's Fiction* (1984). She says:

> Children's fiction is impossible, not in the sense that it cannot be written (that would be nonsense), but in that it hangs on impossibility, one which it rarely ventures to speak. This is the impossible relation between adult and child. Children's fiction is clearly about that relation, but it has the remarkable characteristic of being about something which it hardly ever talks of.[10]

It is not my intention to pursue this argument; others have done that. But it is important to notice that notions of 'the child' in relation to 'growth' and 'reality' or even 'realism' are contested constructs in discussions of children's literature. They are bound to be tagged with the cultural, historical and economic circumstances of their contexts.

There were real children in Charlecote Park in Warwickshire, a Great House that was the home of the Fairfax-Lucy family before the war of 1914–18 swept away the already threatened conditions of upper-class English country life. Brian Fairfax-Lucy and his brothers and sisters were the last children to live there. After the war, so great were the social changes that Brian Fairfax-Lucy wanted to write an authentic historical narrative about their Edwardian childhood, particularly about the House itself and its effects on the lives of all its inhabitants. To do this, while two brothers and two sisters were still alive, meant changing their names, so the first edition, in 1968, was called *The Children of the House*. The House became Stanford Hall in the story. The children are the Hattons, Laura, Thomas, Hugh and Margaret. The reversion to *The Children of Charlecote* came in the 1989 edition, with a preface by Alice Fairfax-Lucy to explain things.

Selection of autobiographical material creates the text of a life that is closer to fiction in its inclusions, omissions and other changes than is often acknowledged. By choosing to write his story as a third-person narrative, Brian Fairfax-Lucy gave himself more scope to present his siblings as characters. It also gave him a novelist's freedom to invent circumstances that turned the actualities of events into plot sequences.

Most classic narratives for children carry some of the deep structures of the author's childhood. If the writer is concerned to be accurate about actual historical events, then the shift to creating a past world for a new generation of children is more demanding than it might at first appear. Thus, the felicitous partnership of Brian Fairfax-Lucy and Philippa Pearce joined the intensity of the originator's concerns with the shaping skill of a highly regarded author, whose book about a garden had already shown that memory is a powerful prompt in storytelling for the young.

Charlecote Park is a closed community; the servants have a kind of power because the lifestyle of their employers depends on them. The children look to the servants for help, tolerance and companionship. The story is about the relation of adults and children, and the growth of the latter in spite of their parents' attempts, for a number of reasons, to extend their dependence, while at the same time complaining about its cost. The depth and subtlety of the text are in words that convey the feelings and responses of the children to what happens to them. These carry the hallmark of Philippa Pearce's understanding of their sophisticated complexity.

Before we proceed, it is interesting to look at the opening scene in both the Brian Fairfax-Lucy manuscript and in Philippa Pearce's version.

> Hugh awoke once again to the familiar furniture of the nursery. The rocking horse with its mild looking eyes and his joy of riding it. It seemed to be a symbol of eternity. You only had to push it and it went on rocking, and when it stopped you just pushed again. His eyes wandered to the pictures on the walls. The white cat and the green parrot was a favourite because the pussy looked so cosy. The little girl with the inscription 'Wait for me' reminded him of the schoolmaster's daughter with her anxious little face. The drawing of W. G. Grace was only tolerable because he was a famous cricketer. Hugh thought it was a pity. It made him look stuffy and inhuman like his grandfather whose portrait hung in the great hall.
>
> He remembered him when he was a little boy. Hugh's father had often quoted him as being a God-fearing man and a great industrialist, which he combined most successfully, adding he always said 'Look after the pennies and the pounds would look after themselves,' which Hugh thought was another way of saying he was a mean man. Unfortunately his own father had carried on that tradition, and was a chip off the old block, hard in his dealings. He believed in work and made others work too, but this was no moment to think about work. The holidays for which he had waited so long had just begun. His only wish now was to stop the clock ticking so fast.

He did not wait to see what time it was, he knew from the sun and the silence it must be about 5 am. There was still no movement in the stable yard and the grooms were not yet about, nor the kitchen maid who was an early riser.[11]

Before going to sleep last night Hugh had beaten his head repeatedly on the pillow: one – two – three – four – five. He must be awake at five o'clock. And now he was awake – or at least half-awake; and he could not for the life of him remember the reason for urgency.

From over the edge of the bedclothes, the nursery looked just as usual. The rocking horse reminded him that this morning he must ride round the farms with Papa. It would be dull, and miserable too: what might Papa say? What might the horse do? – and then – oh *then* what might Papa say?

Beyond the head of the rocking horse he saw familiar pictures on the nursery wall: the white cat and the green parrot staring at each other; the anxious looking little girl called 'Wait for Me', who always reminded him of Victor's sister Evie; the drawing of W. G. Grace. He liked the drawing best because he loved cricket; but what a pity about the black beard! The beard made his hero look like Grandpapa, whose portrait hung in the great hall, a Hatton among the generations and centuries of Stanfords. Grandpapa Hatton had died when Hugh was a very little boy, but Papa still quoted him as a great and godly industrialist. His motto had been, 'Look after the pennies and the pounds will look after themselves'. Hugh thought he must have been a mean man. A careful man. An unadventurous man –

Adventure! Suddenly Hugh remembered why he had to wake early.[12]

The information seems to be the same in both. The second text takes the reader into the nursery to see it as Hugh does in the moment before complete wakefulness. We are already alerted to Victor's sister; she will surely appear again. Something about the second telling, the pace of the looking round the nursery, the children's separate place entices the reader into the House as a companionable shadow of the children who left their childhood there. One difference: Grandpapa Hatton is Hugh's paternal grandfather. The Stanfords are his mother's family, which means that his father is the master-by-marriage of Charlecote.

The House is guarded from intruders by a system of bells, locked doors, designated rooms for its inhabitants: family members and indoor servants. There is stabling for at least nine horses, a huge kitchen garden with greenhouses, and a park with mature trees. A three-mile surrounding wall separates the gentry from their tenants and neighbours. This is the inheritance to be kept entire for the heir, Tom. Hugh is second in succession should anything happen to his brother. Laura, the eldest, is the daughter to be married so as to join this family with another of equal status. Margaret is the unexpected, unwanted, last child. Sir Robert Hatton sees the house as a drain on his resources and ambitions. His wife recalls the Edwardian glories of her youth, and tells the children stories about that time, as if it were recoverable.

Parts of this scene recur in television costume dramas and in romantic historical novels, as a kind of cultural shorthand. Here the details are intended to be accurate. The difference is that novelists who make up stories with this background have the power of deciding what happens. The people in this family may seem to be invented, but they still have one foot in an historical Eden.

The main thread of the story is the alliance of the children and the servants who are sorry for them. They are separated from their parents by custom and staircases. Their treatment as children, bread and milk for supper and their poor clothing are denials of their need to grow, so they seek their own adventures, sometimes dangerously. They avoid the parts of the house where they have been made unhappy, their father's study especially, and seek solace in the back stairs. The servants have their own hierarchy; they know most of what goes on, and give the children warning of what might happen. The children learn from them a kind of adult knowingness, hints about things they only partly understand: their father's quarrel with the schoolmaster who is teaching the village children to think for themselves. As part of their growing up in this domestic polity the children discover the difference between status and relationship. They are protected by well-practised subtlety, the ancient skill of underlings. The scene is sometimes as dark with foreboding as any Greek tragedy. The servants are a kind of chorus, explaining the state of things to the children, mostly about money.

As long as they are bound to each other the children just manage. At the beginning of the holidays they stand at the park gate and make their wishes in the last rays of the setting sun. Hugh's wish is always the same: to grow up as soon as possible and not to have to go into the Navy or the Church. Laura would like to marry and have children, but not before she has 'done' something. Margaret wants everything to stay the same, and always to live near the others. Tom sees only responsibilities ahead when he inherits Charlecote, but he would change things so that 'everywhere there'd be brightness and lots going on'.[13] In these dialogues with their future, the children reflect their longings for things to be different, for childhood to pass away. Their young lives are coloured with anxieties rather than hopes. One of the signs of their growing is their increased explicitness about how they feel. Official signs of growth are the rites of passage: school, hunting, shooting, 'being responsible'.

The children's growth to maturity depends on their escaping the repressions of the House. Their devised adventures, reminiscent of the books they read, are foiled by their inability to calculate risk or danger. The divisions of social class keep them from encounters with other young people. Hugh's friendship with the schoolmaster's son, Victor, is a moving example. Margaret is the one who clings to childhood. She, more often than the others, says: 'Do you remember?' The others prefer to look forward.

The climax is a grand dinner, at which the symbols of power and wealth, gold plates and 'dishes filled with grapes, peaches and pineapples'[14] from the garden are on display. The children finally refuse to wear the clothes of their childhood and to act the part they have grown out of. Tom tells his mother:

> You bring this kind of misery on us, Mama, because Papa is too mean – and you seem to agree with him – to buy us any new clothes. That's not all. We don't get enough to eat. And that's not all. We are kept short of all kinds of things, just so that Papa can keep all the horses he wants and you can live at Charlecote like Grandfather.[15]

Hugh, told to appreciate all the advantages of his station, says he doesn't want a pony. 'I'd rather have clothes that fit and boots that don't let in the water.'[16] Later, Tom says, 'I couldn't help thinking that Mama really agreed with a good deal of what we said.'[17] He had learned to express his feelings as the result of his friendship and conversation with Walter, the butler. The children do not go to the feast, but from their vantage point in the back stairs they see what goes on. Albert, the footman, gives them 'from the remains of the fish course, half a piece of fried sole each'.[18]

The intensity of feeling in this remarkably told tale lies in such details as these. The writing brings the children in the text close to modern young readers, who picture what is happening as their feelings match what they think or imagine. The 'reality' that Brian Fairfax-Lucy wanted to depict, the actuality of the children's growth, is wholly convincing. The imaginative transformation of the ordinary, visible in the Philippa Pearce version of the first page, is both bracing and memorable. There is no sentimentality, only the strength of sympathy and good writing, especially in the final pages, when, with the onset of war, the family has to leave the House. Laura, Tom and Hugh are the doomed youth in a conflict that later evidence shows was the worst war ever. Margaret, who inherits the house, cannot live in it. There are too many memories, which, by being transformed thus, are now a part of the consciousness of many more young people.

Latent sense: *Minnow on the Say*

The first, full-length novel, *Minnow on the Say*, was published in 1955. The narrative has all the authentic markings of an accomplished storyteller, with a sharp eye for vivid details and a distinctive way of bringing together the action and the setting. Recorded accounts tell how the author, confined to a hospital bed during a fine summer, found solace from the heat by thinking of the cool flow of the river that flowed by her home. Later, the river became the focus of the story, the quiet, never-ending flow of time.[19]

The first paragraph draws the reader into the summer holiday adventure of two boys who live different lives on the river bank: David Moss and his close family: parents, little sister and a brother in the Navy; and Adam Codling, whose parents are dead. His aunt and his paternal grandfather are his guardians. The boys are brought together when the canoe that belonged to Adam's father is washed downstream by unusual summer floods to the landing stage at the bottom of David's garden.

Before he discovers that Adam owns the canoe, David calls her the *Minnow*. She represents the possibility of adventure for him. He can swim, and is therefore trusted on the water. Here he is, on his own, free to take the *Minnow* upstream, across an unseen but acknowledged boundary between his house and those in Great Barley:

> Paddling the *Minnow* upstream was like being able to go into some familiar picture. At first, David knew the scenery well, for sometimes, in hot weather, he had swum short distances upstream and downstream from the landing stage. But soon it grew strange, with a special strangeness that came from his seeing close at hand what before he had seen only in the distance.[20]

The author is setting the reader's view of the scene, to watch David discover unfamiliar parts of the river and the delicacy of his craft – a new responsibility. He discovers that 'only one person seemed to have thought of keeping any kind of boat on the river, and that was only a punt'.[21] This sense of the first freshness of things, a particularity of childhood that adults come to take for granted, is one of the author's distinguishing features. Readers who know her work well, or have had the good fortune to be told the author's secrets, would notice that punt and remember it.

What David sees as he paddles is described with a deliberation that puts the river at the heart of the story. When he comes in sight of the mill, the ancient boundary landmark, he turns back again.[22] The current sweeps him fast downstream to a fallen tree he has seen earlier. This time, a voice : 'I can see you.' It is Adam Codling, frantic when he thinks David is about to paddle on past him. He believes David has stolen his canoe. David falls into the water in an attempt to get the canoe to the bank. Miss Codling, who has already been told by the local policeman that David had found the canoe, helps him out. She provides him with dry clothes, Adam apologizes, and they all have tea together.

David already knows the front drive of the Great Barley house. He cycles there to deliver the morning paper in a box. Now he is looking into the house from the back. 'It was gaunt and shabby, with paint peeling off the door and window-frames. The garden-door stood wide open, and he could see right into the house, to the hall, and at the farther end of it, to a front-door with deep panels of glass.'[23] Quite late, after talk with Adam, David walks back home and is greeted by his family, with the welcome reserved for those believed lost.

All this may seem to be a conventional scene setting for the treasure hunt that is to follow, but the reader has to pick up the clues that make David's growing friendship with Adam a series of boundary crossings that are at the heart of much literature in English; the differences that are categorized by social class. Details like the 'deep panels of glass' are shown, not explained. What the reader is to see is a contrast between the genteel poverty of Codlings, and David's close, comfortable home and family, the well-tended garden, his steady parents and their concern that no harm nor disappointment should come to him in this new friendship. Young readers may not grasp all this at once, but the details lay down a feeling tone that continues throughout the tale.

At their next meeting, Adam explains to David that he will have to go to live with cousins in Birmingham (the city, at this time, was still in post-war dreariness), unless something happens to restore the missing family treasure so that he can continue to live with his aunt in the house on the river. His dream is to find the treasure, and the only clue is a short ambiguous verse about its being 'over the water'. The boys take this to mean somewhere they could reach with the canoe, so they work hard to put it into working order.

We know they will be successful, but what lies ahead is a growing point for both of them. Although by this time, the treasure hunt had more or less been rejected as a cliché in children's stories, more is often at stake than money. Think of *The Treasure Seekers* and *Treasure Island*.

In life, as in stories, the young are acutely aware of the limitations and distress that result from the lack of money and the ease that seems to result from its availability. This theme has also run through adult and children's literature at all times. Dickens knew well how to make his readers pay in sympathy. Children nowadays see fortunes derived from chance, but they also know that they are not allowed by law to add to a family income until they are a certain age, or possess exceptional talents. The effects of poverty, real or imagined, are long lasting with children. In stories they are shown as indefatigable seekers after what is lost, if that's what the author wants. There is always some kind of reward. If the happy ending is in the reader's sight early in the tale, then the unravelling of the quest has to be exciting, challenging and unexpected.

David now has a new friend and a share in the canoe. He is happy to go along with Adam's plans for adventure. If Adam stays in the house on the river, they will both go to the same school in September. David's view of the future is changing; it will have new, different people in it. At first, he envies Adam's freedom. What he has to come to realize is that his mother's anxieties about boats and drowning are indications of her care. He is scolded for carelessness and what are seen as pranks, but this is part of learning to be responsible. Nor is his family a closed system; the parents are generous in their attention to the needs of others. The reader is expected to guess that David's father has paid for some of the expensive canoe varnish. He doesn't interfere with David's projects, but he is there as a strong presence. David never hears anyone say: 'I wish milk weren't so expensive', as Miss Codling does. When Mrs Moss asks Miss Codling if she may contribute a cake to the boys' tea, the acceptance seems to convey that Miss Codling is pleased to do Mrs Moss a favour. In fact, there is no money for cake at Codlings.

David's father remembers the heyday of the Codling family, then the melancholy details of the deaths of Adam's parents and the consequent decline of Adam's grandfather, who is still looking for the return of his son who was killed in the war. It is David's father, not Adam, who tells the tale of the hidden treasure. It is not a secret; everyone knows about it but no-one expects it to be found. In this conversation, David is being initiated into local knowledge, the habitus that Bourdieu says is important as the 'active presence of past experience', the things we take for granted and don't even have to mention.[24]

David has been explaining to his parents what happened when he fell in the river and came home late. They have listened in silence. Now the reader has to interpret both sides of this conversation:

> 'And did you see poor old Mr Codling?' asked his father.
> 'Yes,' said David.
> 'He's been queer in the head ever since his son died, long ago. Did he speak to you?'
> 'No.' David said no more.
> 'And they gave you a good tea,' said Mrs Moss. 'That was kind.'
> 'Especially as they're as poor as church mice,' said Mr Moss. 'They say you rarely meet Miss Codling about the village because she's ashamed of being dressed as she is.'
> 'She didn't seem ashamed of anything,' said David.
> 'Nor do I believe it,' said Mr Moss, quite severely. 'The Codlings have always lived in Great Barley, and never had anything to be ashamed of, for being poor isn't that.'[25]

Later, when Adam goes to tea with the Mosses, David is again aware of the social differences between them. Adam thanks Mr Moss for getting the varnish for the canoe. When David looks at Adam with his mother's eyes, he saw him 'looking exactly as . . . a boy should not look. How many times, as Mrs Moss tidied David in exasperation, had she told him she could not endure a boy with a dirty face, with dust in his hair, with a button missing off his shirt, and so on! All these Adam had — and more, for, invisibly to Mrs Moss as yet, his shirt was hanging out of his trousers at the back.'[26] Adam confidently offers Mrs Moss his hand. She hesitates, then on taking it, discovers that it has been seared by the reed and takes Adam off to bandage it. He returns with his hair combed and his shirt tucked in. When Adam eats a great deal at teatime, David first thinks he is greedy. His mother knows better. Adam is hungry.

The treasure hunt brings ever-increasing frustration, especially to Adam, who is wholly bound up in it emotionally. The boys have promised not to look for the treasure, but, as Adam points out, they are still free to go where they like in the canoe. At one point Adam discovers that his grandfather has already found the treasure and hidden it again, so as to keep it for his son's return. Miss Codling had seen it. The clue in the verse is a constant irritant. Also, there are strangers who show interest in what the boys are looking for.

Now David has to tolerate his friend's dark moods. Then, suddenly, old Mr Codling dies. When he sees Adam in the moonlight, returning from another useless search, he thinks it is his son come home. Thereafter the adults take over. Codlings is to be sold to the man in the punt, whom Adam has regarded as a villain but is in fact a distant relative. In a very short time, the boys are initiated into the business dealings of adults. Miss Codling's care for her status and lifestyle becomes more apparent. When the treasure is finally found, she insists that it had simply been 'mislaid', but her hysteria suggests something different. Adam is content that the search is over, but David really knows what happened. He has been watching carefully. That is what children are good at.

The most delicately worked contrast is between the beauty of the river, its quiet flow after the floods, the rural idyll of the passage of summer, and the fairly severe trials for the boys. Adults see their treasure hunt as children's play, storybook stuff, despite Adam's serious obsession, based on his longing to remain in the house by the river. When they become involved in adult business they are not really ready for, the boys are steered into another useless search. David's initial paddling upriver has the joy of his heart's desire, a rite of passage. But it is complicated by his borrowing his father's wheelbarrow end to be a paddle, without permission, then losing it. The real world doesn't create the conditions that coincide with wishes. David still has some growing to do, including the discovery that some adults do not play fair. By the end of the holidays he knows a great deal about people and their lives being different. When the treasure is found, he is worried lest the restoration of Adam's family fortunes might separate them again. The detailed observations of the scenes that enhance the reader's awareness of the thinking and feeling, which run under the action, are characteristic of all the stories that follow this one.

Why is it important to take so much trouble to detail what a young reader encounters in this text? Surely the beauty of the scenes, the boys' enthusiasm for the adventure and their growing friendship are ample signs of maturation for the readers to pick up at this stage. Indeed, but there is more to claim for the author's skill and insight.

A good example comes early on, as David paddles upstream on his first trip in the *Minnow*. The reader reads the scene to form a picture:

> The first that David saw of Great Barley was the spire of the parish church, poking above some distant trees. Then there were two people on the river-bank: a young man lying face upwards to the sun, fast asleep, and a girl – the girl from Great Barley post office – leaning against him as though he were a bolster. She was picking daisies and tossing them over her shoulder, sprinkling his body with white. She stopped when she saw David in the canoe, and laughed and called to him to beware of a very dangerous weir just round the bend. He thanked her and went on rather cautiously; but there was no weir round the corner; nor did he ever find later that there was any weir on the River Say in this part of the country.[27]

David is concerned about his paddling. What then, does the author offer in this scene, more than a glimpse of the river bank as he goes along? What is the latent sense?[28] Remember Philippa Pearce's lessons to the children about the economy of storytelling. David is still too young, too preoccupied, to interpret the scene of the two people who probably believed they wouldn't be seen. The implication of the daisies is not yet part of David's understanding. Then, the girl deflects him from what he might have thought, by warning him about a non-existent weir. Why should she do that, if not to take his attention away from any other interpretation of the scene by offering what seems to be serious advice?

Later, at the moment when, soon after their first meeting, Adam is about to tell David the story of the portrait of Jonathan Codling, his ancestor, it is quite clear that Miss Codling is unwilling that this should happen. She does everything she can to keep them apart until David goes home. Adam then seems to have changed his mind about telling him. 'They parted almost coldly.'[29] The latent sense of that is quite clear.

Although Adam seems the more likely leader of the pair, it is David who finally discovers what really happens to the treasure and tries to tell Miss Codling about it. But she deflects all his questions and, instead, tries to draw him in as a co-conspirator: 'Then never tell, Davy, never tell.'[30] Now there is a growing point that will echo in the memory.

Promise and the heart's desire: *A Dog So Small*

The opening pages of a Philippa Pearce novel are classic instances of narrative spellbinding, that certainty of tone and tread that keeps a reader reading. Here is Ben Blewitt, the middle child of a family that has two elder daughters and two younger sons. He is getting up on the morning of his birthday to go for a walk to fill in the time before the post comes. As he goes quietly through the house, the reader catches a glimpse of the interior, hears some details about a wedding, and knows, by the time Ben reaches the door that his siblings are Paul, Frankie, May and Dylis. The exact number of Ben's years isn't revealed, but young readers rarely miss the significance of each event on this special day. On a birthday, growth in time is declared, maturation is acknowledged. Some part of childhood is left behind.

Out in the 'pinky-yellow light' of a London dawn Ben walks through the streets to the river. He has been thinking about dogs, of all kinds, as he has been doing ever since his grandfather hinted that he might have a dog for his birthday present. Spoken from behind his gnarled hand, Grandpa's words were: 'what about a dog of your own boy – for your birthday, say, when that comes round?'[31] Ben's acceptance of his grandfather's suggestion had made it seem like a covenant, firm enough at least to encourage Ben believe it would happen, despite the lack of any mention of a dog in the weekly letters to his mother. Ben knows that a dog cannot arrive by post, but surely there would be some indication of its whereabouts.

As he makes his way to the river, Ben recalls in imagination all the splendid big dogs he has seen in library books: Alsatians, Great Danes, Mastiffs, Bloodhounds and the Dartmoor Hound of the Baskervilles. The author intersperses his daydreams with indications of life going on around him, as people come out to go to work. Ben scarcely sees them; he is caught up in his imaginary choice of a dog companion. He gazes over 'that amazing length and width of water, here in the heart of London'.[32]

The next paragraphs reveal the aching intensity of Ben's longing. This passage is at the heart of all that follows in the story, which is about Ben's loneliness and disappointment. All young readers know that a promise is a form of words that lays hold on the vague indeterminate future. Here, readers encounter the author's skill in matching words to the sheer depth and state of any child's feelings about a promise. It is worth careful reading to catch the power of the images.

> This is what he had come for. The expanse of the River reminded him conveniently of the enormous expanses of Russia, the home of the borzoi. At school Ben learnt about Russia – what Russians choose to eat for breakfast and what

agricultural implements and crops they use on which soils; he wasn't very much interested. His father read about Russia in the newspaper, and thumped the table as he read. Paul and Frankie read about Russian space travel. But Ben's Russia was different from all this. For one thing, his country was always under deep and dazzling snow. The land was a level and endless white, with here and there a dark forest where wolves crouched in the daytime, to come out at night, howling and ravening. For Ben, it was daytime in Russia. Sleighs had been driven out into the snow, and left. Each sleigh was covered with a white woollen blanket to match the snow. Beneath the blanket – but wait: already men on horseback were beating the nearby forest. Wolves came out. They were rushing past the sleighs. Men concealed in the sleighs threw back the blankets and, at the same time, unleashed their coupled borzoi dogs. Magnificent, magnificent beasts! They leapt forward after the wolves. The wolves were fast, but the borzois had greyhound bodies, their whole bodies were thin, delicately made, streamlined for speed. The wolves were fierce, but the borzois were brave and strong. They caught up with he wolves: one borzoi on each side of a wolf caught it and held it until the huntsman came up with his dagger –

At this point Ben always stopped, because, although you couldn't have wolves, he wasn't so keen on killing them either. Anyway, from the far side of the bridge the moon-face of Big Ben suddenly spoke to him and said half past seven. The wolf-hunt with borzois had taken a long time. Ben Blewitt turned back from the River to go home to breakfast.

He broke into a run as he realized that the morning post would have arrived.[33]

The details of the scene have probably been rehearsed and extended in Ben's imagination over and over again, while Big Ben time and the actual scene where he is on the bridge are not part of his attention. As readers emerge from the incident with the imaginary dogs, they know the powerful grip of the alternative world on this lonely boy, so that the ensuing disappointment is a great blow. Instead of a real dog, Ben's grandparents have sent him an embroidered picture of a Mexican chihuahua. The family tries to lessen his disappointment by telling him that it is difficult to keep a dog happy in London, but this only increases it, together with his sense of frustration at the betrayal of his hopes. He is on the point of refusing to visit his grandparents

ever again when he reads the postscript his grandfather has added to
the dictated words of his grandmother in the letter: 'TRULY SORY
ABOUT DOG.'[34] Ben changes his mind, and goes for a short stay in
the country with them, hoping to discover more about the dog in the
picture.

At this point it is important to see that this is not an action-based
narrative. Instead, it is a feelings-based one. Disappointment is one of
the most painful experiences of middle childhood, all the more so as
it is usually unexpected. Ben's grandparents have let him down.
Here, the feelings are 'searched', as with a wound, to the depths, so
that the reader's sympathetic understanding is engaged in a process of
maturation. Reflecting on Ben's feelings is both a personal and a
reading experience. Ben cannot have his heart's desire. As a result,
when he turns to his vivid imagination to supply the lack of a dog, he
begins to withdraw from the world of other people.

It is also tempting for adult readers to gloss Ben's feelings and
thoughts from a perspective of personal memories or in terms of
psychological criticism. The underlying complexity of the author's
text includes a showing of the relations of young and old. Ben's
family loves him very much, but from time to time they seem to pass
over his withdrawal in their preoccupations with other things. No
single interpretation of these events should detract from the skill of
the narration, which urges readers to sympathize with Ben, while
realizing that his self-absorption is also a failure to see 'the state of
things' as part of growing up.

Although Ben's grandparents are made to react differently to his
state of mind, they both want to help him to get over it. His
grandmother is a realist; dogs cost money to keep and need space to
run about. Grandpa wants Ben to have a dog, a little one that
wouldn't cost much nor take up much space. Ben, now away from
the rest of his family, fails to tell him the real reason why a little dog,
'not even a dog so small that you could only see it with your eyes
shut' wouldn't do.[35] He had been thinking of big dogs before the
parcel arrived. The dog in the picture could not fill the depth of his
longing.

Tilly, the grandparents' old dog, is some comfort. She and Ben go
for long walks together. There is a moving little vignette of the sort
that authors and readers enjoy. On one of their walks near a river,
Ben and Tilly are about to be caught in a thunderstorm. Ben sees a
canoe with two boys paddling fiercely to get home, a little girl and a
dog. Ben feels Tilly responding to the presence of the dog. He hears
the boy at the stern ask: 'What is it Toby?' From the way he spoke,

'Ben knew he must be the master of the dog. With a pang he knew it: the boy was not much older than he, he did not look much richer – even the canoe was old and shabby – but he lived in the country, where you could exercise a dog. So he had a dog.'[36] Later, Ben's grandfather tells Ben what the reader may already know. The boy is Adam Codling; the boy and girl are David and Betsy Moss from *Minnow on the Say*. The dog, Toby, is the father of the pups Tilly had when she was younger. Earlier we were told that the bus driver who brought Ben from the train was Bob Moss, David's father, also from the earlier tale. Spotting these 'echoes' is part of the reading game that authors play with readers, young and old, as part of their growth in reading.

On the evening of the storm, Ben reads to his grandmother, at her request, the Old Testament account of Noah's flood.

> ... She marvelled, without irreverence, at God's infinite mercy to those two, dog and bitch, who had boarded the Ark so that, long afterwards, there might be Tilly and Toby and all other dogs on the earth to-day. So her mind came into the present. 'And you really expected one of those on your birthday, Ben?'
>
> 'It was only – only that I thought Grandpa had promised ...'
>
> Ben's voice died away. Grandpa was looking at the floor between his feet; Granny was looking at Ben. She said: 'And a promise is a promise, as a covenant is a covenant: both to be kept. But, if you're not God Almighty, there's times when a promise can't be kept.' She looked at Grandpa: 'Times when a promise should never have been made, for that very reason.' Now she was looking neither at Ben nor at Grandpa, as she concluded: 'Even so, a promise that can't be kept should never be wriggled out of. It should never be kept twistily. That was wrong.'
>
> Granny in the wrong: that was where she had put herself. There was an appalled silence.[37]

This was the moment to talk about the little dog in the picture. Contrary to his intent to leave the picture with his grandparents, Ben takes it back to London. Before the train leaves, Ben and his grandfather talk about things better left alone, the big dogs, so the pain comes back. Grandpa is urging the case for a small dog. As the train is about to depart, Ben is trying to think 'how he could convince an obstinately hopeful old man'.[38] Grandpa doesn't hear Ben's sentence about 'not even a dog so small you can only see it with your eyes shut'.

This is exactly how Ben sees the little dog in the picture after he has looked at it in the train. The little dog becomes real to him. Just before he meets his family, in the jostle and haste of arrival, another passenger tramples the picture to pieces. A cleaner sweeps it away. Ben is again bereft. Days of useless inquiry follow. The dog so small is now real to him in his sleep and his dreams; his imagination blocks out the 'real' state of things. As long as he knew he was thinking of imaginary dogs, Ben was doing what we know we all do: thinking of two apparently contradictory things at the same time. Now he is in trouble.

Why don't Ben's parents help him? From the beginning of the story we know two reasons. First, families of five children are more pressurized than most by everyday events and especially preoccupied when planning occasions such as a wedding and the prospect of the whole family moving house. Also, the two sisters are close, as are the two younger boys. Ben's isolation is not obvious to those who see him as one of the family. His deep unconscious is well hidden. But he is also absent from what is going on around him. The climax comes when he is almost killed when he is crossing a road.

With poignant subtlety, Philippa Pearce makes it plain that Ben's maturation and an increase in self-knowledge do not depend on straightforward recovery from his injuries and his disappointment. His mother connects the accident with school reports. Why did Ben walk into the road with his eyes shut?

> ... He wanted to explain, but knew that he must not: his accident and May's wedding had been enough trouble to the family without reviving his old longing for a dog. And, unless he began speaking of that, he could never explain ...
>
> ... However, when she cried a little, in a kind of despair, he went so far as to tell her one thing clearly: it would never happen again. He promised. With this simple but absolute assurance, Mrs Blewitt had to allow herself to be satisfied.[39]

This is one of the great paradoxes of middle childhood: not telling because you know that an explanation will not explain what the hearer won't be able to understand.

Now Ben has a chance to have his heart's desire, a real dog, one of Tilly's last litter, a present promoted by Granny to keep the promise. 'All I hope is that he is not due for any disappointment,' she says.[40] The family has now moved to Hampstead, within reach of the Heath where dogs are tolerated. Ben sees the puppy in his grandfather's pigsty soon after it is born. When it is time to bring it to London,

Ben's mother, another realist, tells him that the puppy he saw would now be quite a big dog, as indeed it is. Ben is devastated that it isn't like the dog in the picture and won't respond to Ben's name for it. He hardly wants to bring it home. Ben's maturation crisis is not the event of finally getting the dog he longs for, but his ability to cope with a real dog, not the imaginary one. Granny is the philosopher. 'People get their heart's desire,' she said, 'and then they have to learn to live with it.'[41] This is Ben's hardest lesson; he learns it the hard way. Accept the dog as it is or it will really disappear.

> Then suddenly, when Ben could hardly see, he saw clearly. He saw clearly that you couldn't have impossible things, however much you wanted them. He saw that if you didn't have the possible things, then you had nothing.[42]

One of the hardest lessons to learn in growing up is that the future, or even the next day, may not turn out just as you want it to. Emotional maturity does not necessarily grow with reasoning; it has its own responses to events and to imaginative possibilities. At no point does Ben's creator relax her hold on the notion that children have to confront what adults see as the 'real' world. An escape into a secondary world of imagination and wishes, possible within a story, has to be reworked in terms of the everyday.

At the same time as Ben's creator is showing the dangers of his withdrawal, she is reminding other readers that they should not forget the power and depth of children's belief that adults can make wishes come true. A promise is a performative form of language, an act that children see as effectively bringing something about. 'That's how things are and I'm sorry for it,' says Ben's Granny. 'As she hated to wrap her meaning in politeness or irony or anything but its own truth, Ben knew she was truly sorry.'[43]

The landscape of the hero's inner world, so touchingly explored and pictured in this story, becomes a central feature in those that follow.

Household words: *The Battle of Bubble and Squeak*

Published in 1978, twenty years after *Tom's Midnight Garden*, this is a modern family story; modern in the sense that the characters, parents and three children live in a house on a council estate outside a village. There are vegetable gardens; people cycle or walk; some keep pigeons. Nearby is a neglected woodland where rubbish accumulates. The setting is neither rural nor urban. It represents the housing situation of growing numbers of families whose children, before this time, rarely found themselves in stories. Jan Mark's *Thunder and Lightnings* (1976) comes under the same rubric. The shining clarity of the text is skilfully created by words readers of the same age as the characters would recognize and use. Read aloud, the narrative engages even younger children. The book has an intensity of thought and feeling that usually comes as a surprise to adults.

The children in the story are Sid, Peggy and Amy Parker. We are told that their father died just after Amy was born. His widow, Alice, is now Mrs Sparrow. She and her husband Bill work in a local General Supply Company. Sid goes to secondary school by bus. Peggy is likely to follow him soon. Amy is in the infant class. The 'battle' is a not unusual household argument, initially between Sid and his mother, about keeping two gerbils as pets. Sid has been given the gerbils in their cage by a boy at school, Jimmy Dean's cousin, who has gone to Australia. He has been keeping them in the tool shed, but as the nights have grown colder, he has brought them indoors. Now their nocturnal movements have awakened the household. At three o'clock in the morning the conflict begins.

Alice Sparrow dislikes animals; they need looking after and they make a mess, as children do. After the first encounter with the gerbils, to calm down, she makes herself a cup of tea and remembers the children's father. 'No doubt, if he had lived, the house would have swarmed with cats, dogs, rabbits, guinea pigs, hamsters, budgerigars, and canaries in yellow clouds. What would *she* have been like then? Alice drank her tea slowly and thought all kinds of things.'[44] The careful reader may note that she has also admitted that gerbils don't smell and that they don't really look like rats. 'Their tails were furry for one thing.'[45]

When Sid resists having to take the gerbils back to the pet shop the next morning, his mother says she will. Anything to get rid of 'these rats'. But it is her husband who sets off with them. However, when Alice returns from work the gerbils are still there. The pet shop doesn't want them, but the girls love them, especially Peggy, who discovers how to distinguish them and gives them names. Amy delights in them as live playmates. Sid is less demonstrative, but he is conscientious about their care. Alice remains determined to get rid of them. When they gnaw holes in her best scarlet curtains, her mistrust seems justified. Sid pleads with her; he will buy new curtains with his savings, but to no avail.

'No,' said his mother. 'I'm not thinking of the curtains now.'
'But, Mum listen —'

'No', said his mother, 'no, no, NO! Not another day in this house, if I can help it! They go!'

'But, Mum –'

'THEY GO!'

She would listen to no more from any of them.[46]

When Sid discovers the next evening that his mother has given the gerbils away to two small boys who called in response to a notice she had put in the newsagent's, he rushes from the house, taking with him his father's pruning knife. He wants to separate himself from his mother who is afraid of animals. Later, when his absence causes concern, his stepfather finds him in the woodland, which Peggy's friend, Dawn Mudd, described as 'somewhere to feel awful in'.[47] There is a nasty moment with the knife. Then Bill tells Sid that he hadn't really offered the gerbils to the pet shop but had brought them back home. Now that they've been given to the boys, perhaps Bill and Sid can persuade Alice to let them have two more.

'You mean, in spite of Mum? Against Mum?'

'She'd have to be talked round.'

'And who'd do that?'

'Well, I'd try.'

'Why?'

'I'm –' Bill Sparrow hesitated. 'I'm your stepfather. And, when I was you age, I had white mice.'[48]

Bill offers to put away the pruning knife Sid has been using to hack his way though the dreary bushes. Sid can then ride Bill's bike to get quickly home to reassure his mother. Sid and Bill are now allies.

The mother of the two little boys, unpleasantly polite, gives the gerbils back to Alice, who then has to witness Bill joining in the shared pleasure of their return. In desperation, Alice leaves the gerbils on top of the dustbin. Amy catches sight of the great maw of the collecting machine as the dustman hands the cage back to Alice with 'there's something alive in here'.[49] Amy's frantic despair makes her mother promise that she won't ever send Bubble and Squeak away. Peggy, calmer than the rest, suggests that the pets should stay with Dawn Mudd's more tolerant, easy-going family for a while, 'till Mum gets used to the idea of having them'.[50] Sid agrees. Peggy and Dawn discuss fathers.

Nothing goes easily; every hazard that could threaten the gerbils does so. On their return from the Mudd holiday, one goes missing. Sid stays away from school until he finds it. The next-door cat,

Ginger, is aware of the pets and drawn to the house whenever he is outside. Inevitably, he sneaks in and attacks the cage, knocking it to the floor. In the consequent flurry, Mrs Sparrow is the heroine. She saves Bubble from being mauled by Ginger. But next morning the gerbil is clearly very ill. When Sid and Peggy take him to the vet by bus, Peggy's thoughts are of the kind that occur at times of crisis:

> Perhaps when I'm old, I shall remember this bus ride. Then she thought that, when she was old, Bubble would be long dead, anyway. Tears of hopelessness rolled down her cheeks.[51]

The children sense that Bubble may die, as their father did. The vet says there is a chance: antibiotic injections three times a day for a week. 'The tricky part will be getting him to take it.'[52] When the injections are too much for Peggy, Mrs Sparrow, who has never touched one of the gerbils before, succeeds. Just as the treatment is clearly taking effect, Jimmy Dean's cousin appears at the door. Australia 'didn't suit'. Amy persuades him to have two new gerbils and 'let them have babies'.

> 'Jimmy Dean's cousin was very much taken with the idea. 'But I don't know what my mum and dad would say,' he said.
> 'Pooh!' said Mrs Sparrow. 'They'll just have to put up with it, won't they?'[53]

Over many years I've read this story with children and adults of various ages. The drama of risks and rescues in the life of the gerbils is instantly gratifying. Genuine fear for their fate is balanced by the satisfaction of their recovery. Is Mrs Sparrow a good mother? Does the evidence of her care for her children count against her hatred of animals, or is it the mess that she minded most? Does she see the gerbils as children? What do we make of her question about how old gerbils are when they die? Will there be more children? Bill is appreciated for his generosity and his attempts to put things right. He has to work against the force of the absence of the missing father. He succeeds with Amy who has no memory of her natural father. One of Philippa Pearce's quiet triumphs is her weaving of a latent sense of the missing father right through the story.

There are other distinctions. For example, the children confront their mother, expecting her to be compliant with their deepest desires only to discover that she has become equally implacable in her self-regard. Readers learn to see and feel the characters from the inside, sharing the author's insight. They also discover clues that the author has left for them, something they know that the characters do not do. Peggy tells Dawn Mudd that she remembers how her father gave her his finger to hold, instead of his hand. We already know that Bill does this for Amy. As well as being contributions to a subtle narrative that includes a strong view of the importance of children's imaginative play, these are reading experiences.

In terms of children's growth, we see the protagonists coming to terms with themselves and each other. Gradually they go beyond the wounding words of the arguments. The dialogic presentation of fury, dismay, fear and rejection gives an immediacy to these sensations, which, in retrospect, become a literary understanding of 'getting used to' what may not change. Growth is not something that happens as the direct result of literary encounters. It is more visible as change, something we have to look back on to realize its significance. The children here are presented as unable to grasp the idea that, by standing up to their mother, they are actually helping her. This has to be part of the readers' understanding. Amy shows how this works. Her mother has great difficulty in consoling her after the terrifying incident of the dustbin.

> 'Amy,' her mother said. 'Listen. Listen. Amy. I didn't mean them to go into the van. Truly. I put them on top of the dustbin, not inside. I thought one of the dustbin-men might have a little girl that likes gerbils.'
> Amy wailed: 'I'm a little girl that likes gerbils! I love Bubble and Squeak!'[54]

Gillian Avery says, in her discussion of family stories in *The International Companion Encyclopedia of Children's Literature*: 'Fashion has now made it difficult to write unself-consciously about happy families.'[55] From the complexities of this short but outstanding book we may see how much there is to learn about the children's views of family life. Margaret and Michael Rustin have included *The Battle of Bubble and Squeak* in their profound study of modern authors of children's fiction who show particular sensitivity to children's feelings. Their judgement is:

> 'The author has succeeded in finding a metaphor for an intense experience of conflict and development within a family, in terms which remain wholly within the understanding of young children.'[56]

It is likely, in the course of these discussions, that I shall say more than once that in children's lives, reality and narrative fictions of different kinds are very close together. Adults who read *The Battle of*

Bubble and Squeak are likely to know more than most, but not all, children about 'putting up with things'. The story shows an earlier stage, when children are discovering how to come to terms with the conditions that adults have secured and arranged for them, and also, as Sid does with his gerbils, 'restricting them as best they can'.

Secrets: *The Way to Sattin Shore*

Children discover the nature of secrets when their friends or the adults round about them lower their voices to whisper. In these conversations the words don't seem to come out in the same way as in ordinary speech. Young listeners try to make sense of what they overhear because it often seems to be important, so they stretch their partial understanding into some kind of coherence. Often they make mistakes about the details. These can lead to misunderstandings that the listeners perpetuate, as in the game of Chinese Whispers. But the feeling tones of these communications are rarely mistaken, especially when they convey anxiety, threat or worse. Most families have unspoken agreements about what the elders don't discuss in front of the children. Henry James made much of this in *What Maisie Knew*. Being 'in the know' is a sign of growth.

Intellectual and emotional development is bound up with ways of learning, coming to know. The intellectual approach to ignorance is thinking. The emotional part of it may be worry, especially when children are not sure what it is they don't know. But they rarely mistake the tonal quality of secrets. For a long time in childhood, thinking and feeling are difficult to separate. This is the ground of *The Way to Sattin Shore*, a novel published in 1983, the year of Cynthia Voigt's *Homecoming*.

The complicated plot depends on concealment and discovery. An outline isn't enough to reveal the depth and strength of the narrative in relation to the inner life of its central character, Kate Tranter. See how the author makes sure, in the very first paragraph, that we follow her closely.

> Here is Kate Tranter coming home from school in the January dusk – the first to come, because she is the youngest of her family. Past the churchyard. Past the shops. Along the fronts of the tall, narrow terrace houses she goes. Not this one, nor this one, nor this ...
>
> Stop at the house with no lit window.
> This is home.
> Up three steps to the front door, and feel for the key on the

string in her pocket. Unlock, and then in. Stand just inside the door with the door now closed, at her back.

Stand so, in the hall. Ahead, to the right, the stairs. Ahead, to the left, the passage to the kitchen: in the wider part, by the back door, a round, red, friendly eye has seen her – the reflector of her bicycle.

To the left of the hall, Granny's room.

Kate Tranter took a slow breath. She made herself ready to start across the floor to the stairs – to cross the dark beam that came from her grandmother's room through the gap where her grandmother's door stood ajar.

On a weekday, at this time, her grandmother's eyes were always turned to that door, as she sat in her room by the window. Her eyes looked out through the crack of the door, on the watch for whoever came in, whoever went out. Whoever came in must cross her line of vision to go down the passage to the kitchen, or to go upstairs. Whoever went out was seen, noted.[57]

The pace of this narration is that of Kate's walk, organized by the punctuation and the length of the sentences. The present tense, generally used in children's stories to bring the action into focus for the reader, makes certain that we see her concentrating on getting into the house then safely upstairs. Her grandmother doesn't greet her, but Kate knows she is anticipating her every move. When her mother and her brother Lenny arrive, they go directly to their quarters, Lenny to his room, Mrs Tranter to the kitchen. Kate's elder brother, Randall, has begun to spend much of his time away from home. Unlike his siblings, he is old enough to remember his father.

The beam of darkness is the symbol of secrecy and shadows that pervade the house. Behind routines of meals, school, work and visits from the children's friends is the evasive silence of the adults about something important. From her bedroom window Kate can see the churchyard where her grandfather is buried and his son's death is also recorded as the day Kate was born. Kate has been told that her father died by drowning.

There are hints for the reader that some things create unease. On an occasion when her brothers fight, not playfully, Kate hears her grandmother say: 'Quarrelling – fighting: they inherit it ...'[58] She watches Lenny, as he looks out at the falling snow, hoping it will last till the weekend.

'What then?' asked Kate.

Lenny did not answer, but he smiled and narrowed his eyes,

seeing from between narrowed lids visions of snowy delight, pure Paradises of snow. Watching his face, Kate knew what he saw, although she could not see it for herself.[59]

During the Saturday of the great snow, the family seems to be more at ease. This interlude is one of the beautifully imaged incidents that are the hallmark of Pearce writing. Kate admires, and envies, the toboggan Lenny and his friend Brian have made with the help of Brian's father. She realizes that it is a father she lacks.

When, later, she takes her friend Anna to see the family grave in the churchyard, the tombstone with her birth-date on it has disappeared. She decides she cannot ask her grandmother or her mother for an explanation. When she approaches Randall he becomes fierce with her, but he admits that he remembers their earlier life at Sattin Shore, where their father was the schoolmaster. Kate continues to work things out: by thinking she had at least managed to calm herself. 'By thinking, she had made herself better able to think.' But, in the time that followed, Kate sometimes said to herself: 'I shouldn't have to think as hard as this – not *think* – at my age.'[60] One of the puzzles was about names. She realizes that it was their Uncle Bob, not her father, who was buried in the churchyard.

Why doesn't Kate ask her mother to explain things she wants to know? Somehow, the time is never right, especially when her grandmother is present. In a kitchen scene, Kate and her grandmother watch Mrs Tranter making pastry.

> Rub-rub-rub scatter-scatter-scatter *dip* rub-rub-rub scatter-scatter-scatter *dip* rub-rub-rub –
> 'Mum!' said Kate.
> 'Yes?' Mrs Tranter looked up from her rubbing. Old Mrs Randall also looked at Kate.
> 'Nothing,' said Kate.
> Rub-rub-rub –[61]

The scene continues until Kate pretends she is looking for her cat, Syrup, a strong presence in the story, and excuses herself.

> At that moment of disappointment – a kind of explosive despair – the idea came into Kate's head that she should visit Sattin Shore.[62]

She cycles there, a long ride, alone. Quizzed on her return by her mother as to what she saw and whom she met, she is forbidden to return.

'But, Mum, why not?'

'Never you mind why not!' And Mrs Tranter turned on her heel to march out of the bedroom.

Such a departure takes only a few short seconds; but Kate had time to feel a long despair. She felt it here and now; and it seemed always to have been lying in wait for her; and she saw it ahead of her, stretching before her like a long, long road, like the rest of her life . . .[63]

These are the marking moments. There is no way of avoiding or turning back from what they reveal.

In another tense scene, Kate believes she has seen her father's ghost in her mirror. She is scanning her image to see if she can trace the likeness of him that others say she carries.

. . . The eyes of a stranger looked at her from over her shoulder, from the dim depths of the mirror.

Then a breeze blew, and the window curtain flapped, the door swung back on to its door frame and clicked and was shut.

The eyes were gone.[64]

The reader is now in the know, and will watch to see how Kate discovers that this was no ghost.

Later, Randall fulfils his promise to take Kate for a bicycle ride. She meets her other grandmother. The story unwinds. On her third visit to Sattin Shore, again alone, she meets her father when he least expects to see her. The puzzle finally fits together. But the adults do not escape implied criticism for their attempts to rearrange the past and its transgressions.

Although appreciative of this story in its skilled narration, critics have not been entirely at ease with its depths. If the reader is shadowing Kate with a feeling of protection, her solitariness, her lack of intimacy with anyone in the dark-beamed house except her cat, may not be so obvious as they become at the end, when her parents decide to go as far away from it as they can. Kate's painful growing point offsets the lack of insight in the adults, whose secretive selfishness is at the root of their troubles. Kate faces the future knowing that those closest to her have told stories of the past that they learned to tell so as to be able to live with it. Readers are to understand that there is a darker side to coming to know.

Dreams – and Responsibilities: *Tom's Midnight Garden*

If, as sometimes happens, those professionally involved in children's literature are asked to name a book that typifies their attachment to this kind of writing and reading, the chances are that *Tom's Midnight Garden* will be one of those chosen to represent 'the best'. Since its publication in 1958 it has been acknowledged in canonical judgements as a classic. Children who read it, or hear it read, become engaged in the story in ways that confirm and extend their understanding of themselves and others.

A brief glance at studies of children's books since 1960 confirms the general appreciation of *Tom's Midnight Garden* in both the USA and the UK. Writing in 1995, Roy Stokes says 'my mind kept harking back to one book, which, ever since its publication, I felt assured would endure. Hundreds of books have been written regarding the adroitness of a small boy or girl who is sent away from home to avoid the illness of a sibling – usually measles. Ostensibly Philippa Pearce's *Tom's Midnight Garden* is another run at the same theme. But what transforms it immediately is the style of the writing.'[65]

Ted Hughes said that children grasp a story as 'a unit of imagination' and take possession of it, so that it lingers in the memory of the reader as a virtual event.[66] Returning to it to recapture the feeling of the tale, the reader goes beyond the discovery of 'what happens next' to an understanding of the nature of the satisfaction and 'how the author does it'. The characters captivate younger readers, who admire Tom's daring to creep into the garden to have midnight adventures. Those who come to the book in their early teens become involved in the personal relationships. Discerning adults have continued to admire it for its unique, universal view of childhood. This is the place and time that children inhabit and know a great deal about. It also provides the memories that adults edit to live with.

Margery Fisher, the most percipient and discerning of Philippa Pearce's critics, observed that 'it is interesting to know why an author has tracked back to his (sic, written in 1961) childhood, but it is more important to examine how he does it and what he makes of the journey'.[67] Her account of this novel is probably its best tribute. It is fairly well-known that the setting of the story, the garden, was a significant place for the author in her childhood. As she recalls it, she gives her readers a place to be more themselves. They believe that the garden is real because the writer makes it real.

For readers of children's books in Margery Fisher's generation, and mine – adults in the 50s before the next great flowering two decades later – *Tom's Midnight Garden* had special relevance. It made children's books important. Its very material presence in publishing by Oxford University Press, with Susan Einzig's fine illustrations drawn from family photographs, carried implicit assertions about quality and literary value. This gave encouragement to other writers and artists whose work was often diminished by unrefined criticism and condescension. In fact, adults had yet to learn to read this kind of text with matching insight and understanding.

Here then is the creation of a skilful, practised storyteller, well schooled in the history and texts of her predecessors; a sprightly intellect whose engagement with childhood is mature enough to confront the depth of children's emotions and the philosophical complexities of their gradual understanding of themselves in their search for personal identity. Painful as that may be in matters of love and loss, the story is hopeful, enthralling and brilliantly told. Because the book is closely related in many ways to the author's family home and its familiar landscape, we see her rewriting the text of parts of her life in the text of the book, not as autobiography, but so that her readers can begin to see how to do that for themselves.

In the longer history of children's books in England, gardens proliferate as arcadian metaphors of growth, play, space, freedom of movement and 'natural' child development in safety. Tom's discovery of the garden is the result of his being separated from his brother who has measles. (This is a narrative device, but the disease was still grave enough for quarantine precautions to be common.) They had made plans to build a tree-house in the holidays, so Tom feels doubly deprived and lonely when the apartment he goes to, part of a converted, large old house, has only a backyard. His childless uncle and aunt want to give him a good time in his enforced stay, but they have no inventive proposals for that, apart from giving him exotic food. When his uncle explains to him that he must stay in bed from after supper until breakfast, his tone is more formal than Tom is used to, reminiscent perhaps of his uncle's own childhood. For Tom, the problem is how to be at ease with people whose lives are different from his.

His learning begins after midnight. When he hears the erratic grandfather clock, in the hallway chime thirteen times, he decides that he has an extra hour to explore the rest of the building and outside where, he had been told, there was 'A sort of back-yard, very poky, with rubbish bins. Really, there's nothing to see.'

> Nothing ... Only this: a great lawn where flower beds bloomed; a towering fir-tree, and thick, beetle-browed yews that humped their shapes down two sides of the lawn; on the

third side, to the right, a greenhouse almost the size of a real house; from each corner of the lawn, a path that twisted away to some other depths of garden, with other trees.[68]

The author makes sure that her readers see the garden as Tom sees it. This is where he wants to be, more than anywhere else. After he meets Hatty, a lonely orphan, who lives in the house with her older cousins, dependent on the charity of her sour, ungenerous aunt, Tom wants to spend as much time as possible with her in the garden, exploring its secret places, climbing, taking risks and talking. They are not always careful. When the geese follow them into a part of the garden where they shouldn't be, Hatty has to take the blame. Tom is invisible to everyone but Hatty and Abel the gardener. Abel thinks that Tom is an emanation of the devil.

Hatty sees Tom as a new friend in her Victorian time. Tom believes he is part of Hatty's time scheme until it is clear that Hatty's appearances in the garden are not sequential. On one occasion Tom sees Hatty as a little girl, crying on the death of her parents, then she is clearly growing faster than he is. He examines his ideas of the Past. It is a particular growing point.

> Tom was thinking about the Past, that Time made so far away. Time had taken this Present of Hatty's and turned it into his Past. Yet even so, here and now, for a little while, this was somehow made *his* Present too – his and Hatty's. Then he remembered the grandfather clock, that measured out both his time and Hatty's, and he remembered the picture on the face.
> 'Hatty, what does the picture on the grandfather clock mean?'
> 'It's something from the Bible.'[69]

The words on the clock are: 'Time No Longer'. They find them in Abel's Bible, in the Book of Revelation. Hatty is growing up. Tom begins to realize that he wants to stay in the garden, for it is real to him in a way he suspects it isn't for Hatty. He wants both things at once: to stay in the garden and to grow up. This is the central conflict of growing more self aware.

Throughout the story Tom is trying to work out the greatest puzzle of all: Time. His uncle tries to answer his question: 'What is time?' with abstract examples, without success. When Tom sees time from Hatty's point of view, his understanding increases: 'She might step forward into my Time, which would seem the Future to her, although to me it seems the Present.'[70] He will have memories of

Hatty when he is grown up. He is beginning to realize that the Future contains the Past. When he writes to his brother to tell him about the midnight garden and what happens there, he records, in present time, what happens out of time. This is narrative time; it serves storytelling and memories.

Before the story ends, Hatty and Tom have one extraordinary day in the Past as Present. Throughout the story, as in *Minnow on the Say*, the river flows quietly on, the ever-rolling stream of time. Now it freezes. Hatty leaves the house and garden on her own for the first time and they skate together across the Fens. Although Tom is with her, Hatty appears to be skating on her own. Tom has decided that, after this, he will go back to the garden and stay there. He will exchange Time for Eternity. He wants to tell Hatty so, but the day is so full of events, and their difficulties on their return journey from Ely, where they climbed the tower of the Cathedral, so complicated, that he doesn't. Instead, as he sees Hatty growing ever more faint, fading into her surroundings, he realizes that she sees him less and less. She now looks only at her cousins' friend, Barty.

The end of the book is superb. It sometimes comes as a shock to younger readers who have not anticipated the ending of Tom's childhood, his growing independence and the increasing complexity of what he is thinking about. Tom now has to go back home in 'real' time; the conventional ending of 'time travel' tales. Worse, he can no longer enter the garden; it is a backyard. This causes him great distress. He wakens the neighbours with his crying and has to apologize the next morning to old Mrs Bartholomew, the owner of the house and the landlady. She tells him that he called her in the night. She is Hatty. They have been meeting where their dreams crossed. There is no real time in dreams. 'Mrs Bartholomew had gone back in Time to when she was a girl, wanting to play in the garden; and Tom had been able to go back with her, to that same garden.'[71]

That could have been the end. Instead, the narrator shifts the viewpoint to Tom's Aunt Gwen, who, throughout, has been more insightful and imaginative than her husband. She tells him how Tom, on his way downstairs, raced back up again.

> 'There was something else, too, Alan, although I know you'll say it sounds even more absurd ... Of course, Mrs Bartholomew's such a shrunken little old woman, she's hardly bigger than Tom, anyway: but, you know, he put his arms right round her and he hugged her goodbye as if she were a little girl.'[72]

However many stories there are about the end of innocence and the beginning of responsibility and independence after childhood, this one still stands out. In reading it once more, in the context of the acclaim for current 'other' or 'parallel' world stories for children in later childhood, I confess I am unwilling to think of *Tom's Midnight Garden* as an example of literary fantasy, and to leave it there. For one thing, the actual relations of old and young have rarely been more subtly done. Most clearly, this creation demonstrates what a skilled writer can make for young readers with words, pictures and imagination: a story of outer and inner worlds of the kind all children are the better for, especially at the spots of time when these worlds are changing fast.

Universal praise for this novel confirms its status as one of the most outstanding books for children of all time in any language. Commentators continue to discuss its appeal to readers of all ages, tracing its filaments through the tradition of writing for the young and their own recollections of childhood. They have found in it the story of the Garden of Eden; the balance of *kairos* and *chronos*,[73] and other significances of love and loss.[74] Having read praise and appreciative interpretations of the novel over the years I have selected the statement that confirms my thoughts and feelings about it in the context of this book, where the central topic is children's growth in feeling and understanding. Here is Neil Philip:

'It is a book about time, innocence, experience, redemption. Yet it is triumphantly what it sets out to be, a book for children. The treatment of these themes makes it so, for the mystery at the heart of the text is that the relationship of Hatty and Tom is the same as that between the author and the reader.[75]

In the part of our culture that we reserve for thinking about children and childhood, the continuing presence of writers who value the very transience of this period of dependence is absolutely imperative. If it is the case that 'Culture signifies a link between a specific civilisation and a universal humanity,'[76] Philippa Pearce, a writer who has devoted her life and art to children's literature, is a significant example of this link.

Endnotes

1. L. S. Vygotsky (1978), *Mind in Society*, Harvard University Press, p. 102.
2. James Britton, 'The Third Area, Where we are More Ourselves' in Margaret Meek, Aidan Warlow and Griselda Barton (eds) (1977), *The Cool Web: the Pattern of Children's Reading*, The Bodley Head, pp. 40–7.
3. This is the first story in *The Rope and Other Stories*, (2000), illustrated by Annabel Large, Puffin Books. It first appeared in *The Fiction Magazine* vol. 5, no. 5, July 1986.
4. Ibid., p. 10.
5. Ibid., p. 11.
6. Ibid., p. 14.
7. Ibid., p. 7.
8. Ibid., p. 41.
9. John Goldthwaite (1996), *The Natural History of Make-Believe: A Guide to the Principal Works of Britain, Europe and America*, Oxford University Press.
10. Jacqueline Rose (1984), *The Case of Peter Pan: or the Impossibility of Children's Fiction*, Macmillan, p. 1.
11. Brian Fairfax-Lucy, *The Back Stairs*, unpublished manuscript.
12. Philippa Pearce (1989), *The Children of Charlecote*, Oxford Children's Modern Classics, p. 3.
13. Ibid., p. 28.
14. Ibid., p. 93.
15. Ibid., p. 92.
16. Ibid., p. 92.
17. Ibid., p. 93.
18. Ibid., p. 94.
19. See entry by Mary Nathan in Victor Watson (ed.) (2001), *The Cambridge Guide to Children's Books in English*, Cambridge University Press, pp. 547–8.
20. Philippa Pearce (1955), *Minnow on the Say*, Oxford University Press.
21. Ibid. p. 20.
22. The Mill is a place of special significance for the author. Her father was a miller and she still lives in the village of her childhood. Less well known, perhaps, is the historical significance of the mill; apart from its recurrence in folk tales, and in Chaucer's Tale.
23. *Minnow on the Say*, p. 25.
24. See Pierre Bourdieu (1977), *Outline of a Theory of Practice,* Cambridge University Press.
25. *Minnow on the Say*, pp. 33–4.
26. Ibid., p. 73.
27. Ibid., pp. 19–20.
28. This idea is borrowed from Frank Kermode (1979) *The Genesis of Secrecy; on the Interpretation of Narrative*, Harvard University Press.
29. *Minnow on the Say*, p. 45.

30. Ibid., p. 252.
31. Philippa Pearce (1962), *A Dog So Small*, Puffin, (illus. by Anthony Maitlow (1964), p. 9.
32. Ibid., p. 12.
33. Ibid., pp. 12–13.
34. Ibid., p. 23.
35. Ibid., p. 59.
36. Ibid., p. 44.
37. Ibid., pp. 51–2.
38. Ibid., p. 58.
39. Ibid., pp. 104–5.
40. Ibid., p. 142.
41. Ibid., p. 152.
42. Ibid., p. 155.
43. Ibid., pp. 124–5.
44. Philippa Pearce (1978), *The Battle of Bubble and Squeak*, Andre Deutsch, Puffin (1980), p. 16.
45. Ibid., p. 16.
46. Ibid., p. 31.
47. Ibid., p. 39.
48. Ibid., p. 44.
49. Ibid., p. 48.
50. Ibid., p. 53.
51. Ibid., p. 81.
52. Ibid., p. 83.
53. Ibid., p. 91.
54. Ibid., p. 50.
55. Gillian Avery in Peter Hunt (ed.) (1996), *The International Encyclopedia of Children's Literature*, Routledge, p. 342.
56. Margaret and Michael Rustin (revised edition, 2001), *Narratives of Love and Loss: Studies in Modern Children's Fiction*, Karnac Books, p. 145.
57. Philippa Pearce (1983), *The Way to Sattin Shore*, illus. by Charlotte Voake, Puffin, pp. 7–8.
58. Ibid., p. 27.
59. Ibid., p. 29.
60. Ibid., pp. 56, 59.
61. Ibid., pp. 64–5.
62. Ibid., p. 55.
63. Ibid., p. 81.
64. Ibid., p. 95.
65. Roy Stokes (1996) 'Fn de Siecle,' in Sheila A. Egoff (ed.) (3rd edition), *Only Correct*, Oxford University Press.
66. Ted Hughes, 'Myth and Education', *Children's Literature in Education* (March, 1970), reprinted in Geoff Fox *et al.* (eds) (1976), *Writers, Critics and Children*, Heinemann Educational Books, p. 80.

67. Margery Fisher (1964), *Intent Upon Reading*, Hodder, p. 16.
68. Philippa Pearce (1976), *Tom's Midnight Garden*, Illus. by Susan Einzig, Puffin, p. 24.
69. Ibid., p. 143.
70. Ibid., p. 165.
71. Ibid., p. 215.
72. Ibid., p. 218.
73. Maria Nikolajeva (2000), *From Mythic to Linear: Time in Children's Literature*, Scarecrow Press Inc., pp. 103–8
74. Narratives of Love and Loss: Studies in Modern Children's Fiction, pp. 27–40.
75. Neil Philip, '*Tom's Midnight Garden* and the Vision of Eden', in *Signal*, Vol. 37, January 1982, pp. 21–5.
76. Terry Eagleton (2000), *The Idea of Culture*, Blackwell, p. 54.

CHAPTER 3

The *Tillerman* series

Victor Watson

Series fiction and the growth of character

A series of novels provides a writer with space, amplitude and extended opportunities for representing the development of character. If the protagonists are young people emerging from childhood into adulthood, one might expect maturation to be a predominant theme, providing a narrative structure and a fictional process, determined largely by key rites of passage and appropriate moments of inner revelation.

However, nothing is quite what it seems in these seven novels. The *Tillerman* series undoubtedly represents characters who mature as their lives proceed, but the usual authorial ways of doing this are stubbornly avoided and the clichés of fictional maturation challenged at every point.

It is salutary to consider what the novels do *not* deal with: there is no sex (love is there, especially between Jeff and Dicey, but characteristically undemonstrative); there is no overt interest in religious faith (except, in passing, with Mina); and there is no psychological analysis. Although the consequences of parenting are everywhere present, the narratives are pre-Freudian. This is surprising, since six of the seven novels are everywhere concerned with the consequences of absent or inadequate parents; and also because it could be argued that (certainly for many other writers) the sharpest indicators of maturation in fiction are sex, religious faith and psychological awareness, providing narrative programmes enabling an author to chart maturation into adult life. Even the more outward signs of Dicey's physical maturation are dealt with only briefly, almost perfunctorily. In fact, the narrative seems almost to be irritated by having to pay any attention at all to such self-evident facts of life: Dicey feels 'tricked' into having to wear a bra and 'go around feeling like a dog with a collar on'.[1] Mina Smiths' maturing body is, on the other hand, of central significance in *Come A Stranger* – but it is not primarily an issue of sexuality but of race. Mina can joke about her physical precociousness but, despite her laughter, her strong and highly co-ordinated body has been a problem throughout her adolescence – but only because white people see it as one.

Wolfgang Iser has pointed out that 'the most effective literary work is one which forces the reader into a new critical awareness of his or her customary codes and expectations'.[2] It is not clear what Iser means by 'effective' and I do not believe a reader can be 'forced' into anything. But his comment does provide a way of understanding Cynthia Voigt's highly complex achievement in the *Tillerman* novels. This series works by resisting or undermining fictional norms and challenging readers' expectations. For example, another traditional way of representing maturation is to take protagonists through their changing perceptions of their parents, often involving a sense of loss as well as a wisdom (or bitterness) gained. This theme – under the powerful influence of Holden Caulfield in *The Catcher in the Rye* – has been especially potent in American fiction. It is rarely far from the surface in the novels of Betsy Byars and, in the work of Paul Zindel, becomes a raw adolescent angst, sometimes comic but often bitter and angry, saved only by the self-mockery of the main sufferer. But in the *Tillerman* series there can be no confrontation between the generations because the parents are not there. Indeed, Voigt has transformed this rather threadbare theme by making both parents into an *absence* – everywhere felt but nowhere known.

The series comprises seven novels, the first published in the USA in 1981 and the rest issued at roughly yearly intervals until 1989. They are not a straightforward family chronicle: the first two follow the adventures of the four Tillerman children as they seek a new home and eventually settle in it with their grandmother. The third, *A Solitary Blue*, introduces a new character, quite unrelated to the Tillermans until he meets Dicey about two-thirds of the way through. *The Runner* returns to the Tillerman family, but a generation earlier; it is an historical novel set in the 1960s. The fifth in the series moves to yet another central protagonist, Mina Smiths, though the link with the Tillermans is again eventually established when Mina befriends Dicey at school, picking up on an episode from *Dicey's Song*.[3] *Sons From Afar* returns to the Tillerman family, focusing upon Dicey's younger brothers, and the last novel, *Seventeen Against the Dealer*, completes the series by locating itself almost totally in Dicey's mind.

The sequence outwits the serial nature of series fiction. Despite the linearity of narrative, the *Tillerman* series is circular, expansive and inclusive. Its authorial attention circles around a particular group of people, back in time, and out into other families and communities. But Dicey remains the centre; the series begins with her and returns to her at the end.

In *Homecoming* (1981) the reader is placed alongside Dicey, viewing and understanding the USA through Dicey's developing perceptions. This is a road novel, in which the growth of the traveller is inseparable from the road travelled. Here, movement does not always mean progress but it does always involve meetings with strange people – eccentric, kind, wicked or violent. Dicey's maturation is not simply a matter of observing these people and learning lessons about the USA; she is forced to *become* the USA – capitalist, opportunistic, courageous, worried and sharp witted, a pragmatist defining her family group against the difficulties of survival. Already the attentive reader is being invited to refine popular notions of maturation: the growth of the character is inseparable from the way the community is perceived and lived in; it does not only take place *within* the community but on its terms. The entire *Tillerman* series can be seen as a sustained analysis of the effects of the 'American Dream' as it exerts its shaping power over the tenderest and most private parts of the human psyche.

Journeying has a special significance in the American novel and fictional groups of pioneering travellers seeking to find somewhere to settle have an honoured place in its history. The road novel becomes a novel not only of American life but also of the pioneering psyche – the willingness to travel to uncertain destinations, to tolerate arrival as an ambiguous and insecure achievement, and to expect further demands if survival is to be achieved. *Homecoming* is also a sailing novel – but obliquely. Dicey's understanding of herself accepts that she needs to be by the sea and that she takes great pleasure in the idea of sailing. At one point she rhapsodizes about its pleasures and speculates that 'maybe life was like a sea, and all the people were like boats'.[4] And, at the end of the novel, the fact of having a home becomes, for her, associated with repairing the boat she has found there and perhaps sailing it. But there is something odd here: sailing is for Dicey a frequent metaphor for life, providing an alternative conceptual mode to both the linear journeys by road and the fixity of having a home. And yet (apart from some dutiful in-shore fishing trips) there is no true sailing anywhere in the series. Boats and boat restoration are for her – and for Jeff in *A Solitary Blue* – a matter of refuge and recovery; building them, as we later learn in *Seventeen Against the Dealer*, is problematical and dangerous. But sailing them does not happen – perhaps because it would unconsciously seem like an endorsement of the irresponsibility of the world-travelling absentee father.

The differences between road travel and sea travel frequently occupy Dicey's thoughts, but she remains puzzled and the issue remains unresolved. Readers are not allowed to believe that maturation involves a simple progression from one point along the road to a different one further on; nor are there given any straightforward answers. In the *Tillerman* series maturity is never an achieved state and never a straightforward binary shift. It can be manifest only in unending movement, a meaning defined in an often meaningless flux, with unpredictable outcomes and incomprehensible origins. There is no point at which a character can sit back and say: 'I have achieved maturity.' The grandmother is an illustration of this, and she admits it. An exception, though, is the doomed Bullet in *The Runner*, whose fate befalls him partly because of the time he lived in and partly because he is convinced that he has already done his maturing and the rest of the world has still to catch up.

Language

The experience of reading the series is decisively a matter of how the reader reacts to the author's distinctive language. The style of the first novel, *Homecoming*, is compact and uncompromising, for the most part representing Dicey's perceptions as indistinguishable from the narrator's.

> Dicey knew her sister could read and do sums, but Maybeth always sat quiet around strangers. For Maybeth, everyone in the world was a stranger, except Momma and Dicey and James and Sammy.[5]

Whose observation is represented in that second sentence? It is characteristic of Cynthia Voigt's unpretentious prose that this comment is both Dicey's perception (because Dicey was the subject of the preceding sentence) and the narrator's as well. It also manages (through the childlike repetition of 'and') to be the young Maybeth's perception too.

The distinction usually made between a closed text and an open one seems not to be applicable here. The writing *is* highly controlled, but the effect is to provide a relentlessly faithful account of the realities of the lives of the four children, without sentiment or mitigation. Voigt's authorial voice seems to be saying to the reader: this is realism, this is reality, we must agree to be realistic about it. And, since Dicey is the oldest and has a growing understanding of the three younger children and their predicament as a group, this perception is predominantly associated with her. Throughout the first novel there are two key pronouns, *she* and *they*, indicating two narrative polarities: the inner monologue of Dicey and the narrator's/Dicey's account of what the children do together as a group.

Homecoming is characterized by writing like this:

> Maybeth and Dicey crossed the dirt road from the playground and found the path to the small campground. Another path led to a bluff overlooking the marshes. They walked without speaking through the warm morning. The only sounds were the rustling of the leaves above them and the rustling of their feet on the leafy ground. They emerged from the woods on top of a low bluff that marked the border of the marshlands. Below, the heavy grasses swayed. Narrow canals of water moved gently. *The scene could have been painted in watercolours, so pale was the green of the grass, so subdued was the green of the water.*[6] (emphasis added)

Most of this is effective information-giving; compact, precise and vivid. The perceptions could be the objective narrator's or they could be subjectively Dicey's or – less likely – Maybeth's. But the sentence which I have italicized introduces a new and self-consciously authorial manner: both the aesthetic painterly observation and the stylized repetition ('so pale … so subdued …') are clearly not part of the consciousness of either of the children. There are other examples: 'The air was clear, clean, lucid, lying lightly upon the world that morning'[7] and '… wispy trees looked like weeds grown up'.[8] They invariably occur in the midst of routine reportage, twitching the reader's awareness a little from the faithfully prosaic to a slightly more distanced poetic perspective.

At times, these writerly observations are there to indicate for the reader that a child's own language is never quite going to be adequate to the narrator's requirements. These are not first-person narratives. So, when we are told, for example, of Cousin Eunice's 'silly helpless smile'[9] at their first meeting, we cannot be sure whether the narrator is sharing this observation with the reader, or whether Dicey has already summed up her relative. It is more likely that observations like these work conspiratorially – the character, the narrator and the reader sharing a growing understanding as events take place and words are found for them.

Even in the first novel of the series, Voigt's language often seems to recoil from its own prosaic nature by turning unexpectedly – and with simple directness – into revelatory symbol:

> Maybeth looked up from a pile of stones she was making into a long circle around herself.[10]

or, in this case with less simplicity, as Dicey is working in the circus tent:

> More goodbyes, Dicey thought to herself, coiling up the last rope into a dark brown hoop, piling loop upon loop. 'I am unfond of goodbyes,' she said to herself. All of their goodbyes lay like the coiled ropes on the ground, connected and unconnected, curling silently, finished things.[11]

How things work

To read these novels is to become absorbed in processes. The *Tillerman* narratives are fascinated by the way things work and how things change – how a meal is prepared, how timber can be smoothed and shaped, how four children approach a house and knock on the door, how to order fresh supplies for a butcher's shop, how to fish for crabs, how people operate in groups, how groups inter-relate in cultural communities and ideologies. Nothing, however mundane or trivial, is beneath this detailed authorial attention. Always, the prose works solidly at it, capturing the actuality, the sequence of tiny inter-relating events, the inter-dependence of homely phenomena or the significance of unconsidered actions, and the way past patterns impinge upon current needs.

In *Sons from Afar* there is so much of this kind of description that Cynthia Voigt seems almost to be deliberately risk-taking, pressing her readers into a state almost of boredom. We are given even more here than in previous novels of the multiplicity of details surrounding the protagonists. Sometimes pages of it. In the following example, Sammy is shocked to discover that James has no money:

> 'Why not?' Sammy asked. He had twenty-one dollars left of the hundred dollars he'd started off what James called their fiscal year with. They had a summer crabbing business, he and James, and Jeff helped out when he wanted to which was pretty regularly. They kept the first money they made for themselves, for a year's allowances, a hundred dollars apiece. Jeff didn't keep any, but James and Sammy did. At first, Jeff had agreed to split the earnings three ways, for the days he worked along with

them, but then he'd stopped, refusing to take his share. He'd told them to put his share in a college fund, or get something they needed. Usually, Jeff did what he thought you wanted him to do, but about the money he wouldn't budge. So James and Sammy started out the summer with a hundred dollars and the rest of the profits they gave to Gram. It wasn't a fortune, but it helped. 'You had twenty dollars after Christmas,' Sammy reminded his brother.

'I had to buy a glove.'[12]

Why does Cynthia Voigt do this? This detailed retrospective in-filling of information is certainly dispensable. One reason, I believe, is her fascination with the way needs and immanent phenomena are linked, often unsatisfactorily. Another is that, in this book, the narration, with its insistently detailed minutiae, enacts the psychological condition of these two fatherless sons. In the above extract, the pragmatic and down-to-earth Sammy, trying to understand his reticent and preoccupied older brother, constructs an accurate and sensible equation with the logical outcome that James should still have twenty dollars – only to discover that he had not factored in James' obstinate need to buy a baseball glove for a game which he hates. So this detailed account is not a narrative digression, but a demonstration of how Sammy thinks. Style is both character and understanding.

But not always. The faithful accounts of mundane moments can unexpectedly shift into poetry.

Maybeth sat straight-backed at the piano, wearing an old brown sweater Gram had knitted for James years ago. Her head, *curls the colour of yellow corn ripened in the sunlight*, bent forward a little, and her hands moved over the piano keys. The music *tumbled out, filling the room, generous*. Her hands were what made the music, her hands and Mozart and the piano. James sometimes wondered how it was that Maybeth, who was so slow at everything else, even the cooking and sewing she had a natural ability for, could be so quick and sure with music.[13]

The history of the 'old brown sweater' is precisely the kind of humble detail which gives families a sense of themselves and their continuity. But what follows (italicized) are perceptions of a different order, rhapsodic and lyrical. But whose thoughts are they? They might be the appreciative James', as what follows certainly belongs to his way of working things out – the careful self-correcting is typical of him, as he acknowledges that Mozart and the musical instrument had something to do with the music played. And then the reader is told directly what 'James wondered' about his mysterious sister.

Cynthia Voigt has shaped for herself an authorial voice which retains the advantages of a first-person narrator without relinquishing the third-person narrator's objectivity. As I have already suggested, this works to create the sense of a three-way conspiracy, with the character, the narrator and the reader edging their way together towards understanding. Maturation takes place in this novel on these terms.

In *Sons From Afar*, as Sammy and James search for their father, both boys undoubtedly mature as they discover that they can survive violence and emerge from it with greater self-understanding. But the way that Voigt manages such transitions suggests a discriminating authorial caution, as if she is suspicious of the ways in which narrative grammar can seduce a writer into slickness. James at one point, for example, comes to feel that he is at last free of the obsessive need to find out about his father; he no longer believes he must go on playing baseball to prove he is not a 'dork'; and he intends to sing in the chorus because that is what he wants to do, and because 'it wasn't as if he was going to live for a hundred years'. In fact, he adds, nobody is guaranteed any time at all.

> Figuring that – it was as if a dark shadow that had been riding round on his back all of his life had floated away. There was a dark clinging thing and he had unwrapped its fingers from his throat and tossed it back into the darkness it had come from. *That wasn't exactly true, he knew, but it was the way he felt.*[14]

The 'dark figure' that had been riding around on his back all his life might have appeared in any number of psychological novels of maturation or therapy – but it is characteristic of Cynthia Voigt that she (through James) draws back in the sentence I have italicized from its melodramatic evocations. She invites her reader to share with her the understanding ('That wasn't exactly true') that serious writers may at times need to use words which are not strictly accurate but which may, provisionally, help to clarify. The reader is being asked to contribute, to bring some understanding of the task of writing.

James becomes clearer about many muddled matters in his life. But clarification, though psychologically crucial, is syntactically peripheral. It slips into the characters' consciousnesses at unguarded moments. Understanding and revelation invariably occur at the edges of sentences or paragraphs, almost as accidental afterthoughts; or, sometimes, in a dialogue in which the speakers stumble apparently by chance upon some important perception. In this way, Sammy too becomes clearer about something which had puzzled him, and his perceptions come to him when he is crabbing with his new young assistant, Robin, engaged in 'safe' chat about rowing, traps and outboard motors. But Robin has family uncertainties of his own to deal with and Sammy finds himself unexpectedly discussing fathers – and then mothers too.

> Sammy never talked about Momma; he almost never really thought about her; he just remembered. But floating along in the boat, he wanted to say something. 'She played with me, she was fun. Her hair was long, and soft – it kind of shone,' he remembered that. Remembering that hurt, but it was a good kind of pain. 'I was pretty little when she died, but I think now,' he thought aloud, 'she was the kind of person who might be too gentle. You know?' The kind of person who needed taking care of – he couldn't stop himself from thinking; and his father was the kind of man who didn't take care of things.[15]

The practical Sammy does rather well in this episode. He is unusually articulate – though more gets worked out in his inner speech than is expressed in actual utterances. More significantly, though, he handles the smaller boy's anxieties and inexperience with enormous tact and kindness, unconsciously demonstrating how unlike his father he has already become.

It is easier for James than for Sammy; at least, that is what Sammy thinks. '... James always knew what to think because he was practically a genius, or something.'[16] Voigt seems with the character of Sammy to be fascinated by the kind of mind that does not speculate, and by states of *un*-awareness. Shortly after the above episode, Sammy is mortified to discover that everyone is blaming him for not having noticed that Maybeth is unhappy and that his neglect has contributed to this.

> Sammy had said something wrong, something awfully wrong, and Gram and James knew what, but he didn't. If they didn't tell him, how was he supposed to know? How was he supposed to guess, without being told? And then, the way they were looking at him – like he should know, like they couldn't believe he didn't know. They were blaming him now for not knowing. It made him angry, even though he maybe ought to know whatever it was he didn't.[17]

The graceless syntax, the unanswerable questions, and the awkward way in which sentences recoil against themselves all indicate Sammy's frustration and bafflement. When he eventually understands what it is he has failed to do, he is irritated by the cussedness of time, by the irredeemability of the past. He and Robin had been forced to throw the anchor overboard earlier, and this loss provides Sammy with a homely analogy to help him understand:

> ... The anchor was gone, lost. You couldn't find things you'd lost overboard. The bottom shifted, mud and sand moved constantly, covering up anything that fell in; and then, it was almost impossible to pinpoint any particular spot on the water, because there were no stable landmarks. You couldn't mark anything by a wave. A wave just moved on away; it was just part of a moving pattern.
> There wasn't anything he could do about Maybeth, either.[18]

The physical practicalities of Sammy's daily life provide him with the language with which to understand metaphysical issues. The father he had never had, and whom he and James had failed to trace, the severe beating-up they had suffered in their search, also belong to this incomprehensible and irretrievable past. 'Without a father,' Sammy thinks, 'it was like being lost without a map.' And that cheers him, because 'the picture was exciting, not frightening; it was an adventure. Sammy didn't mind adventures'.[19]

Maturation creeps up on James and Sammy unobtrusively, in afterthoughts, humble metaphors, and chance insights. But, most importantly, it takes place reciprocally. The beating-up which they endure – which comes close to a killing – amounts to a decisive *rite de passage*, with Sammy showing extraordinary physical courage and James employing his intelligence and way with words. But for all its dramatic intensity, Voigt makes it clear that the real maturation occurs afterwards as the two brothers think and talk about what happened. In the closing pages, the two of them acknowledge their understanding of each other – and their responsibility towards Maybeth. In their talk, it becomes clear that the problems of fatherhood have been put behind them; this is a maturing of brotherhood.

Jeff

A Solitary Blue more closely fits the notion of a maturation novel than the preceding two: it is exclusively about character. It is also structurally very straightforward in its representation of personal growth: it is a there-and-back novel, taking the boy, Jeff, further and further into himself until he is at the very edge of breakdown, and then – almost exactly halfway through – bringing him out again, safely back to sanity and stability, with the help of his father.

From the start, Jeff is a lonely little boy, trained in acquiescence and submission, and over-aware of other people's reactions so that he can please them. His wariness is conveyed in extended deadpan descriptions, as if the narrator's voice is located behind the little boy's eyes as he carefully appraises everything that happens to him and every place he finds himself in. This example occurs when Jeff has flown for the first time to visit his mother's family:

> At the luggage claim Jeff picked out his father's battered leather suitcase and went to the waiting area. This was a big room, with two long walls of window and two short walls of ticket counters. He sat on a plastic chair, his suitcase at his feet.
>
> Outside the window to the runway, the sun went down and the sky turned dark.[20]

Jeff is always conscious of two things; the details of place and the changes that occur in those details as time passes.

> ... Jeff kept an eye on his suitcase and on the clock. He wasn't hungry, he wasn't tired. He waited.
>
> And he waited. The room was less crowded now, and the twin headlights drove up less frequently. The air grew quiet ...[21]

Melody, his mother, arrives eventually to take him to her grandmother's house, and when Jeff is left alone in his room, the careful and deliberate description resumes. The reader is given every detail about the bed, the walls, the furniture, 'a little writing table, with a chair pulled up to it', the wardrobe where he hangs all his clothes, how he arranges his brush and comb and where he lays his toothpaste and toothbrush.[22] This description is an inventory of prolonged discomfort, because all the time Jeff really needs to go to the toilet; but, like visitors everywhere, he doesn't know where it is. With Jeff, though, this systematic watchfulness has developed into a chronic and necessary part of his coping, a strategy of discipline and disguise to conceal his inner vulnerability.

In the days that follow, Jeff explores the house and the people, the town and the country nearby, the hierarchy and ethos of a family which is totally strange to him. The orderly prose enacts the orderly way he assembles the details of this new environment he finds himself in. Most of the children in the *Tillerman* series have to make or re-make a sense of family and stability within a place and this is Jeff's first experience of a family with a sense of its own continuity and distinctiveness, a quality which is (much later) revealed as weird, unloving and even cruel. The way of life represented by the old grandmother is 'contented' to be the way it is; he later thinks of the 'spacious indifference' of her house.[23] It is inert, and Jeff literally falls asleep when he resolves to try to think it out.[24]

But he falls in love with his mother, Melody.

> Jeff *sensed* that she wanted him to talk about school, but he was *bemused* by sensations and *couldn't chatter*. He felt as if he had been cold, frozen down to his bones and into the marrow, and suddenly now he lay under the warmth of the sun. He could feel himself growing easy, relaxed, under the warmth; he *couldn't distract himself* from the enjoyment of that. It had something to do with the way his mother held his hand, held to his arm when they walked, touched him with his glance. His sensations were *half remembered*, *memory* growing stronger with every minute he was with her.[25] (emphasis added)

There is more going on here than that rather commonplace cold-and-warmth figure of speech might suggest. Jeff is a thinker, very aware of himself and already able to anticipate what he thinks Melody would like him to do. He is also, secretly, a rather adult boy ('bemused'), and at the same time stirred by fragmentary memories of having been loved by Melody in his infancy. And tormented, too: why can't he 'chatter', and why would he want to 'distract himself' from this pleasure? Already, Jeff is being divided into two selves.

The journey home confirms this division.

> It was not simply going from a warm to a colder climate, or from his mother to his father. It was also going from one self to another. In Charleston, he was Jeffie, Jefferson, Melody's son, the last in a long line of Boudrault men. In Baltimore, he was Jeff Greene, self-sufficient and reticent, no trouble at all, occupying his corner of the world. But he knew now how it felt to be loved, to be happy.[26]

Is Jeff thinking these thoughts? Or is the narrator interpreting for the reader? In the gap between those two possibilities, the reader's own understanding takes possession. Later, back home, Jeff's duality becomes real in a different – more visual – way when he looks into the bathroom mirror and 'catches his own grey eyes'.

He stared at them, his glance going from one to the other mirrored eye, surprised.

These were his mother's eyes. His eyebrows did not arch over them, as his mother's did, but were straight. His hair lay flat on his head; his mouth was broader, thinner than Melody's. But the shape of the face – he almost traced it in the mirror with his finger – the straight, narrow nose, the chin, was very like hers. He looked back into his own eyes, a grey so deep that it did not ever change colours. They were like hers, they were hers. He felt almost as if he could convince himself that he was looking at Melody, that she was with him now. He hugged the idea to himself and went downstairs.[27]

He has made Melody into a secret, dangerously tied in with his sense of his own identity. She is, of course, totally unworthy of his love. Everything she says wrong-foots him and she lets him down at every turn. Cynthia Voigt's creation of this character never falters. The writing seems to be in love with Melody – it has to be because Jeff is – while simultaneously exposing what kind of woman she is. The account of her final betrayal when she abandons him for a month, needs to be quoted in full:

> ... 'Where have you been?' she asked him.
>
> Jeff just let the happiness grow inside him.
>
> 'Nobody knew where you were,' Melody said. 'You shouldn't just go wandering off like that.'
>
> She was angry. 'I'm sorry,' Jeff said. 'I told Gambo this morning.'
>
> Melody stood up and took him out into the front hallway to say, 'You know she can't remember anything. Honestly, Jeffie, I thought I could trust you.'
>
> Jeff felt ashamed of himself, although he couldn't be quite sure why, and he hadn't noticed Gambo forgetting, just not being interested. 'I'm sorry,' he said, and then said it again. 'I'm sorry.'
>
> She wasn't satisfied. 'And I told Max I'd go with him out to Sante Fe, and now I don't know if I can,' she told Jeff. 'All you can say is, "I'm sorry". Just like your father.'
>
> Jeff just stared at her. He couldn't have spoken. He was confused, between guilt at failing her, dismay that she was going away again, and the desire that she not be angry with him.
>
> 'Well?' she asked.
>
> He swallowed. 'When?'

'We have to leave tonight and drive straight through, to get there in time. I had to wash and iron everything, and Miss Opal is so slow – it takes her ages to do anything these days.'

'But Melody ... 'Jeff heard his own voice complaining and saw anger rise in her eyes again. He didn't protest any more. 'For how long?' he asked.

'A month, maybe five weeks. It's a really important chance for Max. And you're here to keep an eye on Gambo for me so it's all right. If you weren't here I don't know how I'd get away.'

Jeff made himself accept it, right then. He knew that if he waited even for a second, he would start complaining, and then she really wouldn't like him. 'OK,' he said.

'Oh Jeffie, I knew I could count on you,' and she smiled into his eyes. ... 'Come and watch me pack? We can catch up with each other. Oh, I missed you, Jeffie,' she said. She looked like she meant it. He felt like she was telling the truth, even though he knew she must be lying.[28]

Jeff's disillusionment is twofold: he can see through Melody's manipulative love for him; and he has been shocked to discover his own weakness.

... He felt ... as if he had been broken into thousands of little pieces. Broken and then dropped into some dark place. Some dark place where he was always going to stay.
... He had never suspected how easy he was to break.
He couldn't think of anything he wanted to do. Ever.[29]

This is despair, not maturation. He seeks solitude on a remote beach, where he can feel 'washed clean, healed'.[30] Eventually, when he returns to his father's house and his old way of life, he takes the idea and imagery of this beach with him, locked into a private place in his mind where he can feel safe. He has become solitary and blue. These pages[31] faithfully chart the disintegration of the self, as Jeff locks himself away from all contact. He is now a seriously disturbed boy, on the edge of complete breakdown. His outer life is a matter of mechanically going through the motions – to ensure that he is left alone with his private inner life left uninterrupted. Jeff has set up a psychological lock-out, an isolation to guarantee that he won't unravel like a 'melody' turning into its meaningless separate components.[32]

But Jeff is rescued. And it is characteristic of Cynthia Voigt that there is no total mental collapse, no therapy, no psychological fireworks. Jeff's father had all along understood more than the reader had given him credit for. He steps in now, prompted by school reports of truanting and flunked courses, and the two of them begin to talk – two males hurt by the same woman, beginning to discover (to their own muted astonishment) that they are both affectionately interested in each other. This delicately written account of the intimacy between father and son, both habitually reticent and undemonstrative, is a supreme authorial achievement.

Maturation for Jeff is recovery from disillusionment – but also from his growing sense that he had no self at all, no identity. He is appalled to discover that, when he tries to recall his earlier years in school, he remembers some of the teachers and some of the children but never himself. 'It was almost as if he'd been a ghost in all those rooms, all those days, a ghost in his own life.'[33] This idea is later picked up and worked out more fully.

> Most of the time, he thought, he practised not being anybody. If you weren't anybody then nobody could – what? Hurt you or leave you behind? Make you unhappy? But then they couldn't make you happy either, could they? If you played it safe, then you kept safe.[34]

This 'not being anybody' accounts for all those long paragraphs of apparently endless description which filled so much of the first half of the novel. Cynthia Voigt's task was to represent life as observed by a consciousness habitually seeking to hide itself. This was style as symptom. The recovery in the second part of the novel is possible only because Jeff is capable of intelligent self-analysis; he does work things out for himself, privately at first, until later this inner speech becomes external and collaborative in conversations with his father. Talk becomes understanding and healing.

Dicey appears on the scene at about this point but his growing friendship with her is difficult because of his experience with Melody. In the concluding section, Melody makes one last appeal[35] to Jeff and almost succeeds in demolishing his recovering sense of self. But Jeff comes through this with the help of his uncommunicative father; and Dicey plays her part too, telling Jeff that her grandmother thinks he is a 'rare bird' with 'staying power and a gentle spirit'.[36] Voigt never uses the words 'maturity' or 'maturation'; Jeff's quietly joyous sense that he has a valued place in the world is both more muted and more dramatic: he feels as if he had just got a letter from 'somebody wise enough to know the truth, from everybody, or at least everybody that mattered'.

'Hello,' the letter said. 'Hello, Jeff Greene, I've been watching you and I like you and I want to know you better. This is just to say I'm glad you're alive in the world.' The list of signatures, he thought, would include his own.[37]

Dicey's reference to a 'rare bird' ties in with the symbolism of the solitary blue heron of the title. It first appears viewed by Jeff from a bus as he is travelling from his mother's home to his father's: it is described as 'unnoble and unbeautiful', occupying 'its own insignificant corner of the landscape in a timeless, long-legged solitude'.[38] The heron reappears later, described in some ornithological detail, but with nothing but its isolation to suggest a connection with Jeff: it is part of this fully and relentlessly described landscape.[39] Later, however, when Jeff and his father are considering a new home, Jeff's mind seems to be made up when a blue heron appears and stares at him. 'Jeff stared back, not moving, except for the smile on his mouth.'[40] When it appears for the last time, its solitariness is again emphasized before it turns its back 'in a stately gesture of dismissal'.[41] The symbolism of boats and sailing in the first two novels of the series has already demonstrated the tendency of symbols in this series *not* to be clear, their resistance to analysis or definition. That is the role of symbols – but Voigt's symbols are so modest and undramatic that they are almost indistinguishable from everything around them. She seems almost to be renouncing them, or exposing their untrustworthiness, the slippery way in which they are both potent and at the same time commonplace. If it were not for the title of the book, the solitary blue heron would be just one of the thousands of observed details of this fictionally realized world.

The closing chapters of *A Solitary Blue* are remarkable because Jeff, his father and Dicey – all individualists given to considerable reticence – formulate within their heads, and occasionally in conversation with one another, a collective understanding of themselves, and of life, love and relationships, which constitute what amounts to a philosophy in which Jeff can find a comfortable place. If this constitutes his maturity, it is made clear to the reader partly in the form of 'wisdom statements'. These are possible because, in the *Tillerman* series, maturity equals understanding. Jeff articulates them, sometimes privately for himself, and sometimes with other people. When, for example, he asks his father if he thinks there is such a thing as a one-woman man (meaning, really, is he – Jeff – such a person?), the Professor replies: 'I wouldn't be surprised if you were; it seems to be in your character. And what's in your character is what you've got to deal with.'[42] And, later, when the two of them are considering whether Melody ever loved Jeff, his father says:

> 'It strikes me that love is just the beginning. If you think about it, Jeff. I think we can't help loving, but what matters is what we do about it. What we do with love. Do for it. What love does with us.'

Jeff does not simply take this statement and apply it to himself; its meaning to him depends on his appreciation of his father.

> ... Jeff could see what his father was looking at: the Professor was looking at his own love for Melody and for Jeff; the Professor was sitting up and away from them, studying them and trying to understand how they worked. The Professor was doing what he always did, using his knowledge and experience to try to understand things as they really were.
> Jeff could do that too ...[43]

In spite of the symbolism of the solitary blue heron, it is in these carefully timed and staged formulations that a stronger sense of mature understanding emerges. Trying 'to understand things as they really were' is, in fact, a constant theme in the *Tillerman* series. Such perceptions are arrived at most frequently as points of dramatic understanding, achieved after considerable suffering and confusion, but sometimes as personal epiphanies. At the end of *A Solitary Blue*, when Melody has said to Jeff that she can never be 'happy' knowing about poverty in Colombia and doing nothing about it, he speculates inwardly:

> Happy, unhappy – Jeff was beginning to think that wasn't the question at all. The Tillermans never worried about that, they worried about ... living right for each one of them, together. He guessed you might call that happy, but he didn't think that was it, he didn't think that was the half of it.[44]

Perhaps 'epiphany' is not the best word to describe such insights. The language – and the ellipse – suggest something much more cautious, more provisional, more exploratory. There is no such thing as a fully-achieved wisdom.

Bullet

The Runner, however, shows that maturity can go wrong, and understanding can readily turn into cynicism and rejection. It is an historical novel, a flashback to the generation before Dicey, to the time when the US was beset by two momentous issues – civil rights and the Vietnam War. Anyone reading the novels in the order of publication already knows that the main protagonist, Bullet, is killed in Vietnam. So a different kind of reading is required, with a renunciation of the right to a happy resolution, an acceptance that the narrative leads not towards adulthood and an imagined possible future, but to an early death. Everything in this novel is obstructed and the reader, from the start, is caught up in this. It is a narrative driven by destructive and frustrated energies. Bullet's name is his fate.

Bullet, full of adolescent physical energy, is an unlikable hero – aggressive, uncommunicative, rebellious, cruel to his dog, unresponsive to all appeals to his better nature, indifferent to the two big issues of his day. The emphasis throughout is on his separateness. He is realistic about life and people, and proud of his contemptuous understanding of everyone else's foolishness. He can see through everyone and everything.[45] Maturation is impossible for him because he thinks he is already 'grown up' and everyone around him has been left behind.

> ... Bullet knew what had happened – he'd grown up. His classmates talked about being grown up and realistic, but they didn't have the first idea about what was really involved in it ...[46]

What is involved in being 'grown up', for Bullet, is a proud and contemptuous acceptance that what happened to most people was 'nothing, at best, and getting wiped out, at worst'.[47] This perception is the basis of his untroubled and calculating confidence, which expresses itself both in his conversations and in his physical fights.[48] He opts out of everything: he loves running but doesn't care about winning; he loves sports meetings but despises the camaraderie and is dismissive of the sportsmanship ethos. 'He didn't run to win races, or to beat anybody. He ran because his body was built for it. He ran for himself. Simple as that.'[49] He is described as 'absolutely unconnected'[50] and later this word is taken up against him as a reproach.

But Bullet does show some 'connection' in private – his unexpected feelings of grief and self-reproach when he kills the Old Dog; the short intimate time he spends with his mother afterwards; when he admits that he wishes Liza hadn't gone away;[51] when he accepts that his friend Patrice is 'coloured',[52] and – perhaps most significantly – when he notices and appreciates the beautiful black girl athlete and privately acknowledges her.[53]

But, contrary to all the expectations of the maturation novel, these apparently transforming perceptions transform nothing. The most significant example of this is the issue of racism in the school. Bullet is not deceived by the principal's time-serving hypocrisy as he addresses the assembled students. He simply stands up and leaves, very publicly. It looks for a moment as if he has – at last – made a stand, and certainly his friend Tamer believes he has the kind of charisma which might have swayed the opinions of the assembled students. But Bullet's outspokenness is not ideological or in any way principled; it is an expression of his personal indifference. He just walks out.

> He waited, to see if [the principal] had anything else he wanted to say, not nervous, not uncomfortable, just waiting. He didn't care, and that seemed to sink in after a while – he didn't care about the principal up on the stage, or about Tommy up there blowing it, or about the students sitting turned in their seats to watch him. None of them could make him do anything, and he knew it.[54]

Bullet takes action but he does not take sides. He rejects the principal's hypocrisy only because he personally despises it, but he does not see beyond that to its wider ethical or ideological implications. Everything about this novel is self-defeating and circular. The circularity is not inclusive and embracing but imprisoning, and its energies are reminiscent of a caged animal. It is energy with nowhere to go. His running – always returning back to exactly where he started – gets him nowhere; it is highly trained and disciplined young vitality with nowhere to direct itself. Either because of his own temperament or because of the time he lived in, Bullet can make no progress. Enlisting for him is not a matter of commitment but of acquiescence, of finding an arena for his tough and disciplined physical energy.

Related to this is the Housman theme, introduced by Bullet's English teacher, 'the old wind in the old anger'.[55] This is what Voigt is interested in: representing the combination of adolescent anger and energy and power, the Tillerman stubbornness tragically located in a time in US history when the young were trapped, their futures cut off, their ideals confused and blocked, so that maturation can develop only in distorted ways. Bullet thinks he knows all about it:

> Growing up meant you knew what you wanted and you worked for it, and you didn't let yourself get in your own way.

> Not dreams, not memories – he knew he could allow no
> weakness in himself if he was going to win free. He could feel
> the danger of his father's will closing in around him, and he
> could feel his own strength too. It would cost him, but what
> didn't cost something?[56]

He sees growing up in terms of conflict and triumph. And, with a
tyrannical and aggressive father like his – and an uncommunicative
mother who will not take sides between father and son – how else
could he understand maturation? The contrast with Jeff, in *A Solitary
Blue*, is striking: Jeff found himself recognized within a small group of
loved-ones; but Bullet is challenged for supremacy. His family
conflict is connected in his thinking with the other great conflict –
Vietnam and the draft.

> They were all, Bullet knew, frightened. Fear sat behind their
> eyes as they looked at one another. Fear for themselves, fear for
> one another. They really didn't know, Bullet thought; and
> *maybe you had to grow up in a family like his to know what was really
> worth being afraid of.* They said they argued from moral
> conviction, labelled it an oppressive war, a dirty war, an
> imperialistic war, a war for the big corporations – but he knew
> fear when he smelled it. The way he figured it, you were going
> to die anyway . . .[57] (emphasis added)

The bitter implication of the statement I have italicized is that
growing up in a loving family incapacitates a young man and leaves
him too frightened to take either one side or the other in the big
issue of Vietnam. The others, he realizes near the end of the novel, all
want to avoid the draft and the danger altogether.

> But that was the one choice they didn't have, because you
> didn't choose the time you were born in.[58]

If that perception is the climax of his wisdom, the question arises:
what constitutes maturation? Self-knowledge? Acceptance of the
need to 'connect'? But Bullet only half-learns his many lessons – or
learns them but fails to follow through the learning. This is a novel of
frustration: of energies blocked off, of anger, of connections
thwarted, of a character who cannot mature because of the time he
was living in. Whether Bullet's unsentimental appraisal of the divided
world he belongs to amounts to a flawed maturity, or a complete
failure of maturity, is a matter of opinion. Perhaps it is the only kind
of maturity possible at such a time in American history.

But that is not quite all. This novel is more complex than a chronicle of social or individual moral impotence. A young man not lucky enough to have a father like Jeff's, or a brother like Sammy and James, and unlucky enough to have been growing up at this particular period, still has his energy to somehow contain and direct. The adrenalin and muscularity of youth, the super-heroic testosterone of young men, does not quietly dissipate, leaving the rest of society at peace. *The Runner* also celebrates that adolescent physicality – its amoral and uncompromising daring.

In some ways, this novel is an elegy for a generation. Perhaps that is overstating the matter; but certainly, when Abigail Tillerman takes the phonecall telling her that Bullet has been killed in action, that he was 'a fine soldier' and 'a letter would follow', and she takes a cleaver and 'slices through the connection, where the wires came out from the wall'[59] she has silenced the perennial voices of cliché. As her son was, she now becomes 'disconnected' – until, of course, her four grandchildren arrive a few years later and reconnect her.

Mina Smiths

Come A Stranger (1986) is a novel about communities visited by significant strangers. Tamer Shipp is an important one, then the Tillermans (providing an agreeable frisson since they are not strangers to the reader), and finally, in the closing pages, Dexter Halloway. The stranger theme is tied in with the exploration of race and the issue of 'colour' and, for the first time in the series, a girl's physical maturity is a central point of interest.

When Dexter remarks that Mina doesn't look fifteen, she replies: 'I never looked fifteen. I looked ten for a while, then I started looking twenty-eight.'[60] This is characteristic of Mina: she is articulate, funny, and – for most of the time – relaxed, unembarrassed, at ease in her world, and very aware of the ridiculous. But, for all her joking, she knows (and the reader knows) that her physical precociousness was earlier in the novel used as a pretext for removing her from the ballet summer school. Mina compares the process of physical growing-up to an insect shedding its chrysalis or a crab its skin,[61] though with typical perspicuity she pushes the cliché beyond its usual limits by acknowledging that that is when a creature is most vulnerable to attack. This is timely, for the attack on Mina comes a few pages later, when she is expelled from the ballet class because she has allegedly 'failed'.

When she first arrives at the school, Mina realizes that she is – for the first time in her life – a stranger herself, a black girl among the whites at the summer school. 'They were seeing the outside of her,' she thinks.[62] She laughs out loud at the thought that she is 'the only little black girl there'. The word her thoughts pick up on is not *black* but *little*.

> ... Little? Well, she wasn't any too little any more. There were bras and a box of Kotex she'd unpacked with the rest of her things. She guessed, if they thought she was little, in any way, they were underestimating her. She guessed she was going to have to make friends with them all over again. She stretched her arms out, her broad shoulders up, and flexed her fingers. She didn't mind that. She always liked making friends.[63]

In her classes all the students are surrounded by mirrors. There is no escape from them. They reflect 'Mina's blackness back and back, among the white skin of the other girls'.[64] But in spite of its emphasis on the insistent facts of skin colour and difference, *Come a Stranger* does not allow the reader to settle on personal image or physical maturity; the narrative goes inwards, showing how an intelligent and sensitive black girl awakens to the racial injustices of her own day and the past, and also to other minorities. Maturation for all of the main characters in this series is a matter of understanding; but for Mina, this understanding has to be arrived at in terms of race – who is a stranger to whom, and why, and with what consequences.

The issue of her dancing is not oversimplified: Mina admits it has become clumsy and she has been clowning around. 'Your people develop earlier,' the principal says, unwittingly confirming Mina's status as 'stranger', and then going on to expose the ambivalences within notions of maturity by adding: 'The trouble is, you're so mature.'[65] Mina is told that she must leave – 'It's always hard to admit that you've failed.'

> At that, Mina was so angry that she did burst into tears. She was so angry she just wept. She was weeping so hard she couldn't speak. Just growing wasn't failure, you couldn't say someone had failed because her body grew bosoms and hips and the muscles worked differently.[66]

This is a bitter experience for Mina.

'Strangers are a fearful people,'[67] says her father in one of his sermons, speaking of Jonah having to go and live among strangers in Nineveh. Mina 'folds her hands in her lap' and listens attentively. However, she is at this stage – before her humiliation at the ballet school – untroubled by her position as a black girl in a white world:

and so when she wins the dance scholarship and her father asks if she was the only black girl there – and why? – she replies blithely:

'I was the only one good enough, I guess.'[68]

She is resistant to books about black history, pointing out to her mother that 'except for slavery, nothing ever happened to black people'[69] and, later, grumbling that whereas white people had the great classical myths, 'all we ever had was Brer Rabbit. And the Ananse stories'.[70]

She was, of course, recruited to the ballet school to ensure federal funding; but the words *token black* are not actually articulated until Tamer Shipp arrives in Mina's community. He has come to meet her train the day she returns home. He takes her to a restaurant and asks her how it feels to be a 'token black, retired'.[71] This turns her tears into sudden laughter but – as a check to simplistic readings – there is an incident immediately afterwards in which Mina is given a gentle lesson about other ways in which people, not just blacks, can become strangers in their own community. Mr Shipp concludes that the waitress, who is weighed down with weariness and who is probably a single mother since she has 'the ghost of a wedding band' on her finger, should have an extra large tip.

> 'Because you feel sorry for her?' Mina guessed.
> 'Because I know about how she feels,' Mr Shipp corrected her.
> 'But Tamer,' Mina said ... 'you're not divorced, are you?'
> He shook his head.
> 'Have you been a waiter?'
> He shook his head again, smiling, teasing, waiting for her to work it out.
> 'And you're not a woman, and you're not white.'[72]

Tamer Shipp isn't black either, he points out. Mina is for a few brief moments embarrassed by this strange assertion, but Tamer leads her into a conversation about shades of skin colour, pointing out that 'blacks, it's what we call ourselves, so that's all right' but that, in fact, they are all different kinds of black.

> ... She thought about that, about all the colours the blacks were. There was dark, like Mr Shipp, dark, dark brown so that in certain lights you could see the purply black that went into it. Her skin was like a chocolate candy bar, a Hershey bar to be precise. Kat's had coppery tints in it. Some blacks were so light

they were beige, almost, and some had golden tones and – She started to laugh, because he was exactly right about it.[73]

By the end of their conversation, she and Tamer Shipp are friends. Mina is good at that, making strangers into friends.

In the next chapter Voigt describes Mina at church, watching the congregation from her position in the choir, attending carefully to Tamer Shipp's sermon. It is a contented chapter, describing a community coming together, comfortable with themselves, safely contained in their church, with no strangers amongst them. But the present is not the whole truth; Mina is an enquiring girl and the history of black people in the US inevitably begins to draw her. In a conversation with her old neighbour, Miz Hunter, she comes to realize that they are still only a few generations from slavery. Voigt does not deal in abstractions: Miz Hunter tells Mina how her great-grandfather – 'that big handsome black man'[74] – ran away and probably died a horrible death in the swamps. The big handsome black man in Mina's life at that moment is Tamer Shipp, and so the imaginative connection is made.

> But Mina's imagination was stuck there in the green swamp, with a man who looked like Mr Shipp ...
>   She put her glass down, even though her mouth was dry. She couldn't have swallowed anything. She couldn't have gotten anything down past the anger and misery, the pity and the bitterness all mixed up in her throat. She was looking with a long eye, and that man lay too close to be forgotten about.[75]

For Mina, growing up also involves 'a long eye' looking at the history of black people. In all the *Tillerman* novels, there is a strong awareness of physicality, a visual and tactile appreciation of bodies. It is apparent in descriptions of the young Sammy in *Homecoming* and *Dicey's Song*; it is there in the accounts of Jeff in *A Solitary Blue*; it is strongly, almost bitterly, a part of *The Runner*, and savagely present in the fight in *Sons from Afar*. In *Come A Stranger*, this awareness of the physicality of colour, size and growth becomes acute and, for Mina, inseparably enmeshed both with the past history of black people and with her own personal history of dance and her expulsion from the ballet school.

> And herself? Mina looked at her legs, lined up neat, two strong thighs and the knees flexed at the joint, long calves and big feet. She registered her bust under the bathing suit and knew she looked much older than she was. A hundred and fifty years ago,

it wouldn't have mattered how old she was; she'd have been treated like a woman grown. Broken to slavery from day one of her life.

She'd have been entirely different. She'd never have had a chance. There were so many people, then, who never did have a chance, no choices to make, not about what to eat or where to go or what to do. She'd never even have had a chance to make her own mistakes. A black girl who was t-roub-le didn't make anybody smile a hundred and fifty years ago. And all because of the colour of her skin, all because the skin covering Samuel's bony back at the far end of the porch was dark skin.

But the blood under it was red, and the bones were white.

Looking with a long eye, Mina saw how close they sat to a hundred and fifty years ago, and fear ran along her blood.[76]

This is fine writing, passionate and precise. The discourse on skin colour leads, unexpectedly, to Maybeth. Mina becomes friendly with Jeff and Dicey, and is quickly at ease with the whole Tillerman family. Maybeth provides her with a characteristic Voigt epiphany: Maybeth, who throughout has been a transformer and a touchstone for others, doggedly persistent at studies she can't understand, the beautiful girl amusingly described by one character as 'a Botticelli angel, snapping beans',[77] a vulnerable, mysterious and talented child 'all wrapped around within the music'.[78]

...[Mina] tried to name for herself the colour of the girl's cheeks. It was like nothing she had ever seen, except milk maybe. It was rich white, tinted with some creamy colour underneath. It was a beautiful colour.

Looking at the little girl, her mind wandering, Mina just barely stopped herself from jumping up and yelling, *Whoo-ee*. Oh, Tamer Shipp, she thought, you're right. Coloured does cover just about everything.[79]

Tamer Shipp has come to stand in for Mina's father at their church in a precisely Freudian way. And part of Mina's understanding of herself – this twelve-year-old girl with the body of a mature woman – is to realize what has happened in relation to him.

During the trip down from Wilmington that July afternoon ... Mina had fallen in love with him. She'd fallen so fast, she didn't know until now how deep she'd fallen.[80]

That, too, is part of Mina's maturation. It is perhaps worth bearing in mind what this novel does *not* do. There is no exploration of sex with an under-age child, no abuse, no harassment, no guilt and misery, no scandal, no 'exploration of female sexuality' and no embarrassment. Here, and in all the novels of the series, Voigt sidesteps the easy expectations of genre and challenges narrative cliché. Her love for an older married man is treated as an issue of understanding rather than hormones. What counts in this novel is what Mina feels and thinks, and how her understanding is the basis of what she does. Everything, Mina realizes, is connected – her first real thoughts about skin colour and poverty had started at the same time as her love for Tamer Shipp, only a few hours after her expulsion from the ballet school. Now the bitterness of that has gone, leaving only a determination:

> ... But she did know for sure that she'd go where she wanted to go – in this world that had Tamer Shipp in it. Not just go where somebody else said she had to ...[81]

The final chapter acts like a coda; and because it takes place at Jeff's graduation two years later, Mina is thinking a good deal about him. She appreciates the details of his body – 'like some Greek statue of what a young man should look like'[82] – and her heart is touched by his devotion to Dicey:

> ... part of the rush of feelings she felt was a sense of freedom, of being ready to grow upwards even farther from the strong tangled roots of her life.[83]

As in all the *Tillerman* novels, growth is never an achieved condition. It is *freedom* and *readiness* that Mina feels, and a grateful appreciation of the 'tangled roots of her life' which make further growth possible – her family, her community, her church, her widening circle of friends, and the strangers that have come into her experience. There are difficulties everywhere, and race is one of the biggest. But ordinary human intercourse – considered, affectionate and thoughtful – is repeatedly shown as capable of transcending the so-called barriers, welcoming the arrival of strangers.

Whether you are a stranger depends to a large extent on where you are. Mina is never a stranger in the enclosed safety provided by her family, her neighbours, and – most importantly – her church. So, when the entire Tillerman family turns up at Mina's church one Sunday, the novel has its own small victory over the divisions of race. Mina, in the choir where she can see everything, enjoys the moment immensely: her mother who 'looked at Mina with an eyebrow raised', Mrs Tillerman 'with her chin up high', and the congregation's polite and pleased amazement when they hear Maybeth singing out the harmony. There are other victories too – link after link is made, each one a small healing. The sermon, which is about the grief that 'many of us still carry' for 'our sons, our brothers, sweethearts and husbands',[84] seems by chance to be specifically addressed to Abigail Tillerman, with reference to her son. Yet it is not entirely by chance, for Tamer Shipp had had Bullet in mind all along.

> ... Abigail's eyes were smiling. 'I thought of him, when you spoke.'
> 'I thought of him, writing it –'[85]

And one more (light-hearted) twist is given to the theme of strangers and colour.

> 'I liked the singing. I'd like singing in your choir,' Maybeth told Mina.
> Mina thought she was asking. 'You can't, even though I'd sure like to sing in a choir with you.'
> 'I know, I'm the wrong colour,' Maybeth explained.
> Mina couldn't help it, she got a fit of the giggles.[86]

Flux and uncertainty

I have a number of times referred to the density and detail of Cynthia Voigt's narrative manner in the *Tillerman* series. However, in spite of the apparent certitude and reliability of realism, this fictional world is not composed entirely of fixed phenomena and known relational structures. This is a world of uncertainties and mysteries, where change is a condition of being and where all wisdom is to some extent incomplete and provisional. In such a world, maturation must inevitably be exploratory. The language of these novels is shot through with suggestive colourations that never quite settle into defined meaning. There is a shiftiness in the narrative universe, a slight fuzziness at the edges of apparent certainty.

Ideas and images are employed poetically, strung throughout the seven narratives in extended clusters. One of these clusters has to do with music. The 'song' of *Dicey's Song* is partly explained when we are told that Dicey likes simple beginning-to-end things like songs; the journey in the preceding book was like a song – you began at the start and stopped when you reached the end. And she describes her mother as walking 'like a song sung without accompaniment'.[87] She thinks of experience as a complicated piece of music, but comprehensible because she can grasp one melody at a time.[88] These musical analogies begin in the privacy of Dicey's thoughts but they extend throughout the entire series like a motif with variations: Dicey's song–Momma–Maybeth–melody–Melody–guitar–Jeff–hymns. These variations do not work like equations and they do not resolve anything; they provide links and resonances, ways of understanding often working below the level of the characters' conscious thought.

Another analogy Dicey uses to make sense of her life has to do with wind and sea. Travelling on a train, sitting with her hands wrapped carefully around the box containing the ashes of her mother, she:

> ... felt as if a wind blew through her hands and took even Momma away.
>
> What did that leave her with? The wind and her empty hands. The wind and Dicey.
>
> As if Dicey were a sailboat and the sails were furled up now, the mainsail wrapped up around the boom, and she was sitting at anchor. It felt good to come to rest, the way it felt walking up to their house on a cold evening, seeing the yellow light at the kitchen window and knowing you would be warm inside while the darkness drew in around the house. But a boat at anchor wasn't like a boat at sea.
>
> Except, Dicey thought, a boat at anchor wasn't planted there, like a tree. Furled sails were just waiting to be raised, when the sailor chose to head out again ...
>
> How was Dicey supposed to understand?[89]

The boat/sailing analogy leads to no conclusion; but it does help Dicey to contrast the different realities of movement and fixity. Contradictions bother her. She has been baffled before about the apparently oxymoronic meaning of the phrase 'home and gone'. Now, standing quietly as they bury Momma's ashes, the phrase again comes into her thoughts.

> Dicey stood alone and unmoving. But inside her head her own voice spoke clearly: 'Gone and home'. Those were all the words to speak over Momma, all the songs to sing.
>
> Home and gone. It didn't seem possible that both of those words could be true, but they were. Dicey shivered in the wind and went inside.[90]

This brings together her two favourite similes, singing and sailing (a metaphor submerged in the *wind*). But she returns to the safety of the house. In spite of everything – her need to be near the sea, her boat-restoring – Dicey's natural place is home and hearth, and the security of being in a family. The Tillermans and their friends are marginal people living along an irregular coastline with unclear boundaries between land and sea, where there are marshes and fogs, and an unremarkable flora and fauna. Dicey herself shares this ambivalence: she is preoccupied with repairing and building boats but never goes sailing, as if driven by a work-ethic deriving from her grandmother but never able quite to follow her father and go to sea.

And that brings us to the last novel in the series.

Father and daughter

'Just because you work hard doesn't mean you'll get your good ending,' Maybeth says wisely to Sammy,[91] none of them realizing how sharply true this is going to be for Dicey too. The 'good ending' to this remarkable series proves to be both ambivalent and uncompromising, as unlike the formulaic closures of teen romances as it is possible to be.

The narrative language which *Tillerman* readers have become accustomed to has always served especially well with obsessives. In *Seventeen Against the Dealer*, it compels the reader, grimly and insistently, to see life as it is seen by a young woman so preoccupied by physical work of her own choosing that she neglects everything else that matters. The details of planning, calculation and hard physical work are not just described, but enacted and shown, placing the focus, day after day and chapter after chapter, on Dicey's solitariness, her determination and constant muscular tiredness. The slightly self-conscious touches of poetic description have disappeared. The reader is shown how overwork in a consumer society leads to a neglect of intimacies and a dislike of people. In fact, people are seen as interruptions to the main business and their claims are a distraction. This is doubly true of the self-employed, who become enclosed in a particular circularity of their own choosing, suggested here in the way the phrasing turns back on itself:

> She had always got things done; working hard, and harder, was what worked for her.[92]

Business is seductive to Dicey; this is partly because she has always been a person who knows how to focus on a job and see it through until the song, or journey, or job has reached the end; and partly because business does provide its moments of excitement, triumph and jubilation, and its deceptive promises of success, as Dicey finds when she unaccountably gets an order – and the money – to build a boat.

> There were a dozen things to do, and she wanted to get to work
> on them right away, but first she had to go to the shop and
> unload this wood. She'd never felt less tired in her life.[93]

Working out how her capital, her energy and the limited space in her
cramped workshop can best be used and balanced against each other,
Dicey becomes unwittingly trapped in the processes of capitalism.
The language is that of commerce and business: setbacks, profit and
loss, investment, capital, problem–solving, time management, all of it
happening in Dicey's psyche – not in her mind exactly, because she is
hardly aware of what is happening to her.

> Dicey leaned her head on her hands, and looked at the numbers.
> Looking at them, and how they didn't change, at their balancings
> between debits and credits, she made herself look again at
> Claude's offer. You had to balance time and money. She had to
> weigh the time she'd have to waste working on Claude's boats
> against the money that work would bring in.[94]

Dicey's studying of the books, this 'balancing between debits and
credits', is a kind of voluntary myopia. She buys into the central
capitalist deception in which free choice and compulsion are
inseparably confused, perfectly suggested in the choice of words
and the shaping of the syntax in comments like:

> She was going to do what she had to do, because she had to do
> it in order to do what she wanted to do.[95]

She gives her assent to the circularity of this economic treadmill
because she is convinced that she is tougher than the system: 'Things
weren't easy, they never had been; in fact, things were often pretty
hard. But Dicey was harder.'[96] But her illusory independence and
freedom to be her own woman is itself shaped by economic realities
and the consequences both on her body and her mind of this
obsession with physical work are spelled out.

> ... Her arms ached from the circular motion of sanding and the
> stroking motion of painting. Her shoulders ached from the
> hefting around of plywood boats. Her back and the backs of her
> legs, too, ached – from bending over, to sand and paint, long
> hour after long hour.[97]

The syntactic shaping of those sentences, and the repetition of
'ached', reinforce the effect of this checklist of exhaustion and effort.
But the consequences for her inner life are even more serious. The

novel began with an episode in which Dicey savoured the 'familiar gladness'[98] of hearth and home and family, and Chapter Three was devoted almost entirely to a celebratory occasion when almost the whole cast of the series are brought together. But Dicey is in danger of neglecting all that she most cherishes as she loses herself in the preoccupations of business.

> Maybeth and Sammy were studying for exams ... but Dicey wasn't much help, either. She couldn't remember the things you had to know for American history. She could barely remember two days ago. She wasn't even sure whether it had been a week, or more, and if so how much more, that Gram's deep cough had lingered on, after the stuffed nose and runny eyes of the cold itself. Dicey kept forgetting exactly when it was that the exams would start. She kept forgetting in the evenings to return Jeff's phone calls, and not remembering that she had forgotten until the next evening, when she was too tired to remember not to forget again.[99]

Again, especially in the final sentence, there is the circular language Voigt has become so good at, where words turn back upon themselves and an uncomfortable meaning is squeezed out of repetition. Dicey thinks she knows herself, that work is what matters and what she can always make herself do. Yet her family demonstrates the wrongness of this certainty – Gram can't work because she is ill; Sam can't get to study tennis because they are not rich enough; and Maybeth can't pass her courses because she is not clever enough.

Into this situation comes a handsome middle-aged drifter, constituting perhaps the most mysterious feature in the entire series. He is shifty as a character and shifty as a narratorial device, indicating – as I suggested above – that the reality so solidly described in Cynthia Voigt's reliable prose is not as reliable as it is made to seem. The seven novels of the *Tillerman* series define a central problematic absence: the father. There was no father in the first two novels, though his desertion of their mother was a constant theme. Sons and fathers have been explicitly faced, positively and benevolently in *A Solitary Blue*, with failure and frustration in *Sons From Afar*. There are an absent father, two loving fathers and a cruel father. The series is concerned with fathers and their role in maturation.

We know of Dicey's missing father that he had thick dark hair, light eyes and a lean body; he liked gambling, stole money and enjoyed telling stories about his adventures at sea, especially among the Pacific Islands. The puzzle for the reader – and once, just, maybe for Dicey too[100] – is this: the smooth-talking drifter who comes into Dicey's life also has thick dark hair, light eyes and a lean body; he too likes gambling, steals money and enjoys telling her stories about his adventures at sea and the sexual pleasures of the Pacific Islands. Readers also know that, in *Sons From Afar*, James did a good deal of research about his father and learned that there was something special about him, that he had a kind of charisma that was irresistibly engaging. In the words of a former schoolteacher:

> ... He was such a bright little boy, you see, and he looked like an angel, big eyes and curly hair and such a sweet face. Not a goody-goody angel, but the kind of little angel who could make God laugh.[101]

He makes Dicey laugh too. An odd kind of intimacy is established between them as they work, eat and talk together in the tiny workshop.[102] He has a lively face, made for fun. He quotes Shakespeare, knows more than she does, and is interested in more things. Dicey suspects she is 'telling him more than she was telling him'[103] and he suspects she doesn't think much at all.

> 'You know, Miss Tillerman, in all respect, I'd say you don't think much as a general rule.'
> Dicey, taking off her jacket, hat, and scarf, shook her head. 'You'd be wrong. I'm always thinking about what's next. I've got today all thought out.'[104]

But there are different kinds of thinking, and different things to think about. A first-time reader will be suspicious of him and a re-reader knows that he will eventually rob Dicey of her last $839. But Cisco is an *alternative*, not just a villain. He offers a different view of life, irresponsible, perhaps, but one genuinely based on curiosity about a wider world than the narrow one Dicey has enclosed herself in.

> 'You ever gamble?' Cisco asked.
> 'I can't afford to lose.'
> 'But that's the time when you should,' Cisco told her.[105]

This is a key statement, offering the exact reverse of success as seen in an enterprise culture. This advice is handed over to Dicey by the man who reminds her of the old gambling song, 'Never hit seventeen, when you play against the dealer'[106] – the same man, perhaps, who gave her a gambling name when she was a baby.

Dicey has many disappointments and makes many mistakes, but it is Cisco's theft of her money which finally brings her to her senses. That he should do this is entirely in character – but it is also a father's gift, forcing her into an understanding of the trap she has enclosed herself in. This is the kind of father he has been all along, unacknowledged and operating negatively. He gives her advice about the work ethic;[107] he prompts her into realizing that she misses studying;[108] and he advises her to make a more determined effort to keep the love of Jeff. True, his advice comes in the wordly wise and cynical manner characteristic of traditional male thinking: 'My advice is: switch tactics ... Try chasing him. Try it, I'm serious. Unless you want to get rid of him?'[109] Of course, he misunderstands his daughter: Dicey is entirely innocent of 'tactics' in her relations with Jeff. But his advice is – or might be – a disguised expression of regret that Momma, all those years ago, did not try harder to keep him.

There is no way of being totally sure that Cisco is Dicey's father. But that does not matter; he is a father figure who comes into her life, representing a particular kind of masculinity, disruptive, challenging, uncomfortable, and with a certain genuine under-standing of the ways of the world and his own limitations within it. Whatever his motives for stealing Dicey's money, its effect on her is decisive and benevolent.

An achieved maturity?

A reader approaching the final chapters of the last novel of a series whose main character has grown into a twenty-one-year-old woman might expect to find indications of achieved maturity. They are, in fact, stacked with wisdom statements and they come, mostly, in the form of moments of perceived self-understanding. First, Dicey feels shame:

> ... Dicey recognized the feeling she was feeling and knew its right name. Shame. She was ashamed of herself, for all the things she hadn't done right; she figured she should have known how to notice them.[110]

She has tried to achieve economic maturity and failed. (So much for the popular idea that if you want something passionately enough you will succeed in it.) Dicey's desire has been so strong it has become an obsession, all-absorbing to such an extent that she has probably lost both Jeff and Gram through neglect.

> The idea [that she had lost Jeff] had got into her head. It was sinking through all the levels of her understanding, like a stone

through thick water. When it hit bottom, she'd feel it. When it hit bottom, she'd know everything that no meant.[111]

The curiously constructed phrasing of both those quotations, with their repetition, alliteration and internal rhymes, is typical of Voigt's manner as she finds words to suggest the numerous ways people have of not knowing things, or half-knowing, or denying that they know, or realizing that they will in time come to know what they know already. Similes, too, are important to Dicey's way of thinking; she tells herself that Jeff is like a plant – 'he'd just go on with his own growing, the best he could do in whatever the circumstances were'.[112] Maybeth she sees as 'a patch of marsh grass, rooted in the mud, letting the water wash over it'.[113] Metaphors of rootedness are important in the *Tillerman* series but not quite enough; hearth and home are even more important:

> ... There was an echoing hollowness inside her – not hunger – it was in her chest, not her stomach, and empty hollowness locked inside her rib cage. Like an empty house.[114]

Dicey might be forgiven for telling herself that she had been the victim of an unusual amount of bad luck; but, in the wave of self-knowledge that sweeps over her, she admits 'that she was one of her own enemies'[115] and that she is, in effect, a gambler, true to both her name and her father's careless philosophy.

> Big dreams, she'd had big dreams. When big dreams exploded it was worse than when little ones got lost ...
> It was as if she'd been playing her hand out, against everybody, gambling on herself.[116]

In fact, despite Cynthia Voigt's resolute cliché-busting, Dicey does achieve a happy ending with Jeff – but strictly on the terms established through this long series of seven novels. The *hearth and home* metaphor is insufficient if the person you want most is not there; and the *roots* metaphor is inadequate because plants can make no effort to change their situation. Dicey, though, can. She goes to see Jeff and everything is quietly resolved in a process of mutual self-knowledge – though characteristically the language of Dicey's thought keeps apologizing for itself:

> She couldn't explain. She couldn't even begin to explain. There were too many reason, all too woven tight together into a cloth that was too ... beautiful, or thick, or right, or complicated, she didn't know what – she knew only what its value was. She

couldn't even begin to put words to it. And then Dicey knew, from looking into Jeff's eyes, that not being able to explain was the right answer.[117]

Woven into their decision to get married are Dicey's determination to build a boat one day in the future, and Jeff's announcement that he has a ring for her (which readers will recall from *A Solitary Blue*) which links both of them to the past.

As I suggested above, the entire series is to some extent based on the insufficiency of language to represent human experience, teaching its readers that that they must accept a provisional and tentative uncertainty as they share with the narrator and with the characters the task of edging cautiously towards understanding. In spite of that, in the closing pages of *Seventeen Against the Dealer*, the voice of self-knowledge in Dicey's head seems to have found the confidence of revelation.

> ... But when she thought of all the things she wanted to do, and do right – do right by, do as well as they could be done ...
> It was all so risky, because there were no guarantees. You couldn't be sure that any of the risks would pay off. Even if you studied, and planned, and worked, even if you did the best you could, you could still lose out. There was no way to walk away from the truth of that, that's what no guarantees meant. But even knowing that didn't make Dicey feel any different about anything – which puzzled her, because it didn't make sense that it shouldn't. Then she understood – it wasn't guarantees she needed, or any of them needed, but chances, chances to take. Just the chance to take a chance.
> And the eye to recognize it, she added.
> The hand, to reach out and hold onto it – that too.
> And the heart, or the stomach, or wherever courage came from, she thought.[118]

Maturation is represented as a gaining of wisdom, an acceptance of the chanciness of the world and a knowledge of oneself within it. But, if that understanding is to be articulated, then characters can mature only in terms of the language they have – and Dicey's formulation is made in the language of gambling borrowed from Cisco. The difference is that Cisco was a chancer and a loner, reckless of other people; Dicey's maturity has been earned with the support of her family and Jeff. But 'earned' is not the right word, for it implies something achieved, a process complete. Gram knows better that there is no end to the learning:

... Dicey wondered, coming back into Gram's room to play a cutthroat game of cribbage, how old you were before you began to get things settled. She looked at her grandmother, wondering. In my experience, older than dead.' Gram told her.[119]

Maturation in the *Tillerman* series is a serial process; it is never a straightforward transformation into a new and better state, and it rarely occurs as a single moment of breakthrough. Her characters do have such breakthroughs, sometimes an epiphany occurring mid-book or in the closing pages; but their real maturation is a slow unending achievement of small reality truths, one of which is that the only constant is change, that maturation is forever happening. Another is that individuals are always capable of being astonishing, especially under the influence of the people they care about.

This is what maturation finally means: an acceptance of certain hard truths about self and life. To explain it in these terms is almost to reduce it to the simplicities of platitude, but in these novels such truths have been earned and substantiated by the densely convincing solidity of these fictional people and proved upon the pulses of their readers by a perfectly developed and sharply meticulous realistic manner employed in the representation of the inner and outer life. The hesitant language and the insistent prosaic detail 'creep up on' the reader as inevitable parts of lives closely and substantially lived in all their concrete and minute detail. The maturation of these characters dawns slowly upon the reader, gradually and incrementally, in the unpretentious accounts of the pulse of existence, comprising thousands of small and carefully-observed private moments and points of interchange.

However, a bigger theme has been lying there implicitly all through the series. The individual boy or girl has to mature against and within the potentially tragic and confused nature of humanity, and the huge unstoppable forces of history. Dicey's understanding of the realities of life begins early; her induction is uncompromising and has nothing to do with the pious popular simplifications which assume there is an answer for every problem, a cure for every tragedy. For example, when Momma is dying in *Dicey's Song*, the reader is taken resolutely through the unavoidable fact that this is (it just *is*) an incurable condition, Dicey's anger and grief, her ways of finding comfort – finally arriving at the moment when she unaccountably and illogically begins to feel a little better.

Maturation in these novels is close to *realization* and being *realistic* about life. It would be easier to develop a matured understanding if the characters existed in a fixed and predictable universe. But human experience is not like that – which is probably why the apparent authenticity of Cynthia Voigt's realism is constantly shot through with puzzles: the never-resolved uncertainty about Momma and Maybeth; the mystery of the father; and the implied promise associated with boat-building and sailing.

Despite her Americanness, Voigt's language reminds me of Daniel Defoe, who believed that a plain and direct style betokened a plain and direct writer; and her characters remind me of Thomas Hardy's – peripheral people, rural and humble, and far from the great centres of commerce and culture; often poor and socially unimportant, interested in unsophisticated ways in art, history and literature as a source of a wiser and richer understanding of the fullness of life. The fullness of life for the *Tillerman* characters is in the living of it, with understanding and with the people they love. As for maturation, that consists of living and learning as you live, so that you can live better.

In the *Tillerman* series, readers are given an extended tragic vision of the human condition which sees knowledge of the way things are, and understanding of self, as the only bearable ways of coping; and which accepts that these kinds of understanding take one by surprise in the form either of private revelations or of wisdom statements from other people, often older but in search of understanding themselves; and that the style and structure of the narrative enact and exemplify this vision. Maturation – like reading these novels – is collaborative and exploratory.

Endnotes

1. Cynthia Voigt (1982, 1984), *Dicey's Song*, Collins, pp. 83–4.
2. Wolfgang Iser, quoted by Peter Hunt (1991), *Criticism, Theory, and Children's Literature*, Blackwell, p. 100.
3. *Dicey's Song* p. 131.
4. Cynthia Voigt (1981, 1983), *Homecoming*, Collins, pp. 221–5.
5. Ibid., p. 11.
6. Ibid., p. 67.
7. Ibid., p. 22.
8. Ibid., p. 27.
9. Ibid., p. 128.
10. Ibid., p. 24.
11. Ibid., p. 265.
12. Cynthia Voigt (1987, 1988), *Sons From Afar*, Collins, pp. 58–9.
13. Ibid., pp. 37–8.
14. Ibid., p. 202.
15. Ibid., pp. 265–6.

16. Ibid., p. 259.
17. Ibid., pp. 274–5.
18. Ibid., p. 280.
19. Ibid., p. 287.
20. Cynthia Voigt (1983, 1985), *A Solitary Blue*, Collins, pp. 30–1.
21. Ibid., p. 31.
22. Ibid., p. 37.
23. Ibid., p. 102.
24. Ibid., p. 52.
25. Ibid., p. 44.
26. Ibid., p. 56.
27. Ibid., p. 61.
28. Ibid., pp. 95–6.
29. Ibid., p. 96.
30. Ibid., p. 109.
31. Ibid., pp. 96–116.
32. Ibid., p. 114.
33. Ibid., p. 138.
34. Ibid., p. 142.
35. Ibid., p. 138 *ff.*
36. Ibid., p. 215.
37. Ibid., p. 216.
38. Ibid., p. 56.
39. Ibid., p. 100.
40. Ibid., p. 125.
41. Ibid., p. 186.
42. Ibid., p. 185.
43. Ibid., p. 212.
44. Ibid., p. 219.
45. Cynthia Voigt (1985, 1986), *The Runner*, Collins, p. 26.
46. Ibid., p. 29.
47. Ibid., p. 26.
48. Ibid., p. 34.
49. Ibid., p. 103.
50. Ibid., p. 70.
51. Ibid., p. 185.
52. Ibid., p. 151.
53. Ibid., p. 210.
54. Ibid., p. 176.
55. Ibid., pp. 180–1.
56. Ibid., p. 18.
57. Ibid., p. 30.
58. Ibid., p. 196.
59. Ibid., p. 221.
60. Cynthia Voigt (1987), *Come A Stranger*, Collins, p. 234.

61. Ibid., pp. 72–3.
62. Ibid., p. 63.
63. Ibid., p. 63.
64. Ibid., p. 65.
65. Ibid., pp. 74–5.
66. Ibid., p. 77.
67. Ibid., p. 16.
68. Ibid., p. 41.
69. Ibid., p. 47.
70. Ibid., p. 51.
71. Ibid., p. 82.
72. Ibid., p. 87.
73. Ibid., p. 90.
74. Ibid., p. 103.
75. Ibid., p. 105.
76. Ibid., pp. 119–20.
77. *A Solitary Blue*, p. 182.
78. *Come A Stranger*, p. 204.
79. Ibid., p. 204.
80. Ibid., p. 128.
81. Ibid., p. 129.
82. Ibid., p. 230.
83. Ibid., pp. 230–1.
84. Ibid., p. 223.
85. Ibid., p. 225.
86. Ibid., p. 223.
87. *Dicey's Song*, p. 128.
88. Ibid., p. 213.
89. Ibid., p. 214.
90. Ibid., pp. 220–1.
91. Cynthia Voigt (1989, 1990), *Seventeen Against the Dealer*, Collins, p. 132.
92. Ibid., pp. 14–5.
93. Ibid., p. 55.
94. Ibid., p. 71.
95. Ibid., pp. 72–3.
96. Ibid., p. 81.
97. Ibid., p. 86.
98. Ibid., p. 19.
99. Ibid., p. 87.
100. Ibid., p. 152.
101. Sons From Afar, pp. 86–7.
102. Seventeen Against the Dealer, p. 1096.
103. Ibid., p. 114.
104. Ibid., p. 119.

105. Ibid., p. 123.
106. Ibid., p. 146.
107. Ibid., p. 161.
108. Ibid., p. 186.
109. Ibid., p. 224.
110. Ibid., p. 177.
111. Ibid., p. 192.
112. Ibid., p. 200.
113. Ibid., p. 200.
114. Ibid., p. 216.
115. Ibid., p. 233.
116. Ibid., p. 234.
117. Ibid., p. 251.
118. Ibid., p. 254.
119. Ibid., p. 239.

CHAPTER 4

The Fiction of Jan Mark

Margaret Meek

Prologue

Jan Mark's impressive skill as a storyteller and her incomparable qualities as a writer make it both impossible and unnecessary to set her books in a single, summative category of children's literature. Her range of topics and narrative modes – each story is a distinct, writerly artefact – keeps the adventures of narration close to the pleasures and challenges of reading. Maturation, in the sense of growth, is appropriate to describe how her characters and the situations they inhabit become part of the reader's increasing self-conscious awareness of their own involvement in this process. She writes for her youngest readers with the same scrupulous care as for adults, a notion that the latter sometimes find disconcerting.

When her first novel, *Thunder and Lightnings*, was published in 1976, children's literature in English had acquired a reputation as a distinctive form of narrative fiction worthy of serious critical attention. A new market for 'quality' publishing had attracted authors who wanted to write more complex novels for confident readers and to experiment with different textual kinds, including those that displaced the conventional relationship between the teller and the told. There was also a deal of interest in newer kinds of fantasy, derived from child psychology, and other tales that shadowed adult metafictions, where the reader's awareness of the reading process is part of the narration. It was a good time for new writers.

The most significant model for Jan Mark's early books was the unpredictable, idiosyncratic and emotionally powerful work of William Mayne, who has remained faithful to a young readership in his explorations of the felt life of childhood. Sympathetic critics called his writing 'new realism', a well-meant but somewhat diminishing description of his love of language and what it makes. Jan Mark says of Mayne that he encouraged her to write the way she wanted to. He had already shown how dialogue – conversation – could be an active force in storytelling. Narration was beginning to move forward in modulated speech patterns. She also learned from him how to 'position' her readers in relation to events in the texts. In her more speculative novels she has interests in common with Ursula LeGuin. Over twenty-seven years Mark has written a great deal. Critics appreciate her work and find in it both different and renewed sources of satisfaction, notably in her technical mastery of narrative, her wit, intellectual toughness and her subtlety of apprehension in dealing with the universal experiences of childhood and thereafter.

In what follows we shall examine how Jan Mark represents, shows and interprets children's expanding notions of identity, and their concern with 'how I wonder what you are'. This should be related to other aspects of her work, sometimes too little regarded: for example, her challenging of conventional wisdom and values, and her concern for the scholarship that underpins her critical acuity. It should be possible to show how, with an author's help, children discover that people in stories are sometimes easier to get to know than people in real life. The person in the story who has to endure suffering, hardship or loss 'might be me'. Maturation, as coming to terms with emotional difficulties, is often more complex than the ability to survive in dangerous circumstances.

There are at least 75 titles in Mark's bibliography. Innovations in content and narration make conventional categories inappropriate. Some books are recorded as being out of print, others are being reprinted. Selection has been inevitable. There will certainly be something new to come.

Exploring childhood: picture books

Jan Mark was an established author of books for older children before she wrote texts for picture books. As a trained artist, a sculptor, she knew how much the illustrator depends on the author for clues about the setting of the story and the appearance of the characters. Shirley Hughes says that writers leave

> a shadow of themselves that runs through everything they write, like the letters in a stick of rock candy. You read and reread and mull it over, get the scent like the hound dog shown somebody's old shoe. The better the book, the stronger the scent.[1]

Jan Mark's stories are interpreted by many artists who respond to the latent as well as the obvious sense of the telling.

In 1986, Charlotte Voake created the drawings for *Fur*, Jan Mark's first picture book. Here are all the words:

> Thin Kitty grew fat. She made a nest in my hat, another in the kitchen cupboard and a third on Mum's skirt. But she liked the hat best. All night she purred. And now my hat is full of fur. Kittens![2]

The feeling that comes with the text is enhanced by the texture of the drawings; the straw of the hat contrasting with the fluffiness of the kittens. In good picture books, the words and the pictures 'enhance and extend each other'.[3] In a book like *Fur*, early reading is visually memorable. Children come to expect, and then to know, that the words and pictures in a book are the same every time you read it. Their book friends are there, waiting for the next meeting. The feeling is recaptured with the sense.

The association of this kind of reading with children's imaginative play has been extended by recent research, including new technology for tracking eye movements, that examines in detail what children do when they read pictures.[4] Yet nothing has displaced Margery Fisher's conviction that if children are to become willing, competent and sensitive readers, 'enjoyment must come first'.[5] The competition from other visual stimuli is strong. But the discovery of how to pore over a page at will is, literally, an eye opener to the familiar and the strange, the comic and the tragic.

The virtue of picture books includes an offer of dual virtuosity in storytelling, as with music and verse in songs. Sometimes there is comic excess. In *Strat and Chatto* (1990), illustrated by David Hughes, the written text and the pictures are formally more complex. The architect's drawings on the endpapers suggest a formal complication will appear in the text. It may be only a housing difficulty for a rat and a cat. The 'voice-over' of the text begins formally; is it comic or serious?

> A rat ran up the fire escape and rapped at the cat flap. A cat looked out. His name was Chatto and it was his flap.
>
> 'Good morning,' said the rat, with his tail over his arm. 'I hear you have a mouse problem. Can I be of assistance?'
>
> 'I certainly have a problem,' said Chatto. 'However, excuse my mentioning it, but aren't you of the mouse class yourself?'
>
> 'I am a rat,' said the rat, and you may call me Strat – short for

Stratorat. I'm a high flyer.' He tried to look modest but his whiskers twitched.

'Oh, a bat,' said the cat.

'No, a rat,' said Strat. 'But some of my best friends are bats. We hang out together.'[6]

The word play is in both sound and meaning; a rat-a-tat-tat for all the 'a' sounds and a *double entendre* for 'hang out'.

Strat's engagement is to rid Chatto's house of a mouse that drops lentils on his head. He engages helpers: bats, cockroaches, silver fish and a toad, who not only intervene but also take up residence. Chatto is relieved when they all clear out again, leaving him with the mouse, and Strat as a new lodger.

The particular kind of wit that goes with the mock-heroic tone and conversational clichés is beyond the discernment of the youngest readers. But they know something is afoot when they hear from someone reading the text aloud the particular way of saying 'we vermin must stick together'. The reader has begun to know that words mean more than they say. This is one of the most important reading discoveries for nearly fluent beginners, whose understanding is usually in advance of their reading aloud with confidence.

A more intricate tale, another that displays Jan Mark's witty versatility, is *Carrot Tops and Cotton Tails*. Tony Ross's pictures begin with a Victorian gentleman at table with two balefully scowling children who sit with their arms folded, staring out of the picture. The gent is holding up a carrot on his fork. He is about to tell the story of why carrots can no longer talk, a tale of conflict between a colony of peaceable rabbits (shown in Puritan attire) and a 'band of gallant carrots'. We are told that the rabbits ate the grass, ('kept its hair tidy'). The carrots came out at sunset ('when carrots look their best'), to show themselves off to the other vegetables. Only the rabbits fail to admire the carrots, who then provoke the rabbits with jeers.

'Why do you have such silly ears?' And the next night: 'Why do you have such silly tails?' And the following night: 'I say, I say!' The carrots called: 'You there, with the silly eyes', and so on. The carrots' scorning of the rabbits reaches 'such silly teeth'. Provoked beyond all bearing, the rabbits turn on the carrots who then meet the full force of the teeth they have disdained.

When night fell, the garden was laid waste. And since that time, no carrot has been safe in the presence of a hostile rabbit, and all other vegetables fear their terrible teeth. But the rabbits ... still live in peace and harmony with grass.[7]

A modern fable like this one involves a different kind of collusion between the teller and the told. When the rabbits try to defend themselves, the carrots 'fall about laughing'.

This kind of hauteur that implies nods and winks on the side, comes again when the narrator says the story came from 'a seafaring sheep with one eye'. He may have been lying. The illustration of the sheep suggests this might well have been the case. Story-telling depends on such ambiguities. The reader has to learn to distinguish a reliable narrator from the rest.

A more sinister note is struck in *Fun with Mrs Thumb*, illustrated by Nicola Bayley whose miniature scenes are instantly recognizable from their detail. The scene is set in an exquisitely furnished dolls' house. A ginger cat, whose head scarcely appears in full at the window, invites Mrs Thumb to play hide-and-seek. The well-appointed rooms are overturned; Mrs Thumb falls downstairs. From the illustrations it is clear that this is more menace and *mayhem than play*.

Do you like
hide and seek?
Let's play you're
A mouse –
I'll bite, you squeak.

Real mice
squeak and skip
when I nip,
so ...
When I pounce,
you bounce.

Cheer up.
Here's one last swipe
Before they shut you in.
I have to go now,
someone is opening a tin.[8]

There are echoes of Beatrix Potter from time to time; from Mr McGregor's garden, for example.

'Doing the voices' is one of Jan Mark's repertoire of skills in giving texts, verse or prose, a distinctly tonal quality, especially in those which come with overtones of others. In *Haddock*, a more straightforward but no less subtle traditional tale, we hear siren songs, perhaps the Lorelei. A haddock falls in love with a mermaid, but he cannot follow her when she meets a fisherman called Stanley whom she wants to marry. Stanley wonders what the neighbours would say.

'I love you', the haddock said. 'My heart belongs to Stanley,' the mermaid said.

'Stanley eats people like you for breakfast.'

'I know,' said the haddock sadly. 'Fishwives cook us with rice and call it kedgeree.'[9]

The fishwife, Moll, in serge and a bustle, also fancies Stanley. The mermaid decks herself in fishnet to impress him. She wins. But when Stanley seeks to kill the haddock for his wedding breakfast, the mermaid and the haddock return to the sea. They have thousands of children.

Picture books are a place for authors and artists to stretch their skill as best pleases them. They can recast conventional kinds of writing; invent worlds, realist or surrealist, as long as the story draws the readers into the created world without losing sight entirely of the real one. Jan Mark joins in the fun with the artists. The more serious side of this play has to do with the activities of the reader's imagination, the 'what if' of fantasy. We remind ourselves that, in childhood, the real and the fantastic are close together.

Retellings

When Jan Mark retells stories, she is not only giving her readers, adults as well as children, something different. She is also extending their repertoires of narratives into older kinds. There's a distinguishable whiff of its Apocryphal origin in the way she tells *The Tale of Tobias*.[10] This is the story of the journey Tobit's son made to reclaim the money his father, now old and blind, left with a friend in a city far away. The narrator is Tobit's dog, who comments on people and events en route. Their travelling companion is Azarius, the angel Raphael in disguise. He tells Tobias that the intestines of the fish they caught for supper will be useful in dealing with demons during Tobias' stay in the house of his prospective father-in-law and, later, when the mission is accomplished, in curing Tobit's blindness. The moral is, your good deeds will be remembered and recompensed. The dog is the only one spoken well of in the Bible. Jan Mark's version has the economy and straightforward clarity of the original, and a less easily described heart-warming quality. Rachel Merriman's illustrations, on fine cream paper, set the biblical scene.

In the following year, Walker Books went for gold in the illustration, design and production of *The Midas Touch*, a cautionary tale if there ever was one. From time to time, publishers are urged to ensure that children know the fables of Greek mythology. Here Jan Mark makes the classical past approachable. She uses the device from the oral tradition that takes the reader into the confidence of the storyteller, this time about wishing stories that all end the same way. The wish backfires. Midas asked for something that he did not need and had not wanted until that mad moment.

He said to Dionysus, 'Let everything that I touch be turned into gold.' Dionysus smiled a terrible smile. He did not say: *Everything*. He did not say: *Are you sure*? He did not say: *Think about it*. He only said, 'My pleasure,' and he meant it.[11]

Folk tales, fairy tales and legends count as the past in storytelling for the young. In addition, Eve Bearne suggests that readers and listeners, entering the world of the storyteller and understanding the wider relevance of the tale, (friendship and faithfulness in Tobias, greed in the case of Midas) have the chance 'to stand both within and outside of themselves' in the way traditional tales 'uniquely offer'.[12]

Although designed for older children, Jan Mark's version of the Old Testament, *God's Story*, illustrated by David Perkins, fits neatly into this section. The emphasis is on the Bible as a store of narratives which attract different kinds of commentary from adults, but are rarely read nowadays 'as stories'. Not many devoted readers, re-tellers and commentators see them as part of a longer story, of

> ... how God made the Universe and then, when he had finished it, he created Mankind to enjoy all the other things that he had made, only to discover that no matter how much he loved his humans they could rarely be bothered to remember him, much less worship him or even thank him. God was frequently on the point of giving up on his disappointing creatures, and wiping them out before they ruined everything else that he had made.[13]

To separate the Bible stories from the commonly read texts of the Old Testament, Jan Mark used the Midrash Rabbah – the scholarly commentary or 'investigation' of the Torah.[14] She has brought exceptional narrative skill to the task of making a coherent whole of the well-known incidents, up to the return of the Jews from exile in Babylon. The relation of Biblical texts to children's growth is a cultural matter as much as a personal one. Jan Mark suggests that her readers should not become embroiled in the debates about how God should be worshipped and his Law obeyed, but 'stop here with the words of one of the first great rabbis, Hillel, who said, "Do nothing to other people that you would not want them to do to you."' Although experienced Bible readers will recognize the characters and the incidents associated with them, even those well-acquainted with the common English versions and translations will gain some different insights from this portrayal of God's reasonableness and the folly of those he is good to.

We began with picture books which encourage young, even very young, readers to explore childhood. In the next section we see how other children and adults help with this process.

Short books

At the same time as they are learning to read, children begin to encounter more of the world outside their homes. School becomes the extension of social life. Many experiences there and elsewhere have a 'first-time' quality before they become routines. The first day at school is only one of a series of new experiences. Looking back on incidents that linger in the memory we recall not only what happened, but also what we felt at the time. Nearly always, something changed afterwards. Amongst these recollections lurk the stories we encountered in books at that time. Learning to read both words and the world, especially the world of school, is a distinctive growing point.

'Short' books are a publishing convention linked to perceived progress in children's reading after picture books. Sometimes called 'chapter books' because of the contents list, they encourage readers to read continuously, so as to become accustomed to the thrust of a narrative, its shape, characters and 'the sense of an ending'. The readers are encouraged to read silently, singly, so as to become both the teller and the told.[15] Andrew Melrose describes these books as 'amongst the most rewarding things that a new reader can be offered. The sense of achievement is immense.'[16]

As we shall see, Jan Mark takes short stories very seriously as a literary kind. Some critics regard them as her best work, making comparisons with Henry James and William Trevor as they do so. Her introduction to *The Oxford Book of Children's Stories* (1993) is a scholarly history of the form, as are the carefully chosen examples. She is also concerned that children should not be short-changed in what they are encouraged to read.

> Most animals are 'children' only for weeks or months. A human is a child for years, continuously learning. Whether or not children's authors intend to teach, they know perfectly well that their readers are in a learning mode. Most hope to leave their readers at the end of a novel or short story with some idea, attitude or opinion that they didn't have when they began reading, even if they are unable to articulate this. Young children are not analytic critics, which is why so many adults are prepared to be critics on their behalf.[17]

In writing short books for young readers who are just beginning to be independent, Jan Mark not only adapts her choice of words and length of sentences, she also makes the complete story a reward for the effort of reading it. The reader's discovery that 'texts make meaning' is the beginning of the insight that relates the content of a story to readers as persons. No study of intellectual growth should omit the fact that memory treats story characters and events as actual happenings. Fictive narratives also extend young readers' views of what reading is good for. Other components of these texts are: an increased use of the past tense, longer dialogues, a change in the voice of the narrator to the first person, the surprises of 'what will happen next', and the implied judgements of the characters' actions. Most of these things slip into well-told tales as the reader's understanding brings the world to the book and the book to the world. Francis Spufford's writing about *The Child that Books Build* is seriously exact.[18]

Short books are commonly used in the 'text' fragment of the Literacy Hour, which is the standardized, obligatory time for the teaching of reading in England during the first two years of school. 'Big books' are stories in large type designed to be read by the class as a group. I read *Worry Guts* (1998) in this format. The blurb on the cover says it is 'a provoking story'.

The setting is a primary school classroom. On Monday morning the class pet is missing. Ciaran 'had a nasty feeling that he had been the last person to touch the guinea pig's cage'. As it turns out, he is right. He'd been giving Herman a piece of carrot when Mrs Collier had told them to hurry up and go to the hall for hymn practice. Ciaran has a list of things he worries about. Sophie, the clever girl, asks why his list has SATS on it. She tells him: 'It isn't for months and months and months.'

Sophie's cure for worrying is a collection of tiny 'trouble dolls'.

'They came from Guatemala; that's in South America. You can tell them your worries at night and put them back in the bag, and they take care of your worries during the night. You can only give them one worry each.'[19]

Kershild's worry is about learning Arabic (presumably at his religious school at the weekend). He says:

'I don't suppose we're allowed to use things like this, anyway. It's a what's it, a superstition.' Sophie is sure: 'They look after my worries.'[20]

To displace his worries, Ciaran makes a SATS monster out of yellow plasticine. He says it's yellow because SATS sounds yellow; the way that September sounds light brown. 'Somehow, having the trouble monsters where you could see them made the troubles less threatening than they seemed when written down in the list.' When the teacher discovers that everyone is making SATS monsters 'covered in warts and boils', she decides to have one classroom monster, made out of chicken wire and newspaper, to displace all worries about SATS. When told that they were worrying too soon, a child retorts: 'It's all very well for you. You haven't got anything to worry about.' Mrs Collier's reply is: 'Our trouble monster is called *inspection.*'[21]

The school children's feelings, strongly evoked by the text, are reflected on the faces of the characters in the illustrations. The readers in the real classroom are looking at themselves in a book. They are facing themselves and their worries. They can talk about them, and thus distance them, as part of their concern for Ciaran. Kershild's reading worry is something that inner-city pupils know about. They see him calling up a word he knows, 'superstition'. Now the readers learn it, if it's new. Jan Mark's highly rated realism is at its best when she depicts the 'stringy, sticky mess' of Ciaran's hand in the plasticine. The pace of the sentence includes his effortful 'twiddling at it'. But it is the shared feelings of slight disgust that predominate in those learning to read. They are locked into this powerful tale, as if they were acting it out, for real.

Ten years before the composition of this multilayered text, Jan Mark was singling out incidents of childhood growth to transform into chapter books. Where the picture book has a conventional 'dual address', a level of awareness for adults reading the book to a listener, the short book undertakes to enlarge the young readers' under-standing of the feelings behind what the characters do, notice and say when they are reading on their own. Here now is a selection of examples, each with a particular insight into readers' increasing awareness of themselves and others.

The Dead Letter Box was published in the Hamish Hamilton Antelope Series in 1982. We are told:

> Glenda and Louie were best friends, but Glenda was Louie's only friend, while everybody was Glenda's friend. Glenda might start talking to almost anyone, even if Louie were already talking to her.[22]

These few words convey the uneven reciprocity of the relationship.

Glenda's impending move to a bungalow near the sea where she will be able to have a pony, will leave Louie without a friend. (That is, if you don't count Wayne, who 'wore his snorkel jacket indoors and sat with the hood zipped up so that he looked like a ship's ventilator'). Louie knows that 'you couldn't go round saying to people, "Will you be my friend?" They would giggle and say "why?"'[23]

During the six weeks before Glenda leaves, she distances herself from Louie. Meanwhile, Louie is devising a way to keep in touch with Glenda. She proposes a 'dead letter-box' in a book in the town library, where they will both go even if they do not meet. Louie selects a book that is not often taken out and hopes Glenda will leave her letter in reply. The reader already guesses that she won't; she is not keen on writing. Disappointment is added to Louie's sense of loss. When there is no reply, she expresses her feelings in another letter, this time telling Glenda: 'I think you are a Mean Rotten Old thingy and I never did like you. I'm GLAD you moved. I wish you moved years ago.'

Another girl, Jane, is on a mission of her own in the library to display copies of her mother's books where they will be noticed and borrowed. She sees Louie posting her letter to Glenda in the dead letter-box book. After Louie has explained her plight, Jane robustly tells her that Glenda wasn't worth caring about. Instead of expecting to hear from Glenda, Louie should advertise for a pen friend by leaving a note in more than one book with her address. This becomes a collaborative project; Jane puts in messages of her own. The result is a huge increase in visitors to the library. Louie knows that, when Jane goes back to London, she will still have a faithful pen friend who will appear again in the school holidays.

Sharing Louie's pain, which includes resentment at being let down as well as a genuine feeling of loss, the reader comes to know that this was inevitable from the beginning of the story. Glenda always spoke of herself first.

The Twig Thing (1988) is a common incident, treated gently. A father is moving house with his two daughters. Their unhappiness focuses on the fact that the new house has no garden. The reader intuits that the children are missing their mother. A small consolation, with some hope, comes when they find a twig to plant and a cat to adopt. They can now look forward. The description concentrates on ways of seeing: 'At the top of the stairs was a door. It was lying on its back in the middle of the ceiling.'[24] Behind these small incidents is continuing unhappiness that children understand but don't always have the words to explain.

The three stories, published by Walker Books as Sprinters, join home and school. The movement between them lets the characters demonstrate their growing independence and responsibilities. Feelings become more complicated. In *The Snow Maze*,[25] Joe finds a key. His first puzzle is to find the door that it opens. His domineering classmate, Akash, has told him: 'Keys are no good unless they open something.' Joe remembers a gate in an old doorway that stands by itself. Once open, the gate lets Joe on to a path that goes round and round a field in circles. It's a maze. No one can see the path from the road, so that when his classmates see Joe running in circles they say he is mad. How is he to convince them of the existence of the maze unless he lets them come through the door? Then the maze would stop being his maze. He tells the others that it is a secret maze and only he can see it. Urged on by Akash, the other boys call him names and say he is mad.

Joe thinks about his friends. Akash and Tim are big and strong, but Joe decides he would rather be like Irrun, 'small and brave'. Irrun says, 'I'd rather be crazy than nasty.' Now Joe is beginning to see how people differ, especially in their approach to others. When Irrun asks to see his maze, he remembers how she had supported him and shows her how to run round it. The onlookers laugh at them both. The snow comes and begins to cover up the footprints left in the frost so there is a chance that no one can see the path. So as to keep the maze after the snow melts, Tim's dad, a builder, puts sand on the path. 'When the snow melted, the sand would still be there.' Later, when no-one is looking, Joe unlocks the gate and leaves it open, so that anyone could run into the maze whenever they wanted to.

In this tale, feelings and attitude count for more than action. Joe's are as complicated as the situation he finds himself in. He is ambivalent about letting his classmates see the maze. Being kept out makes them jealous. Gaps in the text invite the reader to join Joe in his wondering. If you want to be one of the group, what is the right way to share things?

Friendship between Jane and Andrea in *Taking the Cat's Way Home*[26] (1994) has none of the underlying jealousy that spoils the relationship of Louie and Glenda. Although Andrea is a year older than Jane and in a different class, they go to school together, accompanied by Jane's fine cat, Furlong, who returns home by a different route. William, a new boy, doesn't like cats. When he throws a stone at Furlong, Jane hits William and is hit back in return. The headmaster arraigns them both. William then tells Jane he'll 'get her' after school – that horrible threat. So she and Andrea take the cat's way home along the top of the walls of the gardens. When they lose their way, they call for Furlong, who comes then leads them home. The girls have overcome their uncertainties and gained a sense of daring and confident independence. They have seen people in their back gardens, which are all different. William follows but has no such luck. He is genuinely lost and afraid, no longer the bully. He still needs adult help. Since this book appeared, the menace of bullying has moved to the top of the list of topics for books of this length.

In *Lady Long-Legs* (1999) bullying is more evident, but quickly dealt with. Nisba is a new girl. The others in her class have been there for three years and a term, so they can't imagine she doesn't know the rules, both formal and informal. Nisba asks the headmaster where the heating comes from and discovers there are hot pipes under the floor tiles, which often come unstuck. There are superstitions about the tiles: bad luck if you walk on the white tile in the middle of the doorway, for example. 'People said that if you stood on a blue tile and on a pink tile at the same time, all your teeth would fall out.'

Nisba is very tall. When she walks down the corridor on the green tiles she is told by Lucy, an overbearing character, 'Only people in Year 4 can walk on green tiles. Everyone knows that.' Nisba suddenly understands. 'They were angry because she could reach the green tiles, not because she did.' Then, someone hooks a foot round her ankle and she falls. The recovery ritual is the application to the painful spot of the *Hand of Peas*, a white plastic glove with frozen peas in it. Nisba doesn't want to walk on the green tiles all the time, 'but Lucy was a bully, and bullies must never be allowed to win'. Over the weekend, grey tiles replace the discarded ones. They are too far apart for anyone but Nisba to step on them. The others have to jump. Lucy tries and fails. Nisba admits that she won't walk only on the grey tiles.

> 'There,' Mr Martin said. 'Do you understand? You don't have to do something just because you can.' If Nisba stops walking on the grey tiles, will the rest of you stop trying to? They all nodded, but Lucy hissed, 'Daddy-long-legs.'
> 'Nisba can't be a daddy,' Neesa said. 'She's a girl.'
> 'She'll be a lady, not a daddy,' Aisha said.
> And Nisba said, 'That's right. I'm Lady Long-Legs.'[27]

Although the pictures of Nisba distinguish her by her colour and clothes from the other children, no reference is made to her appearance, except to her long legs as she strides across the tiles with ease.

Almost beyond the reach of adults in their attempts to socialize children into everyday realities, lie the stories that children tell themselves about the world and how things happen. Various early systems of belief: not stepping on lines between paving stones, responses to the activities of the tooth fairy and Father Christmas, chants, rhymes and superstitions as ancient as touching wood and crossing fingers and notions of 'good luck' or the opposite, related to the unexpected are still powerfully active when children go to school and learn to say prayers in assembly.

Kasey, the central figure in *The Lady with Iron Bones* (2001), has encountered too much reality in her ten years. She now has to look after her baby brother and her mother in post-natal depression, as her older half-brother has left home to look for work, and his father, in Birmingham. No wonder then that Kasey is both volatile and difficult in school where no one fully realizes how seriously she takes her caring role. In contrast, her thoughtful friend, Ellen, has an orderly, fuller life with her working mother. They both do their best to help Kasey.

Ellen shows Kasey how she takes a short cut to and from school through the bottom of a neighbour's wilderness garden. In her exploration of this enchanting place Kasey finds the battered statue that Ellen calls the Lady with Iron Bones. After a discussion of the function of statues, Kasey turns to the Lady in the hope that she will help her; the church she had prayed in had singularly failed to bring back her absent brother.

Then begins a series of propitiations and votive offerings, including her earrings, that Kasey leaves in the bowl that is part of the statue. They disappear and Kasey insists that the Lady has accepted them. When Kasey's brother rings up to say he is coming home, Kasey insists on thanking the lady. So a pattern develops, petitions are followed by appeasements.

Not content with giving the Lady a rose, a pair of earrings, a handbag mirror and a silver bracelet, Kasey is now anxious that the lady should know that she is grateful. There is still the gnawing fear in her that unless the Lady is kept happy she will vengefully undo all the good that Kasey thinks she had done. How long was this to go on? It was like blackmail, only Kasey was blackmailing herself.

Kasey's brother comes home; her mother is seen to be much better. But Kasey's faith in the powers of the stature has overridden her strong grasp of reality. At some point she asked the Lady to punish her teacher, Mrs Bean, out of vengeance for admonitions about being late. Mrs Bean has a car accident involving a child on a bicycle who is believed to be critically ill. Kasey thinks she is responsible. Her next plea is echoed by Ellen: 'Make it all right. Don't let him die.'

The person who hears this is Mrs Sayer, the owner of the garden, who has seen Ellen crossing the wilderness part of it for two years without stopping her. She asks Ellen questions that bring the whole situation to light. The Lady is a statue of Calypso, a nymph who lived on an island in the Aegean Sea and detained Odysseus for seven years as Mrs Sayer remarks: 'Bird baths do not work miracles.'

Mrs Sayer then confronts Ellen with this and asks what she believes has happened. When Ellen says she went along with the pretence of believing for Kasey's sake, Mrs Sayer then remarks that she is sure Kasey knows as well as Ellen does that 'she is worshipping a bird bath, by putting a face to what she believes in, only she doesn't know what she believes in' Kasey has been 'ill-wishing' in response to 'the feeling that there's nobody in charge, nobody taking care, nobody putting things right'. Mrs Sayer asks Ellen:

> 'Do you read fairy tales?'
> 'Not any more.'
> You ought to. Think of all those stories where people get their wishes granted. Something always backfires, doesn't it? Because they wish for things they shouldn't have.'[28]

The same moral as in King Midas. There is no direct mention of superstitions, but the sense is clear.

By now it must be evident that the range of content and style in Jan Mark's stories is their outstanding characteristic. They offer developing readers a repertoire of textual understandings that have their origins in actual events common to childhood, but made particular in each incident. In her portrayal of friendship, the first encounters beyond the family, her readers discover how other people can be different without being strange, and how the most ordinary events can spring surprises. She also lets old stories beget new ones.

Take a more recent book in this survey as an example. *Long Lost* (2002) is a chapter book for newly confident readers – a scary story in a series called Shock Shop. The godparents are E. Nesbit, the expert on treasure hunts and long-lost relatives, and M. R. James, the master of the ghost story. Their bequests to this tale are an inheritance, and the unseen, guessed-at menace of the imagined horror. Here it is a sinister curse. The overtones of the text indicate the author's close acquaintance with its predecessors in this kind.

The family that benefits from an inheritance left to their dead father consists of George, Elsie and their mother, who live in genteel Edwardian poverty in Hackney. When their circumstances and prospects change, they are invited to visit the home of the current baronet in Chertsey. The early chapters of the story sort out for modern readers the nature of 'heirs and assigns' and the details of primogeniture and the difference in lifestyle between 'rich' and 'comfortable'. For Elsie and her mother the visit is a great success. George finds in Fred an ideal friend. Bertram, the heir to the title, is eerily different; 'everyone seems to be on their best behaviour in Bertie's presence, even his parents'. His smile at Mother and Elsie 'had gone nowhere near his eyes'. He is, in the terms of his time, a rotter.

Bertram's great skill is mental torture; the kind that uses innuendo, vague threat and the sophisticated bullying that works by suggestion and hints. He tells George that the eldest sons in the family have a shadow. It follows them everywhere. They die young. Bertram claims he is free from the threat; an older brother died in infancy. He makes sure that the idea of the shadow is never far away from George's thoughts. 'Just because you can't see anything,' Bertie said, 'it doesn't mean there isn't anything to see.'

George begins to look behind him rather a lot. Summoning courage to talk to the baronet about the missing elder son, perhaps reminding Uncle Gib, whom he loved like a real uncle, of some tragedy he had bravely tried to forget.

> 'I think we'd have noticed another child,' Uncle Gib said cheerfully. 'I'm sure my wife would have done. No, Bertie's the next baronet. Don't say you've been worrying about *him*, you chump. Save your sympathy, he's the hardest nut in the cluster. He never wastes his sympathy on anyone else. Bertie takes after the Milnes and they were all soldiers and pirates.'
> 'Pirates,' George said. 'That'll be something to tell the chaps at school – having pirates in the family.'[29]

George faces what he fears. When Bertie 'was at his old game, staring over George's shoulder as if he could see something there', George 'felt very grown up'. He doesn't hate Bertie; he despises him. It's such a good read, more subversive than it appears about snobbery and class, and quietly witty.

The short books are little packages of rich reading experience. Displaying the author's amazing versatility, good sense and abundant skill, they are bound to be good models for children learning to write. The dialogues in which the characters engage with their peers and elders are represented with artful simplicity. The pleasure principle is strong and continuous; insights abound.

Short story collections

In her Patrick Hardy lecture in 1993, Jan Mark shared with her audience some of the things she discovered while compiling *The Oxford Book of Children's Stories* – an enterprise which involved investigating 250 years of children's fiction. The book includes no extracts from longer works, no translations, no tales which had been written for adults and annexed by children; the contents are short stories, written in English *for* children. The publishers chose their editor wisely. By that time Jan Mark's reputation was well established. She told her listeners that

> the skill in writing short stories lies in recognizing material that needs to be dealt with tersely, but while we had to wait for Kipling for the adult short story, most writers for children understood very quickly that they were dealing with readers and listeners who had a limited experience, short attention span and a notoriously low boredom threshold.[30]

It is Jan Mark's view that

> Over the last thirty years the children's short story has become indistinguishable from the modern adult short story, a sharply focused examination of an illuminating moment, a story that will, moreover, find its own readership regardless of the publisher's recommended reading age.[31]

The stories in Jan Mark's Oxford collection have a great deal to say and show about growing up, the embarrassments and difficulties of later childhood and the period we now call adolescence. The contents include a dialogue of later stories with earlier ones.

My view is that, in the short stories of this anthology and in the collections Jan Mark has made of her own examples, older readers will find incidents they recognize as part of their own experience. Their recollections run alongside as they read. Students of children's literature now have to hand an anthology of examples which provide more direct evidence of the concerns and competences of their authors than are to be found in compressed histories of the subject. It is likely also to play a part in the maturation of those who write books about books for children.

The story of her own that Jan Mark chose to include is *Dan, Dan, the Scenery Man* (1989). On Friday nights June's dad, Keith, goes to rehearsals for the village dramatic society's Christmas pantomime, where he does walk-on parts, creates and sorts scenery and is seen as generally indispensable. His wife has no time nor liking for acting; she irons on Friday nights. When the parents of a dancing rat decide to go away for Christmas, Keith wheedles his wife into agreeing that June should replace her. June has already danced on stage and could learn the part in time.

From her school drama lessons June has learned that 'there is more to acting than pretending to be somebody else. You had to turn yourself into somebody else, be them and think of them, even if it were only a few minutes at a time.' June is sure that she can see the village actors as the really are, even when they are acting. But when she goes to watch the rehearsals she sees her father become a quite different person – Dan, Dan the scenery man. On the way home June begins a conversation by asking why the actors call him Dan when his name is Keith. Her father says it started as a joke. June then gets into a tangle. She has started something she can't stop. She asks:

> 'Is that why you pretend?' And tailed off, not quite sure what she had meant to ask.
> 'I don't pretend.'
> 'But you aren't like that, really.'
> 'What do you mean by really?' Dad said. 'Think what I do for a living: sell shoes. I don't have to be Dan, Dan, the Scenery Man in Dolcis, do I? I couldn't be.'
> 'You aren't like that at home.'
> 'We don't need Dan at home either,' Dad said. 'Your mum sees to all that.'
> 'Are you acting, then?'
> 'I can't act. If I could, I wouldn't be doing the scenery, would I?'[32]

Later in the conversation, June's father suggests that he and all the others were perhaps more themselves when acting, 'different selves'. Having got this far, June wrings from her father the confession that he likes being Dan better than selling shoes. The conversation moves to the point where they both admit that they are not happy 'all the time'. Then it takes another leap. Keith tells June:

> 'I can't say you'll grow out of it because you're just growing into it.'
> 'Into what?'
> 'Well!' He seemed unsure. 'Just growing up, really. You

don't change as you get older, but you learn to seem different when you need to, when you want to be.'

They were almost home. 'Mum doesn't,' June said. 'She's always the same.'[33]

Keith then takes Jane round to the back of the house to look in. Her mother is watching television and drinking coffee. When she meets June and Keith at the door she is carrying a stack of sheets. June discovers that the iron is cold.

The pretending has a long history. It is prefigured in the opening sentence:

> The first time June saw Dad on stage she was only six. He turned up in the middle of a fierce row as a bent old man, wearing a thin white beard and even when Mum nudged her and hissed, 'There's Daddy,' June could hardly believe it.'[34]

This unmasking of parents, a small movement in a conversation like a tongue exploring a tooth with painful consequences, changes June's view of both the past and the future. In the real world, things would never be the same again. This is now part of the reader's awareness and understanding.

Nothing to be Afraid Of

My personal debts to Jan Mark go back a long way. From the start, what impressed me in her work is what Valentine Cunningham, referring to Roland Barthes, calls 'the intermediate nature of signs and texts, poised between reference inwards and outwards, always stuck with and between words and the world – nothing less than the troublingly dual textuality of narratives'.[35] Good storytellers make the most of this duality. Readers discover it in the play of the text. Another occasion for growth, one that no reader can avoid in a Jan Mark story, is not so much a chance to read about different people and thus discover the otherness of others, but to read about people, differently.

'William's Version', with generous permission, has lived in *How Texts Teach What Readers Learn* since 1988. The story is an intertextual *tour de force* in dialogue between William and his granny who are 'left to entertain each other for an hour while William's mother went to the clinic'. The resonance of the last word sets the scene for the subtext, which emerges as William and his Granny read the story of *The Three Little Pigs* and discuss their divergent interpretations of it. The third text is a book that William consults from time to time: *First Aid for*

Beginners. William objects to every detail in his Granny's version of *The Three Little Pigs*. At each interruption, William's interior narrative about his Mummy's baby slips out.

> 'Tell me a story,' said William. 'Tell me about the wolf.'
> 'Red Riding Hood?'
> 'No, not *that* wolf, the other wolf.'
> 'Peter and the wolf?' said Granny.
> 'Mummy's going to have a baby,' said William.
> 'I know,' said Granny.
> William looked suspicious.[36]

Negotiations about the story continue; Granny gets as far as the load of bricks.

> 'So the little pig took the bricks and built a house.'
> 'He built it on the bomb site.'
> 'Next door to the wolf?' said Granny. 'That was very silly of him.'
> 'There wasn't anywhere else,' said William. 'All the roads were full up.'
> 'The wolf didn't have to come by bus or tricycle this time, then, did he?' said Granny, grown cunning.
> 'Yes.' William took out the book and peered in, secretively. 'He was playing in the cemetery. He had to get another bus.'
> 'And did he eat the conductor this time?'
> 'No. A nice man gave him some money, so he bought a ticket.'
> 'I'm glad to hear it,' said Granny.
> 'He ate the nice man,' said William.[37]

The climax advances. William's mounting fear and hysteria make him insist that it wasn't the wolf that was boiled in the big saucepan. In William's version the wolf boiled and ate the little pig: 'He had him for tea, with chips,' said William, consulting the first aid book.

> Then the wolf washed up and got on his tricycle and went to see his Granny, and his Granny opened the door and said: 'Hello William.'
> 'I thought it was the wolf.'
> 'It was, it was the wolf. His name was William Wolf,' said William.[38]

This is deep play. Knowing children understand what's afoot even if they cannot explain it in the linear fashion expected in classrooms.

All the stories considered here demonstrate that growth and maturity in readers include the intertext of the reader's unconscious. Stories reveal what we have successfully concealed from ourselves.

The most obvious place to examine aspects of children's advance when they enter more fully into the world of adults, is in school stories that frame interactions between teachers and learners. When young people have settled into secondary school, they are expected to display the autonomy that the institution calls 'thinking for yourself'. Less frequently acknowledged, outside both schools and stories, is the exact nature of the challenges the young offer their elders who, in public ways like examinations, are responsible for their progress as thinkers. In stories for older readers, dialogues with authors become more serious. In discovering new tones, oblique telling and irony, the reader has to be alert to what is *not* said.

In, 'The Choice is Yours', the heroine, Brenda, is in an impossible situation, instantly recognizable. She is a member of both the school choir and one of the hockey teams. The rule for both groups is that if you miss a practice you will be out for good. In Brenda's school, rehearsals and hockey practice usually don't clash, but on this storied occasion they do. Brenda can't go to both. The teachers are clearly bitter rivals. Their spittle-sour insistence that Brenda must choose between them makes choice impossible. The stinging clarity of the mental cruelty posing as reasonableness invites readers to face what they know there is to be afraid of, the unpredictability and power of adults in authority. As she goes from one teacher to the other, Brenda is involved in their antagonism: 'I will not allow other members of staff to disrupt my choir practices.' Running between the teachers who are awaiting her decision, she is reproved by the Head Girl. Then the blow:

> Brenda looked at Miss Taylor, at the music room windows, and back at Miss Taylor.
> 'If I leave now, can I join again later?'
> 'Good Lord. Is there no end to the girl's cheek? Certainly not. This is your last chance, Brenda.'[39]

Teachers in school stories are conventional objects of ridicule, but here their power to make Brenda the recipient of their animosity for each other is more threatening.

A year later, two longer stories in *Hairs in the Palm of the Hand* (1981) are directly about school.[40] The first is about boys and masters trying to outwit each other. Betting, strictly forbidden, is a kind of challenge. In the new game, bets are placed against the anticipated amount of time masters waste in lessons over a week. Part of the game is to lead them into digressions. (No money changes hands so it's semi-legal.) The masters are aware of what is afoot – they are just older boys, really, playing the game by their rules. Time and the hour is what they share. The young catch a glimpse of adult responsibilities and the reader enjoys the wit that makes them endurable. Teachers are people too.

The second story has a familiar setting. On the first day of a new term, builders are still in the hall, painters are in the art room, pupils are wandering in corridors, and classes aren't where they should be. Eileen isn't a pupil at the school; she is on holiday nearby and still has a few days free to divert herself. She does this by sneaking into the turmoil. By masquerade and ventriloquism she makes her way into groups and conversations, increasing the chaos around her. Then, provoked by Eileen, a teacher complains about having to teach in a cloakroom; and a group of girls demands to do woodwork. By keeping one step ahead of being found out by posing as a new girl, Eileen has a school adventure, discovering things about school. Her verdict? 'This school's all right. You can get away with murder.'

In both stories, the link between the realism of the tale and the reality of children's lives is not so close as it was in 1981. But school offers drama, crime and punishment, unfairness and taking sides; competition, comedy and tragedy are inherent in its structures. Children talk a lot in school. They know how to tune the pages of stories like these. Jan Mark's skill lies in making heteroglossic dialogues on the page vibrate like the stichomythic rhythms of a Greek chorus.

Feet (1983), a collection of romantic tales for teenagers, includes 'I Was Adored Once, Too' in which a boy called Birkett is in charge of the lighting for the school play – *Twelfth Night* – because he was considered no good for anything else. Given a part, he might mangle Shakespeare. When Andrew Aguecheek fails, the lighting expert takes his place. 'He had then to play the fool that the others take him for.'[41] The words 'stayed in his mind like the dust in a net curtain'. Thereafter the Head, as producer, has much revision to do. The extension of a reader's sympathies for classmates must count as a new form of awareness of change in others who have always seemed to be the same person.

School stories of this time, just before the end of the century, now seem to be historical fiction. But there is something immutable in the relations of young people and those who instruct them in institutions designed for their learning. Reading Jan Mark's work of this period is like listening to gramophone records that capture something that later performances lack. These short stories for accomplished readers include particular kinds of sharpness that create some unease in the readers; they feel as if their thoughts have been read, or they had somehow been caught out. It is a moment of revelation, reflexive understanding at least, when you discover that the book has been reading you. There are also incidents that make stronger intellectual demands on readers to consider the social consequences of growing in awareness of others.

There is no doubt, however, about Jan Mark's power to move her readers beyond discomfiture. As we shall see in *Thunder and Lightnings*, her stories about family life explore the soft part of human sensibility, where the important things are ordinary living, even when the characters seem to draw their breath in pain. When it appeared in 1986, *Frankie's Hat*[42] was a different kind of 'in-seeing' of early adulthood. At seventeen, Frankie is facing the strains of motherhood. Her younger sister comes to visit and sees the difference between her married sibling and the one who shared her childhood. When her sister-in-law offers to baby-sit for a day, Frankie changes clothes with her sister and they both go off on an outing. It's a summer's day in Oxford. Frankie buys a hat for £2.50 and loads it with fripperies. At one point, it falls into the stripling Thames and has to be brought out. The narrowly hopeful ending and the resilience of the young are something of a relief. The current generation of readers recognizes this theme as a matter of increasing social concern.

Two other tales in this collection, 'Like It Is Round Here' and 'It Wasn't Me', are examples of what Neil Philip notes as Jan Mark's skill: 'she can invest the trivial details of life with resonant meaning'.[43]

In her historical account of family stories in *The Cambridge Guide to Children's Books in English,* Jan Mark considers the polarization of this topic: the family as a convenient, ready-made unit of children of varying ages, versus the family as microcosm, the small universe in which children learn to be social animals and become adults. This latter kind is her particular domain, especially when the plot turns on the public knowledge that adults take for granted and children have to learn both in school and in the world outside. Popular novels and TV serials have colonized 'the family' in terms of family problems. In books, the short story has the advantages of greater intimacy, subtlety and complexity; a kind of shared confession or revelation negotiated between author and reader in the pace and detail of the telling.

Can of Worms has some of the best stories for adolescents. The title tale shows a family of three women: grandmother, mother and Dora, who has found a holiday job she enjoys in a charity bookshop. She (and the reader) learns a great deal about bookselling. One of her first lessons is that people steal books. A list of suspects is taped to the inside of a cupboard door. When her elegant, mildly dipsomaniac grandmother gives Dora expensive new books to sell for charity, they are, in fact, some of those recently stolen. When her grandmother appears as a customer, Dora sees that, in her grey cloak, she fits the description of one of the thieves.

> Gran looked back, smiled and nodded and walked away down Lower Dukes Lane in the cloak that Dora had not known she owned. It was a friendly look, candid, impersonal, and held not a hint of guilt or duplicity, or recognition.[44]

The little moment that changes a relationship forever.

'Front' is a first-person narrative that details a contrast of loyalties in family and friendship. At the centre of it is The Crescent, a terrace of three-storey houses, embodying notions of grandeur as remark-able, in the eyes of the narrator when she was a schoolgirl, as the Gardens of Babylon. Her next visit is the result of an invitation to tea from Pat, a schoolfriend. Their acquaintance, growing slowly, includes the narrator's and her mother's curiosity about exactly where this friend lives, and what her father does. The surprise comes when Pat takes a different route to The Crescent. But all is not as it seems. The details give a hint of things to come, as the guest looks down into the area inside the gate.

> What had I expected to see? A kind of plunge pool, perhaps, boiling with leaf and stem. Instead the steps went precipitously down into a sump of old prams, bicycle wheels, two more dustbins, tea chests, lath and plaster-part of a ceiling. Out of it emerged a door under the steps and a cracked window hung with a yellow net curtain and swags of cobwebs more substantial than the curtains. A few ferns drooped out of crevices in the wall.[45]

The inside of the house is equally dilapidated. Between themselves the girls weave a tapestry of good manners that lets them believe they are behaving as the occasion, located in The Crescent, demands. All the domestic details and the view at the back of the house, carry a strong emotional charge of poverty and neglect that increases when Pat's mother, accompanied by a little boy, comes home and discovers that Pat has used the last of their coal to boil water for tea. Here is the guest's reaction.

I had seen her before. I recognized the coat. I had seen her a
dozen times, walking down Stanley Street, waiting in the Post
Office, queuing in the fish shop; and I had seen her before a
thousand times. She was every refugee, in every newsreel, in
every war film, dressed in the only clothes she owned, all
character erased from her face by the same blow that had
smashed all hope, all resilience.[46]

The houses in The Crescent have been condemned. The common
understanding is that no-one has lived there for two years. After
the visit, the girls 'were not *that* friendly. I wouldn't have known
how to proceed knowing what I knew, but she didn't seem to
expect it.'

In her showing of the relations between adolescents and adults, Jan
Mark makes good her contention that short stories, as she writes
them, are for reading by those who can read them. Most of the
stories contribute something to adolescent growth in understanding,
glimpses of what it is like to be an adult. The author provides specific
details for her readers to engage, as fully as they can, with a chosen
incident of seeming ordinariness. Sometimes events, probed in
depth, are threatening, as in this story of a girl who risks having her
friend to tea. The storyteller's fanciful view of the grandeur of The
Crescent and its actual, ordered squalor is a shattering contrast. The
cost to the girl who lives there is confirmation of what, in the rest of
her life, she has to contend with. School is her way out.

Some of these stories, and others in the collections from which
they come, are not in print. There are several reasons why this is to
be regretted. As short stories for younger children have come to play
a significant role in the teaching of reading in the early stages, so
might many of the stories for adolescents play their part in reminding
those whose reading diet is not rich in realistic fiction that
imagination is a powerful force in all learning. Jan Mark's stories
where boys are the protagonists are a special case in point.

Two stories

At the centre of Jan Mark's success as a storyteller is a dynamic force
of the kind that urges writers to think about what they have to think
about writing. This is evident from the work time she spends in
schools, workshops, lectures and seminars. The result is a textual
power, rich in dialogue, allusive references and stories within stories,
visible in a range of fictive and narrative elements. No two stories are
alike. Any account of her 'style' must begin with the notion of

difference and continue by considering her 'redescriptions' of reading and the configuration and refiguration of her protagonists' views of growing up.

From time to time, writers whose books win favour with young, competent and sensitive, readers are likely to become aware of pitfalls in writing for this audience. Inexperienced adults are apt to misjudge the apparent simplicities of the texts as indications of immaturity in the writers. There is also an ever-increasing number of would-be authors of fantasy tales who cling to a romantic ideology of childhood framed by recollections of their own early reading. Their intentions are honourable, but their idealism, which may include a lack of contact with actual children, prevents their discovery of the terrifying nature of innocence.

When Jan Mark was Writer in Residence at Oxford Brookes University she wrote *Two Stories* which the University's Inky Parrot Press published in 1984. These stories challenge the English romantic myths of childhood by deconstructing writing for children as a single narrative genre with child protagonists created by a solo author who does all the telling. They are an example of what Bakhtin called heteroglossia – variety of voice and discourses in a textual polyphony, all the more intriguing because, in the first tale, the protagonists are not human but are presented as if they were. The alert reader finds traces of other narratives, parody, hints and words that 'make interpretive closure impossible'.[47] Both tales can be read as reading and writing lessons for adults. The vocabulary has been deliberately heightened to create a newer realism.

Mr and Mrs Johnson

Who would not envy Mrs Johnson her lovely home? Possibly some sophisticate would say that it looks like Shanty Town in microcosm, but Mrs Johnson's experience of domestic architecture is limited. Anyway, she has Mr Johnson and two lovely children, and Elizabeth. Life is good.[48]

Mrs Johnson relies heavily on Elizabeth. If not for Elizabeth, in fact, the Johnsons would scarcely have a roof to call their own. It was Elizabeth who collected the shoe boxes and assembled the messuage; Elizabeth who scavenged for furnishings and fittings; it is Elizabeth who stands between the Johnsons and daily threats of demolition. True, Mrs Johnson cooks over cotton reels and serves the result on the upturned lid of a fish paste jar, but if Mr Johnson is satisfied thereby, so is she. Her world revolves round Mr Johnson.

Mrs Johnson was once married to a clothes peg with pipecleaner arms. She 'finds it difficult to explain to strangers that her first husband died by being split up the middle'.

Mr Johnson is ex-army: 'ochreous in complexion and slightly rubbery'. The children were 'conferred upon' Mrs Johnson 'without benefit of conception', and that, for all Mr Johnson's 'representation of active manhood', he is 'missing certain corroborative detail that would add verisimilitude to an otherwise convincing imposture'.[49]

He has many changes of clothes. Clive King's illustration shows that Mr Johnson bears an uncanny resemblance to Action Man. 'His flak helmet has not become a hive for bees, but Mrs J. finds it a convenient pudding basin.' The Johnson children sail in a boat that rides at anchor on 'blue acrylic billows'. The Johnson's new activity is going to the toilet in a new bathroom – another shoebox. A more secret form of reading growth is recognizing words and phrases first encountered somewhere else.

The tale continues in this mock-heroic vein of black humour to chronicle the arrival of Mrs Teddy, who first suggests that someone might take away the new baby, and then hints that Mr Johnson is not always at his office (in the sideboard), and might be 'seeing other ladies'. A ferocious row breaks out; ending with Mr Johnson assaulting his wife with words he must have heard elsewhere. Everything in this representation of family life is exactly what is not expected to be in stories for children.

Childermas

After an uneasy discussion about fairies with his class of junior schoolchildren, Paul looks in his garden for something to put on his nature table. He hopes he might chance upon some atavistic specimen for the classroom of a more stimulating nature than the over-familiar urban weeds and Carl's repetitious contributions of freeze-dried earthworms, peeled daily from the frosty pavements. It is February. What he saw at the bottom of his garden was not the 'lordly ones' of the The Enchanted Hour but instead, nacreous blind creatures like maggots, 'disinterestedly coupling'. The recollection of this makes him sick when he is given pilaf for supper. Paul sketches what he remembers from his encounter in the garden. 'In every one were present the low furrowed forehead, the elliptically domed and almost glabrous cranium, wrinkled neck and hunched shoulders, prominent thorax and abdomen. They were all, as he rightly recalled, incaudate.'

Searching for a live specimen to examine, Paul goes back in the dark to the tunnel where he knew the creatures would be.

They poured out in the sense that treacle pours, in a torpid sludge, slithering over each other down the shallow slope of the ditch, as one amoebic entity, croaking distressfully and probing the alien air.[50]

Distressed and horrified, 'weeping with repugnance and shock' by the invasions of his body by two of the creatures, one overnight, Paul wonders if he could breed them. Could he, single-handedly, revive the realm of Faerie and restore to mankind the dwellers in the hollow hills? A line of bite marks up his leg drives him to smash the creatures in their lair; 'he smashed and smashed and smashed', a different scene from his earlier careful, temperate explorations of the 'scapular cavity of each veiled by the parchment fronds of ragged vestigial wings' from the writer's imagination.

This slaughter of the innocents demonstrates the capability of language to create what actually goes beyond language, the stuff of nightmares. When, do you think, children recognize the nature and power of imagination? One of Paul's pupils draws for him the picture of a fairy, an exact representaton of what Paul had seen at the bottom of his garden. He faints.

Despite the fact that these two stories are not intended for young readers, they are an important learning encounter for those who work with readers and texts in this domain.

First appearances: *Thunder and Lightnings*

A family: parents, Andrew (nearly twelve), his baby brother (eight months) and their guinea pigs have exchanged their house in Kent for a cottage in Norfolk. Andrew's first surprise is the extent of the sky, and the silence. Suddenly, the quiet is shattered by sonic booms and the noise of low-flying aircraft. These become the repetitive ground bass of the story. Moving house is usually an upheaval with repercussions, but Andrew and his parents have done this several times before. His parents have post-1960s portable careers: his father is a computer engineer, a new skill at this time; his mother is a librarian. They are not house-proud but amiable, comfortable. This time, Andrew discovers more about the world, other people and himself.

Recollecting his experiences of five previous schools, Andrew dreads another beginning. The details of the shortening of the time before this event, lightly sketched, are perfect for the tension of anticipation. The school is in the pre-vacation slowing-down, but there is time for Andrew to make a new friend, Victor. He is clearly

the strangest boy in the class, armed against the world with layers of clothing that distort his appearance, cheerful, with no obvious aptitude for book learning. Explaining Victor to his mother, Andrew says: 'He's like the Archers, sort of. But real instead of pretending.'

On Sports Day, Victor wanders about looking at aeroplanes and being steadfastly inept at most things. Andrew becomes 'ashamed at being ashamed' when Victor takes off his clothes and enters the mile race. To everyone's astonishment, Victor sprints at the end and comes in third.

'How come you were third in the mile when you were so bad at everything else?' said Andrew.

'That take a long time to run a mile,' said Victor. 'I had time to think.'

'What did you think about?'

'I thought about how they were all expecting me to come last. They thought that was a joke, me running the mile,' said Victor. 'Old Skelton's soft in the head. Nothing between the ears. Brains in the feet. So I have, though, if that's what makes me run.'

Andrew looked sideways at him and saw that his everlasting grin was a little fiercer, less amiable than usual. 'Were you angry then?' he asked.

'I suppose I was,' said Victor. 'That's a good fuel, anger.'[51]

The reader's understanding of both boys gains another dimension in this exchange. Andrew is scarcely generous about Victor's success, but he discovers, and is affected by, what lies beneath the surface of his friend's usually genial appearance. Victor does care, very much, about what others think of him.

The boys exchange home visits. In the mildly anarchic interior of Andrew's house Victor is quickly at home. 'I like houses a bit dirty. They smell nice and warm.' In his own house his mother wages incessant war against dirt and untidiness, but leaves Victor's room alone in its idiosyncratic detail. Paper models of all kinds of aircraft hang from the ceiling. A fifteen-watt reading lamp is a bomber's moon. Victor's library consists of two bales of well-read aircraft magazines kept under his bed. Andrew notices that, at tea, no-one talks. Victor's father's comment on his son's Sports Day success is a curt dismissal.

In the boys' growing friendship, Victor is the expert when they go to watch planes taking off and landing at the nearby airbase. Andrew soon realizes that Victor is in no sense 'backward'. He knows and understands more about aircraft than most adults. So why does he not capitalize on this knowledge and experience when he does his school project?

> 'Why don't you do your project on aeroplanes?' asked Andrew. 'Why do horrible fish when you could do aeroplanes? You don't even go fishing.'
>
> 'I don't know,' said Victor. 'Yes I do, though,' he added, after thinking hard for a minute. 'If I started doing that for school, I wouldn't be interested in them any more. I don't care about fish, so I don't mind doing them.'
>
> 'Why wouldn't you be interested in them at school?' said Andrew. 'I thought the whole point of the projects was to do something you liked.'
>
> 'Ah, yes,' said Victor. 'But it would be having to like aeroplanes instead of just liking them. Every time a Harrier went over I wouldn't be thinking, there go a Harrier, I'd think, there goes my project. Then I wouldn't want to look at it. School's like measles. That spread.'[52]

This scene, which shows Victor's reflexive competence in a new light, has passed into the lore of teacher education. Andrew offers to scribe for Victor; they will do the summer holiday project together, for themselves first. Victor continues to teach Andrew about planes. A book illustrator sketching in the churchyard proves to be a Lightning enthusiast; he provides demonstrations and sample sketches.

> 'I'll have another go at drawing that Lightning when we get back,' said Victor. 'Now I know how that's done.'
>
> 'I thought you didn't like learning things,' said Andrew.
>
> 'That wasn't learning, that was just finding out,' said Victor. 'We found out quite a lot, didn't we? About drawing and aircraft and priories, though I've forgotten that bit. What a good thing the library was shut.'[53]

They move on to a cemetery where 'enemy' airmen are buried. Victor is critical of the representation of war in comics. He says: 'Perhaps they don't want people to think what really happened. War is supposed to be fun.' To which Andrew replies: 'It's only fun in comics. But in real life it hurts just as much whatever side you die on. And you're just as dead afterwards.'

In their conversations the boys are discovering how to discuss probabilities. The reader becomes more sure that Victor's pragmatism will help him to tolerate the imminent departure of the Lightnings, now too old to be useful and about to be replaced.

Andrew wants their project to be a memorial to the Lightnings, but Victor will have none of it. He cannot see writing as record. Andrew's mother explains: 'Victor doesn't like people to see him as he really is.' Andrew tries again:

> 'But don't you care if people think you're stupid?'
>   'No I don't,' said Victor. 'Why be miserable just to make other people happy.'⁵⁴

The climax of this fairly quiet plot is as devastating as it is unexpected. When Victor's mother's washing machine breaks down, Victor takes the clothes to the launderette, and then calls for Andrew on his way back. Together they wheel the washing bag to Victor's house. Andrew carries the bag to the back door while Victor puts his bike away.

> Victor opened the door and took the bag from him. The top sheet was squeezed out of the bag and fell onto the path. Victor sidestepped in a desperate rescue bid and put his foot on it. When Andrew picked up the sheet he saw that one side was freckled with mossy green spots while the other was heavily imprinted with the sole of Victor's boot. He looked up and saw Victor's mother standing in the doorway
>   She looked at him, at Victor and at the sheet, then, without saying anything, she smacked Victor hard, three times across the side of the head. Victor rocked on his feet and put his hand to his head, but he said nothing either.
>   Andrew was shocked by the silence of it.

Andrew recounts the incident to his mother, explaining that he was responsible for the accident. His mother says: 'It was probably you she wanted to hit and she took it out on Victor instead.' Andrew says, 'It isn't fair.'

> 'Nothing's fair,' said Mum. 'There's no such thing as fairness. It's a word made up to keep children quiet. When you discover it's a fraud then you're starting to grow up. The difference between you and Victor is that you're still finding out and he knows perfectly well already. He doesn't even think it worth mentioning. I bet you've never heard him say, "It's not fair", have you.'
>   'I suppose not,' said Andrew. 'But she shouldn't have hit him.'

The reader has to think about this too.
    As they become more aware of the ways in which people differ,

the otherness of others, so apparently simple to grown-ups, the boys become friends in ways that are not discussed in the text, but lie at the heart of the novel. Each becomes part of the other's consciousness. Andrew tries explicitly to shift Victor's view of himself, without realizing that his baby brother and Victor's guinea pig, which lives in a special cage at Andrew's house, have already contributed to this. A pattern of significations, extra meanings, surfaces in these incidents. Victor is clearly the central character.

My proposition is this: it is possible, and even satisfying, for readers to read past the text, to go ahead anticipating events once Jan Mark has replaced the image of Victor as a country bumpkin with Andrew's understanding of his love and knowledge of aeroplanes and of country lore and language. That's how their friendship will develop, isn't it? If, in addition, one reads not past the words, but down into the next layer of meaning, then reading itself becomes a different experience. If they are to please their readers and satisfy their writers, narratives for the young need to have both what Jill Paton Walsh once called the 'rainbow surface' and a distinctive kind of depth, sometimes quite dark.[55]

In what came to be called 'the new realism', Jan Mark provides narrative, texts that create different kinds of growing points, especially reflexive thinking. We shall see more examples of this in later works. Here, this extended summary is to show how this first novel, awarded the Carnegie Medal and the Guardian/Penguin Prize, foregrounds friendship as an important feature of adolescence, a theme Jan Mark returns to again and again, to penetrate its complexities. A common assumption is that stories for the young have to be problem-centred if they are to be about growing up. It is more rarely acknowledged that an increasing maturity in under-standing both the outside and the inside of experience is a writer's gift to a reader.

Under the Autumn Garden followed a year later. The setting is similar, as are the ways in which the author's oblique narration, conducted largely in dialogue, organizes the reader's response to the intricacies of family life. Matthew is in his final year in primary school. For part of the first term he is Head Boy, with extra responsibilities. Adults expect more of him. His mother is the dinner lady; she knows all about his school work, the project on the history of the village. The children are to find out when their houses were built and what they are built of. Matthew thinks this is boring. He wants to discover something more tangible about the past, so he begins to dig in the garden of the empty house next door in the hope of finding some remains of an ancient priory. There is a legend of a local ghost. But the teacher wants facts not fantasy. His father lets him borrow his digging tools, but scorns the idea of the priory with the admonition: 'You do something else for your school work and do it properly.'

Responsibilities begin to mount and to weigh heavily. Matthew fails to write anything and is taken to task by his teacher and his parents. The girl children of the builder who is joining the two houses together usurp his first digging site and turn it into a playhouse. His second attempt is blighted by one of the builder's sons, Paul, who steals the only evidence to prove anything, a bottle. It is broken in a scuffle. With all the distractions caused by this intrusive family and the failure of his digging, Matthew is unable to add anything to the class project text. The only adult who helps him is a neighbour, a real historian, who gives him the information he needs about the monastery and its ghost, and later explains that the builder's wife has left him. He offers Matthew the 'unpalatable truth' that the older boys were simply humouring him to amuse themselves. Matthew's defence is: 'Nobody tells me, they just mutter.' About Paul:

> 'But he's my friend,' said Matthew.
> 'Is he?'
> 'I thought he was going to be friends at first,' said Matthew.
> 'You aren't friends,' said Mr Bagnall. 'Be honest. You don't even like him.'
> 'He looks nice.'
> 'Of course he does,' said Mr Bagnall. But that doesn't mean you have to like him. I do, but why should you?'[56]

I return to this novel for its examples of how Jan Mark can 'crystallise a fiction of excellence out of ordinary, almost eventless everyday life.'[57] Here she offers her young readers the challenge to become more self-aware as they see the characters from the inside. This is more intellectual effort than response or empathy. It also involves an appreciation of verbal acuity of the kind that allows the young reader to understand the jokes the characters make.

With these as her first two novels, Jan Mark became an established writer from whom to expect many more examples of the relation of reading to social and intellectual growth. While it is possible to select the books in terms of perceived kinds – fairy stories, family stories, non-fiction and the like – it seems more in keeping with the theme of this study to consider them in terms of a reader's progress, aware that this too is no more than a convenient device. Jan Mark's narratives challenge the very notion of genre.

Novels: mostly girls

Erica Timperley, the heroine of *Handles*, is the Jan Mark character who, in my opinion, fits most closely Victor Watson's description of a protagonist 'whose approach towards some kind of adult status is represented alongside her own capacity to shape or construct her own motivation using whatever material is at hand'.[58]

She is a pre-teenager of her time. When the novel appeared in 1983, discussions of adolescent development portrayed in books that had become a special category of children's fiction were still current. Feminism was well on its way, together with theories of sexual difference in gendered reading, writing and criticism. In children's books heroines were acquiring a different kind of status. Erica wants to be a motor mechanic. She spends her free time in motor-cycle parking lots and goes around with a crowd of like-minded young people, most of whom are still too young to have a licence. She knows she cannot discuss this decision with her father as a prospect for her future. He would see her desire as 'almost as unnatural as men having babies'.[59]

What gives the novel its compelling force is not only Erica's determination to carry out her plan, but also Jan Mark's exceptional clarity in her realistic depiction of the conditions of life, in town and country, that both constrain and challenge her protagonist. We meet her on the first page in the buzzing August traffic in Norwich. She is directing tourists and telling them that the Castle really is the building right in front of them and assuring them that the Guildhall really is as old as it looks. This is the author's ruse to set the scene, with Erica on the wall of the motor-cycle park, watching machines and riders, and to hint at her low opinion of tourists who can't read maps, and ignore the help they have asked for.

Erica's family lives on the third floor of a four-storey building. The description of it lets the reader take note of the family details, includes a brief scene in the 'little square hall' behind the front door. Erica's brother is about to go on holiday with a friend. When Erica comes home from the cycle park, she finds the hall:

> ... full of lanky Craig, standing on a *suitcase*, while Mum knelt at his feet, trying to close the catches.
>
> 'You're not camping with a suitcase, are you?' Erica said. 'I thought you were supposed to have a rucksack and things like that, for camp. Jason'll think you're soft.'

'You be quiet. He won't think anything,' Mum said. 'I can't afford a rucksack specially, not just for one holiday. He might not even need that again. There's nothing soft about a suitcase. You don't want to go around saying things like that.'[60]

The reader also has a view about a suitcase for a camping holiday. The actuality is that the fictive family can't afford to buy a rucksack. More deeply, there is the mother's objection to Erica's view that it's 'soft', knowing well that her daughter isn't referring to the fabric of the suitcase, but a possible judgement of its owner. The reader already knows that Craig quite definitely wants to be a nurse, a 'soft' job for a man. He too is concealing his plan. Erica knows that 'Dad and especially Mum, were always afraid that he really was soft.' Jan Mark's narrative power lies in the multiple applications and exploitations of what she knows her readers take to be 'real', and how they can be enticed to read more into her layered meanings. The events of the story are real in the sense of 'life-like', a convention in writing that also carries a commitment on the part of the reader to see something as real if it is described realistically.

There are hints of other tensions. Mr Timperley is threatened with redundancy, so that his wife's work in a wine bar assumes greater importance. Holidays are 'arranged' rather than paid for. Erica had been looking forward to spending the summer at home, hanging out with the crowd of bike enthusiasts. Instead, she learns that a kind of holiday has been thrust upon her. She has been invited in response to a letter her mother sent to her sister – to stay with her aunt, uncle and cousin in the country. It feels like exile. But Erica sees further.

'What'll you do when I'm away?'
'Oh, I'll manage,' Mum said. 'Don't worry.' She saw Erica's sceptical look. 'I'm not trying to get rid of you,' she said quickly.
Up to that moment Erica had not dreamed of thinking such a thing.
'I'm not, really.'
'No,' Erica said.[61]

The children's absence will be a kind of holiday for their mother.

Life in the country cottage is boring and irksome for a young city dweller. Erica's aunt's family are stolid, conventional smallholders. Cousin Robert is a spoilt, spiteful, lazy and devious youth of no charm. He shirks household chores, is jealous of Erica and gets in her way. Auntie Joan supervises the sale of abundant late summer vegetables, notably marrows, from her garden. Erica takes on this responsibility as a chance to talk to some other people. While she wishes she could go back to Norwich, she was bound not to. 'Vegetables are rampant, vegetables rule.' Uncle Peter is the unwitting agent of her release. His jump-leads are at Mercury Motor Cycles in the nearest small town. Erica goes on Aunt Joan's bike to fetch them and finds a magic kingdom: proprietor Elsie Wainwright, a man who names things.

The repair shop is in a place its owner calls 'the Cave', part of a tiny industrial estate. To Erica it is 'gloriously greasy', with fragments of motor-cycles suspended from its low roof. In these surroundings Erica experiences a platonic relationship that sits within a subtle, delicate distancing created by collaborative work with Elsie, and other cheerful encounters and conversations with the rest of the entourage. Importantly, she gains respect, encouragement and praise. Above all, she discovers aspects of herself that would have remained hidden had she spent all her time within the restricting conditions at the farm cottage.

Elsie has lost Uncle Peter's jump-leads. His efforts to retrieve them grow less and less urgent as Erica's presence in the Cave has more to do with her skill with bikes. She soon discovers that, to be one of the inner circle, she needs to have a 'handle', a variant of her name that announces her distinctive identity.

> She wondered if she could invent her own or if it had to be bestowed by someone else, and whether, once she had it, it would take immediately or have to be grown into slowly, like a school coat.[62]

That is, she would rather Elsie invented it.

Elsie's naming proclivity serves to link the irritations of life on the industrial estate with grander historical disasters so as to produce a comparison of scale; presumably to be glad things aren't worse. A troublesome crack on the kerb is the San Andreas Fault; a crater-like hole is Copernicus. An infestation of frogs after a rainstorm is associated with one of the plagues of Egypt, while the Golden Gate Bridge and the Black Lagoon are results of the flooding after a rainstorm. Yerbut (yer-but) is what he regularly says at the beginning of a speech. Auntie Joan's bicycle is the Iron Cow. Bernard, the assistant mechanic, has been Bunny since schooldays. Some handles are more privately used. 'Old Arrow' is Mr Bowen the dentist. He is not happy that this sobriquet is public knowledge.

Erica's acceptance in the Cave begins when Elsie encourages her to bring some of her Aunt's vegetables to sell and he urges some of his friends to buy them. When she knows her skill in bike maintenance has been recognized she has enough self-confidence to ask if she can help with the bikes. Later, she hears Elsie say to Yerbut, who needed his Suzuki to be mended, 'this is Erica, your mechanic for today. She knows what she's about.' With great satisfaction Erica hears her name included in the list of those to whom Elsie, in one of his dramatic modes, confides his business when he is called out on an errand of mercy. But still no handle.

Erica goes to the Cave in the worst possible weather without her aunt's permission:

> 'Just as a matter of interest,' Elsie said, pouring boiling water into mugs, 'why did you come?'
>
> Erica felt cold. She should have stayed at home.
>
> 'I thought there might be some work – I did say I'd come and I couldn't – not Thursday and Friday – Auntie wouldn't let me.'
>
> 'Oh that's all right then. I thought you might have come storming through the floods for Peter's leads.'
>
> 'I'd forgotten about them,' Erica said, thawing again.[63]

When the Gremlin returns to plague the inhabitants of the Cave and at the same time putting himself in danger of drowning, Bunny turns to Erica: 'You're a woman. What do you with children?'

Erica had never been called a woman before. When Elsie's elegant wife and daughter visit the yard, she is introduced as 'my new mechanic', then hears Elsie upbraided for 'letting the place fill up with other people's kids'. The arrival of Elsie's family has taken away all the magic of the Cave. It now looked like a 'run-down repair shop'.

The drama of the 'personalized' marrows plays itself out at the cottage. Asked over and over why she had 'written' on marrows – they could no longer be sold – Erica says she did it just for fun, but somehow her family can't see the writing as a joke. Elsie accepts his with admiration.

On her last visit to the Cave, before she goes back to Norwich, Erica discovers that Lucy, Elsie's daughter, has come back there of her own volition. Bunny explains that Lucy is jealous of Erica.

> 'Here you are, having a high old time with her dad, *her* dad, remember, up to your eyebrows in grease and muck, counting frogs and giving everything daft names, and where's she? Stuck at home, that's where, keeping her shoes clean and minding the baby. Wouldn't you be jealous?[64]

Lucy's father says of her: she'll never make a mechanic; 'not like you. You've got the feeling for it. You are going to be a mechanic, aren't you?' Erica nodded. Elsie keeps his feelings to himself, but he tells Erica she could be his apprentice, if he could ever afford one. Erica hasn't forgotten the main thing:

> 'I never did get a handle,' Erica said.
> 'Well, you did,' said Elsie, 'but it was such a mouthful I never used it. Good-bye, Eroica Symphony.'
> 'What's that?'
> 'Music by Beethoven, haven't you heard of it?'
> 'No.'
> 'You've heard of *him*?'
> 'Yes.'
> 'That's all right then.' He hummed a few notes.
> 'And that's my handle?'
> 'It is here.'[65]

As a representation of the competence of the heroine to determine what growth could be like and what it could transform, this story is a remarkable feat, subtle yet clear. In the short springtime of pre-adolescence, the unforced acceptance of the young by caring adults is as important as any other time in childhood. Here it is almost poetic in its restraint. Erica is accepted by people who have different views of how to run a motor-cycle business. Elsie's careful silences are a contrast to his fanciful name-making; his choice for Erica is a touching gift. Elsie (L. C.) Wainwright's name doesn't need changing: 'a man who makes wagons' is as strong a handle as any.

Since this novel appeared, many aspects of the social life of young people have changed, almost radically. Although childhood may seem to have shortened, the period of adolescent dependence is longer. The workings of family life that depend on getting and spending are a new kind of economics and also of different expectations. The telephone plays a part in this story, but it has to be sought in a call box or under the ledgers in the Cave. More particularly, if this book were to appear now for the first time, the propriety of Erica's presence, where working men are in the majority, might be called into question, although it makes the case for this to be more usual, not less. Despite these differences, however, readers at the stage of asking 'who am I?' or 'what can I become?' are upheld by this heroine to continue asking, probably with more confidence and insight. They will take the differences of the social scene in their stride. I read the book when it first appeared and I know how much those who have had the good fortune to find a copy to read since then have appreciated it.

Two more novels of this period take up different aspects of this theme within the backgrounds of the families. In *Trouble Half-Way*, Amy's father has died at the age of thirty. Her two-year-old sister is still in nappies; their mother, a careful housewife, has recently remarried a long-distance lorry driver, 'only middling tall and quite lean'. Helen thinks he is her father, and, according to the author, was not the only person to think so. Amy remembers *her* father and misses him. She has learned from her mother that life is unpredictable so it is better to expect the worst. While the reader quickly sees Richard's generosity and patience, Amy keeps him at arm's length and, as is psychologically usual, considers him an interloper. The furniture he carries in his lorry is certainly no match for the careful workmanship of his predecessor, so visible in the home.

When Amy's grandfather is rushed into hospital and her mother has to go to him, Amy can't stay at home alone. She has to go up north with Richard in the van. This means she will sleep in it, eat in transport cafés and use public toilets to keep clean. She has to face all that her worried mother has taught her to worry about: the 'what ifs' of possible disaster. The first has already befallen her; she has to miss the gymnastic competition. Richard promises that he will show her an old cotton mill with her name on it between Oldham and Rochdale. Here is Amy worrying about the mills.

> Amy tried to imagine them but all she could see still were windmills, like they had in Norfolk, with AMY painted on the side in huge white letters. There was something threatening about them, a sense of menace and imminent danger, as if they concealed something not nice, but she could not think why until they were folding the map away, and then she remembered a hymn that they sometimes sang at school: dark satanic mills.
>
> 'There might be a fog,' she said.[66]

Richard is gentle with her and sees to her comfort, but he has work to do. When her constant griping gets him down, he tells her:

> 'Do you know what a pessimist is?'
> 'No.'
> 'Look in the mirror then. Anyone'd think we were going to cross the Alps on roller skates.'[67]

At the same time, he is a good travelling companion. Amy's eyes are opened to the greater expanse of the west and northern midlands of England she sees through the cab windows. The strangers she encounters speak English differently, but they are also kind and helpful. When the unreliable lorry finally breaks down and has to be rescued, Richard insists that Amy should complete the journey to the mill on her own, even if it means changing trains and finding a bus. Richard does all he can to reassure her. Horrible things may happen, but Manchester is 'only a place' and she can't spend the rest of her life expecting her mother to be with her. She says:

> 'It's different when you're grown up.'
>   'I know – but you've got to start growing up, or it won't be. You'll always be afraid.'[68]

The argument continues.

> Richard turned to her and put his hands on her shoulders.
>   'Amy, tell me the truth, why don't you want to go?'
>   'It isn't safe.'
>   'You'll be safe if you do exactly what I told you. If anything goes wrong people will help. They're just the same here as they are at home – nicer if anything.'[69]

The excursion works out exactly as planned, with the addition of much local kindness and support. Amy's change of heart and vision is clear from her response to a strange man who asks her what she thinks of her first visit up north: 'It's all right,' Amy said, 'It's nice. It's just another place.'

Amy's gradual change of perspective comes with the changes in her mode of speaking to Richard. He treats her throughout like a reasonable being. When her gripes decline, a more interesting Amy emerges. With all its bumps and difficulties, the journey has been an important rite of passage. At one point, after a conversation on the telephone with her mother, Amy realizes it has become easier to talk with Richard. Talk is at the heart of the matter. For the most part, the novel is a continuing dialogue, hence its realism and conviction.

In the third novel in this group, *Dream House* (1987), the main characters are deep in their own desires that only their imaginations can satisfy. As usual with Jan Mark, the title implies more than it says, a feature of literary language that young readers grow into when they discover that adults are apt to give too simple explanations for complex actualities.

In the beginning, Hannah is watching a television serial in which an actor called Martin Carter is a war hero, Major Nevard. She is captivated by the way he speaks. Readers are given enough of the scene to make up their minds about what they and Hannah see.

> The major switched off his desk light, walked over to the window where he drew aside heavy curtains and looked out into the night, over the silent city. (The windows were criss-crossed with sticky tape, it must be the Second World War, Hannah decided; they had done the Blackout at school) and the major's view was cut up into triangles. Suddenly, towards a dark horizon, a pillar of light sprang up, eerily swinging across the cloudy sky. Although it was not shining on the major his face showed pale against the window, grim and determined. He frowned, head bowed, and as he drew the curtains Hannah heard the anguished crooning of an air raid siren. The scene went blank.[70]

'Mega-tripe', is the opinion of Hannah's sister, Karen, who is awaiting her exam results in a Walkman music trance, 'like a visitor from another world who mistook human beings for furniture and conversed only with machines'.[71] Tom, their brother, moves across the landscape attached to a pair of binoculars on a stick. He is assumed to be bird watching, but is actually creating in his imagination a road network to cover the whole area. He acts as the reader's viewfinder. As he moves about he sees much of what is happening but refuses to be part of it. The mother of these young people is the administrative secretary for courses on modern arts that are held in a Domesday Book manor house in downland Kent. The course about to begin is on Writing for Television. One of the course tutors will be Martin Carter, so dream stuff will meet the work of creation. Readers have had a taste of what is involved.

While courses are in progress, the House is off limits to Hannah. When it is empty she fantasizes that she lives there. Polly, the course's director, lets her help with the housekeeping chores. Hannah is also good at taking telephone messages and telling would-be students that there are no places left. Her more important obligation is to prevent her almost-friend, Dina, a voracious celebrity hunter, from coming as near as she'd like to people with famous names. Dina hovers around Hannah whenever she can. At the weekends she wears outlandish clothes so that those who see her 'would stop to look at her even if they didn't like what they saw'.

Whatever counts as friendship between these two girls is compromised by these awkward restraints. Indeed the flow and contraflow of friendships are the markers for this story. After the unexpected arrival of Julia Carter, the hysterical, attention-demanding daughter of the hero-tutor, events move as in a sharp, fast theatrical comedy of opening and shutting doors. There is no room for Julia in the House, so she stays with Dina, who gains thereby more direct access to the famous visitor. The ordered running of the House and the relations of those involved with it are upset, especially Hannah's. She wants to be recognized as important to the organization but she is held responsible for Dina and Julia's helping themselves to late breakfast in the kitchen and leaving it in a mess. She also sees Dina's shift of allegiance. All three girls are then banned from the House. Hannah has seen Julia making a scene the night before when she failed to get what she wanted and embarrassed her father. This was Julia's revenge. At this point, friendship is scarcely in evidence.

Hannah had wanted to see what Martin Carter was 'really like'. The first encounter showed that he was anything but 'decisive', his TV characteristic. Climbing up the hill away from the manor she:

> . . . paused to look back, down to the yard. Martin Carter came round the corner and crossed to the stable. He was too far away for her to see how he looked, but from the way he walked she could guess how he felt and now she knew how Dina felt too, barred from Paradise, on the far side of the cattle grid.[72]

When Hannah watches the repeat of the serial episode she had seen earlier in the week 'she no longer believed a word of it'. Every time Major Nevard appeared she saw the 'grey-haired harassed man who leaned out of a window and hid his face in his hands. Major Nevard had no daughters.'[73]

The girls are at the stage in adolescence when hero-worship and uncertainty about their relations with grown-ups produce embarrassment and self-doubt. They expect to be regarded as more than older children, yet they feel they are cast back into childhood when things go wrong. Hannah wants Polly to acknowledge her contribution to life at the manor. She is hurt when Polly says that if she can't keep the other two girls in order they would all 'have to find somewhere else to play'.

Julia wants to be sure of her father's affection. She has left her mother to be with him over a weekend that was his 'turn', but his attention has to be on what he is doing for adults. Only when he shouts at her does she begin to realize that she already has his care and she doesn't have to make a scene to get it. Sadly, Julia has no reciprocal feeling for others; she uses their goodwill to fuel her selfishness. Her departure is a relief. Dina meanwhile has been entrusting her feelings to her tape recorder. As we read the transcripts we see she is more apt for real friendship with Hannah than we might have thought. When both girls are invited to help at the manor, they have a clearer insight into a reciprocal relationship.

Some of the incidents are depicted as television shots. Jan Mark emphasizes gestures to underline the feeling tone of what the reader is to notice. When Dina comes to borrow Hannah's bicycle to lend it (with permission) to Julia:

> Hannah leaned across the sink and knocked on the pane, meaning to wave, but Dina did not hear her, or, rather, pretended not to hear her, although she was only a metre or two from the window. Clearly she did not want Hannah muscling in on her new friendship, but there was something almost furtive about the way she kept her head down, as if she had known that Hannah was at the window, even before she had knocked on it.[74]

To make the most of this well-wrought tale in its smooth, even-paced prose, the reader has to follow the writer's timing to see the effect of the patterned whole. The characters, so subtly drawn, move through the rural landscape with its modern outlines and literary overtones. The notion of going to the country to escape one's problems is even older than Shakespeare. The adults here are not very strong models for the young.

This is a splendid read. There is amazing grace in the balance of description and implied judgement. It is also a book of its time. Young readers of the next generation must have heard their elders bewail the passing of 'safe' childhood with its bike riding, landscape exploring, trust in strangers and other freedoms that seem to be no more. Television may fill some gaps, but growing up is even more complicated than role-play.

The main characters in *They Do Things Differently There* (1994) are at a later stage. They go about in pairs and groups that relate particularly to school, sharing a sceptical awareness of adults that comes from the recognition that their elders are not always what they seem. Boys are now more evident. Some jealousies arise from the recognition of special features, physical and intellectual, even in the case of best friends.

The setting is the formal pattern of a New Town, Compton Rosehay, created, as is often the case in England, by joining two villages. It's other name is Stalemate. Charlotte, who tells the story after the events are long past, is irked by the over-organized, bland life of the place. It's the exam year and she has just quarrelled with Rowena who wants to borrow her notes on Macbeth. Charlotte is tired of dong Rowena's homework and suggests that Rowena should try writing her own notes.

> 'Stuck-up bitch.' 'Snob.' 'Swot,' said our other friends loyally. As far as I could see, the insults had nothing to do with my refusing to hand over the notes before I had finished with them, but it was the spirit of the thing that counted, not accuracy.[75]

Charlotte takes a different way home through Old Compton, which is 'not yet quite extinct'. On her second visit, when she is standing outside the antique shop looking at a block of alabaster with embedded brass 'things', a voice says, 'The Martians made it.' It is Elaine Crossley, a girl in Charlotte's class whom people called a swot, but to Charlotte she seemed 'effortlessly clever in a way I envied as I spent my time trying not to seem clever at all'. A conversation ensues during which both girls speculate about Martians. Elaine suggests they are missionaries.

> 'Forget all that rubbish about galactic domination,' Elaine said, matter-of-factly. 'They came to save us. They were terrible bores, but they were never dangerous.'
> 'I suppose they held revivalist meetings in their space ship?'
> 'At first,' Elaine said, 'but then they built a small tin tabernacle. That was in the days before religious persecution set in.'
> 'One of those chapels along here?' I said, pointing down the street.
> 'No.' Elaine gestured vaguely towards the silhouette of the distant conifer hedge. 'Up there in Stalemate.'
> Why had I never known before that Compton Rosehay was really called Stalemate? What I did know, there and then, was that Elaine Crossley was too valuable to be left to the care of Rowena's mob. It was a matter of extreme urgency.[76]

Adolescents enjoy these coloratura conversations. Charlotte is now less bored. She visits the house where Elaine lives in semi-nomadic comfort in Old Compton. It is as different as it could be from the residences in Stalemate. Charlotte keeps Elaine on the topic of Stalemate as long as possible on the grounds that what they see 'isn't all that's there'. Elaine, who takes the lead in the earlier discussions, says that Compton Rosehay is in a *double* dimension with Stalemate; they occupy the same space.

'But most of the time Compton Rosehay goes about its horrible business and never realizes that it shares space and time with Stalemate. What we've got here in Old Compton is an interstice. Earth's fabric has worn thin.'

'That sounds like Macbeth,' I said, as we walked up the path to Elaine's front door.

'Earth's fabric hath worn thin and so we see the other where beneath.'

'Do you think Shakespeare knew about alternative reality?'

'Sure he did,' Elaine said.[77]

And so begins a friendship of a different kind; the discovery that imagination and language, including borrowings and quotations from those whose words they read, let the girls create together a place that can be emotionally and intellectually inhabited as if it existed. There are two maps to help the reader for whom this is a new kind of deep play.

They discuss different kinds of friendship and ways of behaving to others. Charlotte's rift with Rowena returns to plague her. She has experienced what it is like to be ignored by members of a group she once belonged to. First they would wait for the miscreant, and then, 'talk to each other as if I weren't there', says Charlotte.

'Not to suggest that they hadn't seen me, but to make sure that I knew I was being seen, much in the same way as one sees a pane of glass, you know it's there but you don't actually look at it, only through it.'

Summing up Rowena:

... she had always understood one thing, the value of the pre-emptive strike. ... Rowena got in first and gave orders, drew up battle plans and took no prisoners. Friendship with extreme prejudice was how Rowena operated.[78]

When this mood returns, Elaine has more news of Stalemate. 'Have you ever tried Zen yoghurt?' When Charlotte replies that it's frozen yoghurt from Jangles Coffee House, Elaine moves in quickly with the alternative reality:

'Earth's fabric?' Elaine said, 'It may be frozen yoghurt in Compton Rosehay but we know better. Zen yoghurt is a celebrated delicacy in Stalemate, fermented from the milk of the harmonious sheep and flavoured with harmonious substances. It's a psychedelicacy, actually,' she added, with a flash of inspiration. I wished I could do that.[79]

And so they go on. The aerobics evening class in the school is a revivalist meeting of Martians. Mr Clyster, the bigamist, works shifts at the mermaid factory. Lord Tod collects corpses. A blackmailer, fishmonger poets and combat nuns are called to account for what happens in Stalemate. The reader is teased by names: Sister Eclampsia, the Throats, McCadavers. Obadiah Gleet, Dagobert (le bon roi), Professor Scrapie. All through the Easter holiday while they revise for exams, Charlotte and Elaine go for evening walks through Stalemate. But as soon as they create new characters, they seem to kill them off.

As earth's fabric begins to wear thinner than ever, the number of occasions when Stalemate seems more real than Compton Rosehay is increasing. Now Elaine's family is about to move again. Charlotte wails, 'I can't do Stalemate without you.' That is, they didn't talk about Stalemate. They created it, because they needed it as an alternative reality as part of their growing up. Now, as we so confidently say, they'd 'grown out of it'. I wonder. Novelists, playwrights, poets, to say nothing of musicians, painters, sculptors, architects and others, still hold to 'transitional objects' of their alternative worlds. Enviously, the rest of us have daydreams.

Novels: mostly boys

Since the appearance of *Thunder and Lightnings*, boys have featured in Jan Mark's stories as often as girls, especially in those for teenagers whose reading matter is often interchangeable with that of adults. Current educational concern about boys' reading is not so much about the nature of the texts, as the competence many seem to lack in the early years of school. Direct evidence of boys' preferred texts is complicated by their engagement with non-fiction in other media, including magazines. There is some acknowledgement of their attachment to narrative fantasy, *The Lord of the Rings*, for example, and to modern forms of science fiction. How adolescents read the books they have selected for themselves and the nature of their responses to adult subject matter are not the concern in this review of Jan Mark's oeuvre. Instead we shall see, when her main characters are males confronted by incidents and situations where they need to understand themselves, how they appear to readers.

Two stylistic features stand out in each book; we have seen them already. First, Jan Mark's oblique approach to her characters. She lets the reader discover the complexity of their personalities. Then, her exceptional skill in timing and tuning conversations where speech patterns range from the laconic to obligato spirals of words and quick repartee, between friends and with others. In a Jan Mark narrative, talk is the clue to what is at stake in relationships. Conversation exchanges illustrate the working of the collective unconscious – what doesn't need to be explained in the swift colloquy of peers with common interests. Slang indicates a bond of assumptions about actions and feelings. Some of the best examples of adolescent banter are in *Enough is Too Much Already* (1988).

When *Man in Motion* (1989) was noticed in *Children's Books of the Year*, the critic praised the serious content of the novel: the teenage hero's need to be like others in his new school in a new environment, to have friends and to be seen with them. As he is exceptionally good at games, Lloyd quickly becomes socialized. Then the conflict arises between going out with friends and playing for a team, especially a team that plays American football, his passion. But despite his skill, Lloyd is never chosen to be in an attacking position. He is told, 'You are all over the place.' When Lloyd later meets someone who wants to be friendly, but who is undoubtedly racist, Lloyd must again consider his position.

From time to time Jan Mark's adolescent readers have to tolerate new uncertainties in their engagement with continuous texts, especially when they find themselves in a polysemic exploration of consciousness – what the characters think, believe, explain, propose, relative to what these introspections mean. The structure of each book is different in content and in form. In Barthes' terms, these books are more 'writerly' than 'readerly'. That is, the readers have to be more actively engaged in interpretation. The books draw attention to the way they 'work' as part of what they are 'about'.

In *Finders, Losers* (1990), readers are addressed directly and told that they are responsible for discovering 'what happened' in the episode related by different people, thus providing a simultaneity of different viewpoints of what 'actually' happened between half-past eight in the morning and five o'clock in the afternoon. The narrators describe what happens to them; no-one knows why. Yet they are all in and out of each other's accounts of the same events. Only the reader knows the 'whole story'. Texts of this kind challenge maturing teenage readers to come to know what growing up means in relation to reading. What readers gain is the confidence to go on with a new kind of narration, one that offers different views of 'how the author does it'. They are now at the stage when they can judge the worth of the effort in relation to the success of the experience, just as they did with new texts in their early days as readers.

What about the fox?

Novels written as autobiographical journals or diaries offer readers close-up glimpses of the past when it was the present for the writer. Reading such texts sometimes feels like peering into other peoples' letters or bank accounts. This common, prurient curiosity lifts bygone events into the polyphiloprogenitive realm that feeds both fact and fiction. For novelists to write a fictive journal is to return to the beginnings of their art. The 'I' of the narrator comes close to the reader with a version of events that claims its origin in authenticity. In *The Hillingdon Fox* (1991) Jan Mark creates two diarists, brothers, who keep journals in time of war, eight years apart. This is a text trial of metafictions. The reader takes a step back to discover the nature of the narratives as well as their contents and finds a dialogue between the brothers at the 'present' time that refers to a time past when they rarely spoke to each other.

Gerald Marshall was eighteen in 1982. In April of that year, his last in school, he recorded events over four weeks. The diary was designed to be buried in a time-capsule along with other articles and writings presumed to be of historical interest to young people in 2082. In 1990, Hugh Marshall is seventeen. He says he is writing his journal for himself to fill in the time his girlfriend is on holiday in Boston. That is where his thoughts are, mostly. His transatlantic phone calls are rationed by cost. Another brother, Geoffrey, is a year older than Hugh. The fact is not elaborated, except that Gerald refers to his brothers as 'the children'. Readers may find significance in these details later in the book. Both diarists record that they are writing in a time of war. Gerald records the beginning of the war in the Falklands; Hugh is preoccupied with the activities of Saddam Hussein and President Bush (the elder).

The fictive parts are about the preoccupations of two young men about to leave school; both include current affairs in their records so readers see the synchronic pattern of world conflicts, local scandals, and the diarists' thinking and awareness of growing up in the world of the everyday, at home and at school. As matters of passing interest, readers of this book in 2002 and afterwards will find references to the possibility of another Gulf War and also to official concern with A-level examination results. Hugh is in the first year of those who took GCSEs and will be amongst the first to suffer the new A-level. Here's his entry on this topic:

> The examiners say the pass rate's up, the right-wing politicos
> say that's because the standards are down. It's all politics, see?

No other way does anything educational hit the headlines.

My turn next year. No doubt the pass rate will drop with me in it.[80]

Until he becomes immersed in personal and school matters Gerald writes as if he were making speeches to the future:

I suspect that our daily lives, unspectacular though they are, will be of as much interest to you as the global spectrum, which, after all, will be very well documented. You will already know of the outcome of the Falklands conflict, the Iran/Iraq war and all the other international concerns and upheavals of which I write. But you will not have known that eighteen-year-old Jo-Ann Rugg was weeping in the reference section of the public library at 11am on Saturday April 10, 1982. And even I don't know why.[81]

He also thinks his father is having an affair with his mother's best friend. Gerald is growing on all points at once. He is of an age to go to war, father a child, have opinions of his own and be able to see the world from new perspectives. However, Gerald learns from Hugh that the time-capsule will be revealed after only eight years underground to make way for an extension to the school building. Gerald then asks Hugh to retrieve the capsule without telling anyone. The reader, but not Hugh, knows what it contains besides Gerald's diary: a death threat sent by the brother of one of Gerald's classmates to the father of another. A Pakistani girl wanted to put the threat in the capsule so that 'people will know what it was like for my family in this quiet town with its good race relations record'. Would the irony survive? This is the inescapable maturation crisis for everyone. Gerald wrote at the time: 'She is willing to wait for a hundred years.'

Hugh's first entries are about diary writing. He wants to write about serious matters but his thoughts 'keep getting in the way'. 'I know what I'm thinking – why do I have this urge to see it on paper?' His observations on public affairs show the degree of his political awareness. He reports that the case of the Birmingham Six, 'accused in 1974 of killing 21 people in a pub bombing has again been sent to the Court of Appeal'. His comment is: 'These guys have been in prison all my life.' He sees television pictures of refugees and other horrors far away: 'Who now remembers Afghanistan?' He thinks he has Republican sympathies; 'that doesn't mean I support terrorism'. He has gone further than Gerald at his age in recognizing complexities for which there are no simple solutions. Hugh is clearly attached to his girlfriend and less hesitant than Gerald was in writing about sex. But readers are not made privy to their telephone calls.

Time's ironies in the layer of current events in Hugh's life in school include the return of one of Gerald's contemporaries as a history teacher. Hugh likes her, but thinks she is pusillanimous to come back to her beginnings. It now seems that the burial of the capsule did not proceed exactly as Gerald had described it.

So, what has all this to do with the Hillingdon Fox?

In his diary entry for 1990 Hugh says be can't bear to watch the news: refugee camps upset him. He has grown in understanding of the role of the media and notes when the newscaster, or a newspaper says after a disaster: 'No Britons involved so it doesn't affect us.' He quotes John Donne, remarking:

> ... it was easier in the seventeenth century; there was so much less of mankind for him to be involved with. In the Middle Ages you scarcely knew what was going on in the next village ... As soon as a new disaster happens we forget the last one – we have to.[82]

Hugh remembers the sinking of The Herald of Free Enterprise in the English Channel in 1987, The Hungerford Massacre, the hurricane, the Remembrance Day massacre at Enniskillen and the Underground station fire at King's Cross.

> And yet, one morning that same year, in May I think it was, we went down to London by coach, on a school trip, and just as we were slowing down at the traffic lights by Hillingdon station, I looked out of the window and saw a dead fox lying on the verge. It didn't look injured but it was obviously dead; a car must have struck it. I was upset seeing that, but glad that someone had laid out the fox respectfully and not left it to get crushed. No one else on the coach had noticed and I didn't say anything, but when we came back that evening, I looked out for the fox and saw that somebody else had taken it and laid it among the long grass under the hedge.
>
> Now, a week later, I went up to town again, on the coach, with a friend. We were going to an exhibition, I think. Anyway, when we got to Hillingdon I looked out specially and under the hedge I could see that the fox was still lying there. I could just see his fur.[83]

After that, all through the year, every time he went up to London,

Hugh looked out for the fox at Hillingdon traffic lights. 'That was a terrible year 1987; so many people died, but the only death that stayed in my mind was the Hillingdon fox.'[84]

Hugh adds, 'We aren't meant to feel so much.' The presentation of the incident as memory, in the same context as disasters that call up the need for cosmic sympathy, the reader faces the quandary that adolescents meet for the first time. What can we do about what is beyond our best efforts to sympathize with before cynicism sets in.

New realism: *Heathrow Nights*

One of the continuing conventions about books for teenagers is that they want to read about themselves in situations and circumstances that they can recognize and empathize with. At the same time they want to be in the know about what is 'cool' to read, without too much display. They also have their version of their mother tongue to describe their responses to events.

Authors know that readers in the category once called 'young adults' are constantly on the look-out for something different, even excessive, in what they read: horror, sex and death are preferred choices, hence the attractions of metafictions and fantasies. The novelty often lies in the author's *invention* – what musicians know as *counterpoint*. In narrative fiction this may occur where the laws of nature are fractured and whole universes rebuilt. The current instances are the elaborate worlds of Philip Pullman and J. K. Rowling. The reader is invited to consider different possibilities in answer to 'what would happen if?' and 'what shall I become?' or even, 'what is the truth?'

Most of Jan Mark's stories for adolescents hold steady the main parts of the everyday world. The characters breathe ordinary air, eat human food, sleep, have families. In many of her books teenagers meet the ordinary confusions of growing up. The restrictions of rules, the actions of parents and the problems of right and wrong are enough to be going on with. She is supported in this choice by Ursula Le Guin's assertion that realistic fiction is one of the very hardest media in which to teach children right from wrong, as if evil were a problem, something that can be resolved.'[85] That quotation is in the notebook where I keep such sayings, but I must have been in a hurry or simply careless; the source has been omitted. I could never have made it up, but I recognize the truth of it. Why, I wonder, should the greatest creator of alternative worlds believe that?

At the time of writing, *Heathrow Nights* is Jan Mark's most recent realistic novel. The focal point of the action is in one of the world's busiest airports. Even if they haven't been there, most readers have seen pictures of crowds waiting to be airlifted or emerging on their return, so they will have certain metonymic expectations of the text: 'a landlocked island, an area the size of a small town, where no one lives'.[86] But all who pass through or work there can eat, sleep, drink, wash, sit about and talk, buy newspapers and practically everything to support life, commit crimes, be arrested or given first aid, all in four different places. There are no public beds. As a metaphor for a world it is linked to many other places, including Earthsea and the circles of Dante's *Inferno*.

Three boys, Russell, Adam and Curt, in their last year of school, spend a significant part of a half-term holiday in Heathrow. They should have been on a school trip to Cumbria, but they have been excluded from it as the result of unacceptable behaviour in a theatre during a performance of *Hamlet*. By deceiving their parents, who have made other plans for the same period, the boys come to London, only to be turned away from the flat where they hoped to be offered bed and breakfast between visiting the sights. Their plan changes to passing the nights, unnoticed, in Heathrow, but London and Heathrow are expensive places to be for a week. They face the fact that they will have to kill most of the time between Monday and Friday at the airport.

The boys are a trio by common consent rather than choice. They have become school rejects. Curt is drug dependent; Adam has 'form' with the police, Russell, the narrator, is furious about his mother's swift remarriage after his father's early death – a heart attack in a plane – to the man who was sitting next to him when it happened. He has found it easier to skip school than to go to lessons where he can't concentrate. Identifying himself with Hamlet, he privately calls his stepfather Claudius. He has accepted Adam's rationale of their common condition.

> 'All we need is time,' Adam said. 'The System is going to get us in the end.' He made it sound like a police state rather than what it was, a bunch of furious teachers and another bunch of unhappy parents, blaming themselves, each other: us, mostly. We'd seen it coming for a long while, Curt had been asking for it, but now it had happened. We wanted time to think, time to get ready. Basically, time to lie our way out of it.[87]

The boys have an uneasy week to discover that the option they thought they wanted, lying, isn't the one they need. The loads they carry internally – guilt, blame, resentment, evasion, threat, deceit – is heavier than their luggage. Russell has more insight than the other two. He is aware of the difficulties, not just the practicalities of the London trip, but also into his own situation, hence the displacement of his feelings to those which Shakespeare gives to Hamlet. Shakespeare and Jan Mark give him the words to think with; his assimilation of the play text is evidence of his intellectual capability. It also becomes his prop when Curt is arrested for shoplifting and Adam is collected by his mother. He is alone after only two nights. He has to sort himself out.

When Adam unexpectedly hugs him before he leaves, Russell wishes Adam was 'my Horatio, the closest friend, the absolutely-trusted one', but as I watched him go all I could think of was *Rosencrantz and Guildenstern are Dead.* He then contemplates his friendship, born of complicity with the other two, in terms of Hamlet's involvement with the two men he knew from his youth; 'the sort of friends you have when you're a kid because their parents know your parents'.[88]

He then wonders about influence.

I don't think I am a particular influence, but I am the third leg of the stool. I shore the other two up.

Then:

... so it was ridiculous to think of Rosencrantz and Guildenstern when Adam went down the escalator, except that I didn't care. That's why I was so surprised by that hug. I don't think he cared either.[89]

Most of his thoughts bring him back to his father, his influence and his death. This time it's in terms of 'To be or not to be.' Russell's edition of the play has 'three pages of notes about what that speech means'. He recollects every detail of the period up to his mother's remarriage, seeing his stepfather's thoughtful treatment of her as a form of intrusion, replacing him, Russell, as the man of the house. Meanwhile, in Heathrow, he has to keep himself awake during the day as travellers swirl and crowd round him. He cannot sleep at night, 'a few seconds of the failing sensation in the dark, I'd wake up again with a jolt'. An encounter with a bag lady who offers him a gardening book reminds him of Ophelia.

Most people familiar with airports know that there can be unexpected encounters. One of these reveals that Claudius had put an envelope with fifty pounds in Russell's jacket pocket, the one he knew Russell would wear. Not knowing it was there, Russell had pulled it out and dropped it in the flat where the trio had hoped to stay. Meanwhile this careful, generous man has been in search of him. They meet, then talk and drink together. By this time Russell is ready to admit he has hated someone he simply doesn't know because he refused to let himself come near him, preferring self-pity.

To those who know about helping people to see things differently, to change their opinions and to review their past, Russell's session with his father may seem too swift a conversion to right-thinking. But throughout the story the author has laid a trail of Russell's dissatisfactions with himself and his growing awareness that Adam's earlier explanation of the situation would no longer suffice. His argot paraphrasing of what happens in *Hamlet* shows just how deeply he is probing the play and his awareness of himself. 'Not much of a story', he says, in keeping with his cool throw-away style. 'But I can't just think of them as characters in a play.'[90] By Friday morning he has decided that he and Hamlet have little in common, except Gertrude. 'Hague was no wicked uncle, not a wicked anything. He was just the man my mum had wanted to marry.'[91]

Here's Russell's growing point, a soliloquy after recollections:

> When you're a little kid you don't take it in that people are just like you; they're kind of soft furnishings that move about, part of the scenery. It's a long while before you understand that you are part of their scenery. That's why little kids are so horrible to each other. They don't know how it feels because they don't know that other people do feel. Some big kids too. Adam for instance. And Mum; and Gertrude. (Less than two months after the King was dead she married his brother, his murderer.)[92]

From where Jan Mark places her readers they are enlisted into encounters with ideas and situations that provide evidence for the notion that the power of the imagination is to configure and refigure what we have learned from life and from books. I am re-reading my already much revised version of *Hamlet* through the eyes and words of this character in a novel. It's a recursive process, like learning a language. At the same time I'm thinking about lending this book to my grandson, just slightly younger than Russell, to find out what he has to say about it.

Heathrow Nights shows how Jan Mark's skill as a novelist in the use of speech forms and inner monologues gives the story its emotional complexity and its realistic impact. Beneath the smooth linguistic surface of the style lurk all the invitations to dig deeper into the words on the page. How will this boy turn out? Has he matured after all this thought work he has done and discussion with his stepfather who really should become his friend? What happens to adults who read novels for the young; do they mature? One thing is certain: this is a novel of its time. It could not have been written in 1976.

'Metaphorical Thrillers'

Jan Mark's skill in telling both the outer and the inner versions of a story at the same time is her most powerful way of demonstrating the growing points in her characters so that readers will notice them. In the supple pitch and toss of dialogic and other speech patterns that are consistent features in the novels, behaviour and emotions merge. >From youngest to oldest her readers learn to read beyond themselves because they know the satisfactions they derive from these encounters. With this in mind we now glance, if only briefly, at some of the novels that have proved more challenging.

Neil Philip described *The Ennead* (1978), *Divide and Rule* (1979) and *Aquarius* (1982) as 'fiercely written metaphorical thrillers for older children'.[93] They are all in different ways about friendship. Other commentators have written about the author's 'dark side' (for example, Peter Hunt in *Signal*, no. 31, 1980). While appreciating the imaginative power of these stories, the common judgement has been that the emotional and textual levels are too complex for most readers who had not begun to be acquainted with adult literature. This harks after the notion that all literature is free from what Terry Eagleton describes as 'the actual particulars of existence – gender, ethnicity, nationality, social origin, sexual tendency and the like'.[94] My view is they offer young readers who enjoy the dare of reading something different, a way into a greater range of modern texts. Having read these novels periodically over twenty-five years I am all the more impressed by the author's belief that adolescents deserve books that convey her own degree of social awareness. While critics at the end of the 1970s were engaging with the formal structures of narratives, she was showing her readers that stories are bound up with ideology, in the sense later explored by Peter Hollindale as 'a living thing, and something we need to know as we need to know ourselves'.[95]

Short summaries of the plots are only rough guides to the speculative nature of the contents. The stories are set in severe contexts, a bleak planet, a prison-like temple and a country where no rain falls. That is, the central characters are not helped by their surroundings. They are sealed inside themselves. All the communities are flawed. Friendship is strained and becomes mere expediency.

The Ennead, the place of the title, is a system of nine planets. The action begins on Erato, a star where refugees from Earth are hoping to reconstruct themselves and their culture by learning to be careful of the resources they has previously squandered. The speculations are about systems of belief and values in terms of social and political behaviour. As a modern fable, the tale has obvious symbolic references to asylum seekers. It also challenges the notion of life as sacred.

In *Divide and Rule* Hanno, at eighteen, is the rebellious son of a family in good standing with the authorities in a culture ruled by a temple hierarchy of powerful guardians and fundamentalist believers. From his age group he is selected by lot to be the Ritual Shepherd, a role that takes him away from his family for a year to be immured as part of the temple organization. As an unbeliever Hanno is antipathetic to the whole scene. The twist is, he is expected to be reluctant, so that his protestations are taken as conformity. They are also the source of the power that others have over him.

At first Hanno believes he is strong enough to withstand coercions to make him conform, but the guardians interpret him to himself as 'mistaken in acts of judgement'. They divide him from himself. The reader, taking Hanno's part, sees how the traumatizing works and longs for it to stop. Gradually, Hanno is left entirely alone. No-one can help him because they cannot reach him. He is sure that his first submission had been his great mistake. When he finally emerges from the temple he has done nothing to improve things and is now a lonely outsider.

Viner, the protagonist of *Aquarius* is a water diviner whose skill is not appreciated in an environment where it rains all the time. Escaping a predicted fate, he leaves home, is captured and then taken to a palace where the King dances, without success, to bring sorely needed water to his land. Viner solves his problem and, opportunist that he is, becomes important as the King's friend. At the same time he discovers that: 'Friendship here was a trade, like carpentry or water divining. No; dowsing was his mystery. Maybe he could make friendship also his mystery. He would not practise it as a trade.'[96]

So far, the reader's sympathies are with the dowser. By when the King's fate is to be driven from his palace with his baby, Viner's attachment to him, already established by the author as a love he will not admit, turns into a kind of self-seeking blackmail. Their journey back to Viner's former homeland, where the King is to stop the rain, is full of graphic miseries. The sardonic ending is as bleak as the beginning.

Perhaps the most stern growing point in adolescent novels since the acknowledgement of this particular readership is the loss of the happy ending and the reduction of hope. The central paradox of these speculative novels, which make no concession to life as easy, is to present readers with 'what if things were as bad as that?' The worlds Jan Mark has created in these books present not only suffering and violent death, but also the tragedies of the egocentric, the isolate, the unloving, and the miseries of betrayal as death-in-life. At no point does the author shun the complexities of these speculations. The ethical puzzles they raise are in the same category as those in *Animal Farm* and *Lord of the Flies*.

The Eclipse of the Century

The characters in these earlier speculative novels keep themselves to themselves. That's their problem. *The Eclipse of the Century*[97] (1999) is Jan Mark's novel about *secrets*, what a writer deliberately doesn't tell the reader. This may seem to leave the book outside a category of literature for young people, but gaps in the text are a feature of most children's stories and poems, even nursery rhymes. The entrance clue to this narrative is the dedication to Ursula Le Guin, who knows that what seem to be omissions are, in fact, silences, like those in music that draw attention to what has just been heard or is about to sound.

The important point is that readers should tolerate the usual uncertainties at the outset for a little longer so as to understand the particular infinity and timelessness that are part of the time and place of this work. Readers' expectations are challenged throughout to ensure that they reflect on what they are told. Think then, of an eclipse as obscuring light so that we see it better afterwards.

Keith is a young man who nearly dies in a motorway accident. During a period of suspended consciousness he hears a woman's voice telling him that it is too soon to die and that they will meet again in Kantoom under the black sun at the end of a thousand years. The millennium is only nine months away, so Keith suspends his studies, spends his loan on a ticket to Tashkent and arrives by rail thirty kilometers from Qantoum – a place he has tracked down from a magazine article – a city on the edge of a desert where the sand sings at sunset.

The inhabitants greet him warmly; the immigration officers waive the usual restrictions as he declares his intention to stay, not as a tourist. The first half of the book traces his settling in and his responses to the intriguing people he meets. The centre of social life is the museum. Keith recognizes its curator, the 'widow' Fahrenheit, as the woman in his dream. The others are a motley crew whose appearances connect with the stories they tell about themselves and their histories. These weave a cultural pattern of chance and intent that Keith accepts but, as an outsider, cannot really penetrate. The indigenous people, the Sturyat, have their own clannish allegiances and customs. They do not lock doors; instead they hang up the bones of their ancestors in a canvas bag in the doorway. They intend to leave Qantoum where they recover their soul stones that they maintain are hidden in the museum.

Keith makes friends with a Sturyat girl and comes to know better the soldier turned customs officer, Lieutenant Kije, who has a rifle.The reader assimilates these things as a kind of cultural anthropology, with various twists and turns like the city itself, while wondering why the non-indigenous inhabitants remain there. Some clues emerge, as in the hidden reference to Prokofiev's non-existent, fictive hero, but they don't come together until, with Keith, we are more familiar with the characters. Impressive in this part of the story is the notion of tolerance, acceptance of differences, including a man with a bear, and frogs as snacks as normal as apples. The lowering presence of the explorer whose antiquities furnish the museum is fully maintained. Are all these colourful characters what they seem?

But Keith's visit has set a trend. As the millennium draws near Qantoum, is discovered by groups of enthusiasts in search of the earthly paradise and the eclipse. Troups of Equispherians, Joggers, Sundancers, Sphynxes and Hobbits arrive. Qantoum is the apogee of their hopes. They act out their beliefs in the one place they have been tolerated, but they also bring with them their particular fundament-alisms which provoke strife. This is what Keith has unleashed; it results in a holocaust and the complete breakup of the company in the museum. There is no closure, only riddles and enigmas. In this book, young, experienced readers meet various aspects of the literature of their time and are left to think on these things.

When we look into the books that children encounter as part of their coming to know themselves and the world, what has to be avoided is the notion that writers deliberately leave instruction for the coming of age of their readers. As authors confront the stony blocks of thought and language to carve out the story within, they have other plans. In the case of Jan Mark, this includes remaking storytelling itself and engaging the reader as a potential apprentice writer. What experienced readers do best for their apprentices is to encourage them not to turn away from something they have never tried before, and to go beyond the conventions which they are used to. They should not be coerced but given time – the chance to extend the pleasure books give them.

Jan Mark's reputation rests on expressive clarity that includes wit, humour, intellectual rigor, understated intelligence and a kind of literary glee, all of which her readers can find for themselves. She exploits alternative formulations of experience to show that metafictions and realism are not in opposition but complementary. The next story will be something completely different.

Endnotes

1. Shirley Hughes (2002), *A Life Drawing*, The Bodley Head, p. 129.
2. Jan Mark (1986), *Fur*, illus. by Charlotte Voake, Walker Books. p. 3.
3. The phrase devised by Elaine Moss to encapsulate the criteria for the award of The Kurt Maschler Award for children's books.
4. My acquaintance with the new technology devised for this purpose is at second-hand. I am grateful for my enlightenment to Professor Yetta Goodman of the University of Arizona. The most recent research into children reading pictures is in Morag Styles and Evelyn Arizpe (2002), *Children Reading Pictures: Interpreting Visual Texts.*
5. Margery Fisher (1961), *Intent Upon Reading*, Routledge. Brockhampton Press, p. 18.
6. Jan Mark (1990), *Strat and Chatto*, illus. by David Hughes, Walker Books.
7. Jan Mark (1993), *Carrot Tops and Cotton Tails*, illus. by Tony Ross, Andersen Press.
8. Jan Mark (1993), *Fun with Mrs Thumb*, illus. by Nicola Bayley, Walker Books.
9. Jan Mark (1994), *Haddock*, illus. by Fiona Moodie, Simon & Schuster.
10. Jan Mark (1995), *The Tale of Tobias*, illus. by Rachel Merriman, Walker Books.
11. Jan Mark (1999), *The Midas Touch*, illus. by Juan Wijngaard, Walker Books.
12. Eve Bearne (1992) 'Myth and Legend: The Oldest Language?' in Morag Styles, Eve Bearne and Victor Watson (eds), *After Alice*, Cassell, pp. 143–51.
13. Jan Mark (1997), *God's Story*, illus. by David Perkins, Walker Books.
14. Midrash: (Hebrew for 'interpretation') is a Jewish method of scriptural exegesis directed to the discovery in a sacred text of a deeper meaning than the literal one.
15. When this becomes part of the awareness of young readers their reading competences increase dramatically.
16. Andrew Melrose (2002), *Write for Children*, Routledge Falmer, p. 122.
17. Jan Mark (ed.) (1993), *The Oxford Book of Children's Stories,* Oxford University Press, p. x.

18. Francis Spufford (2002) *The Child that Books Built: A Memoir of Childhood and Reading*, Faber.
19. Jan Mark (1998), *Worry Guts,* illus. by Jeffrey Reid, Longman.
20. Ibid.
21. Ibid.
22. Jan Mark (1982), *The Dead Letter Box*, illus. by Mary Rayner, Hamish Hamilton.
23. Ibid. p. 12.
24. Jan Mark (1988), *The Twig Thing*, illus. by Sally Holmes, Kestrel, p. 5.
25. Jan Mark (1992), *The Snow Maze*, illus. by Jan Ormerod, Walker Books, p. 10.
26. Jan Mark (1994), *Taking the Cat's Way Home*, illus. by Paul Howard, Walker Books.
27. Jan Mark (1999), *Lady Long-Legs*, Walker Books.
28. Jan Mark (2001), *The Lady with Iron Bones*, Walker Books, p. 139.
29. Jan Mark (2002), *Long Lost*, illus. by David Roberts, Macmillan, p. 97.
30. Jan Mark (1994), Patrick Hardy lecture in *Signal*, No. 73, pp. 19–36.
31. Jan Mark (ed.), *The Oxford Book of Children's Stories*, Oxford University Press, p. xix.
32. Jan Mark (1993), 'Dan, Dan the Scenery Man' in *The Oxford Book of Children's Stories*, Oxford University Press, p. 406
33. Ibid., p. 412.
34. Ibid., p. 406.
35. Valentine Cunningham (1994), *In the Reading Gaol: Postmodernity, Texts, and History*, Blackwell, p. 93.
36. Jan Mark (1980), 'William's Version' in *Nothing To Be Afraid Of*, illus. by David Parkins, Kestrel Books, pp. 68–75.
37. Ibid., p. 73.
38. Ibid., p. 75.
39. Jan Mark (1980), 'The Choice is Yours', in *Nothing to be Afraid Of*, illus. by David Parkins, Kestrel Books, pp. 31–43.
40. Jan Mark (1981), *Hairs in the Palm of the Hand*, Kestrel Books.
41. Jan Mark (1983), 'I Was Adored Once, Too' in *Feet*, illus. by Mary Rayner, Kestrel Books, pp. 56–78.
42. Jan Mark (1986), *Frankie's Hat*, illus. by Quentin Blake, Viking Children's Books.
43. Neil Philip (1989) in *Twentieth Century Children's Writers* (3rd edn), Tracy Chevalier and D.C. Kirkpatrick (eds), p. 635.
44. Jan Mark (1990), in *A Can of Worms*, The Bodley Head, p. 89.
45. Jan Mark (1990) 'Front' , in *A Can of Worms*, The Bodley Head, p. 55.
46. Ibid., p. 64.
47. David Lodge (1990), *After Bakhtin*, Routledge, p. 23.
48. Jan Mark (1984), *Two Stories*, illustrated by Clive King, Inky Parrot Press.

49. Jan Mark, (1984) 'Mr and Mrs Johnson', in *Two Stories*, illus. by Clive King, Inky Parrot Press.
50. Jan Mark (1984), 'Childermas', in *Two Stories*, illus. by Clive King, Inky Parrot Press.
51. Jan Mark (1976), *Thunder and Lightnings*, illus. by Jim Russell, Kestrel Books.
52. Ibid., p. 94.
53. Ibid., p. 104.
54. Ibid. p. 15.
55. Jill Paton Walsh (1971), 'The Rainbow Surface' from *The Times Literary Supplement*, 3 December, reprinted in *The Cool Web: the Pattern of Children's Reading*, Margaret Meek, Aidan Warlow and Griselda Barton (eds) (1977), The Bodley Head, pp. 192–5.
56. Jan Mark (1977), *Under the Autumn Garden*, illus. by Colin Twinn, Kestrel Books, p. 162.
57. Naomi Lewis (1989), in *Twentieth Century Children's Writers*, Laura S. Berger (ed.), St James Press, p. ix.
58. Victor Watson
59. Jan Mark (1983), *Handles*, illus. by David Parkins, Kestrel Books, p. 9.
60. Ibid., p. 11.
61. Ibid., p. 14.
62. Ibid., p. 79.
63. Ibid., p. 126.
64. Ibid., p. 155.
65. Ibid., p. 156.
66. Jan Mark (1985), *Trouble Half-Way,* Kestrel Books, p. 42.
67. Ibid., p. 47.
68. Ibid., p. 48.
69. Ibid., p. 49.
70. Jan Mark (1987), *Dream House*, illus. by Jan Riley, Kestrel Books, p. 7.
71. Ibid., p. 9.
72. Ibid., p. 42.
73. Ibid., p. 77.
74. Ibid., p. 80.
75. Jan Mark (1994), *They Do Things Differently There*, The Bodley Head, p. 4.
76. Ibid., p. 31.
77. Ibid., p. 34.
78. Ibid., p. 46.
79. Ibid., p. 47.
80. Jan Mark, (1991) *The Hillingdon Fox*, Stroud, Turton & Chambers, p. 14.
81. Ibid., p. 61.
82. Ibid., p. 124.
83. Ibid., p. 125.
84. Ibid., p. 125.

85. Ursula Le Guin, source unknown.
86. Jan Mark (2002), *Heathrow Nights*, Heinemann.
87. Ibid., p. 9.
88. Ibid., p. 101.
89. Ibid., p. 102.
90. Ibid., p. 82.
91. Ibid., p. 158.
92. Ibid., p 161.
93. Neil Philip (1989), in *Twentieth Century Children's Writers*, Laura S. Berger (ed.), St James Press, p. 67.
94. Terry Eagleton (2000), *The Idea of Culture*, Blackwell, p. 55.
95. Peter Hollindale (1988), *Ideology and the Children's Book*, Thimble Press, p. 22.
96. Jan Mark (1982), *Aquarius*, Kestrel Books, p. 74.
97. Jan Mark (1999), *The Eclipse of the Century*, Scholastic.

Bibliography

Alcott, Louisa May, *Good Wives* (1869) Boston: Roberts Brothers

Alcott, Louisa May, *Little Women* (1869) Boston: Roberts Brothers

Alcott, Louisa May, *Rose in Bloom* (1876) Boston: Roberts Brothers

Austen, Jane, *Mansfield Park* (1814) London: T. Egerton

Austen, Jane, *Northanger Abbey* (1818) London: John Murray

Bearne, Eve, 'Myth and Legend: The Oldest Language?' in Morag Styles, Eve Bearne and Victor Watson (eds), *After Alice: Exploring Children's Literature* (1992) London: Cassell

Blume, Judy, *Forever* (1975) New York: Bradbury Press

Bourdieu, Pierre, *Outline of the Theory of Practice* (1977) Cambridge: Cambridge University Press

Brontë, Charlotte, *Jane Eyre* (1847) London: Smith and Elder

Bunyan, John, *The Pilgrim's Progress: From this World to that Which is to Come* (1678,1684)

Chambers, Aidan, *Breaktime* (1978) London: The Bodley Head

Chambers, Aidan, *Dance On My Grave* (1982) London: The Bodley Head

Chambers, Aidan, *Now I Know* (1987) London: The Bodley Head

Chambers, Aidan, *Postcards From No Man's Land* (1999) London: The Bodley Head

Chambers, Aidan, *The Toll Bridge* (1992) London: The Bodley Head

Cleary, Beverly, *Fifteen* (1956) New York: Morrow & Co.

Cole, Michael; Vera John Steiner; Sylvia Scribner; Ellen Souberman (eds.), *Mind in Society* (1978) Cambridge MA: Harvard University Press

Coolidge, Susan, *What Katy Did* (1872) Boston: Roberts Brothers

Coolidge, Susan, *What Katy Did at School* (1873) Boston: Roberts Brothers

Coolidge, Susan, *What Katy Did Next* (1886) Boston: Roberts Brothers

Cunningham, Valentine, *In the Reading Gaol: Postmodernity, Texts, and History* (1994) Oxford: Blackwell

Defoe, Daniel, *Colonel Jack [The History and Remarkable Life of the Truly Honourable Colonel Jacque, Commonly Called Colonel Jack]* (1722)

Defoe, Daniel, *Robinson Crusoe (the Life and Strange Surprising Adventures of Robinson Crusoe, of York, Mariner, Written by himself* (1719)

Defoe, Daniel, *The Fortunes and Misfortunes of the Famous Moll Flanders* (1722)

Eagleton, Terry, *The Idea of Culture* (2000) Oxford: Blackwell

Eliot, George, *The Mill on the Floss* (1860) Edinburgh: William Blackwood & Sons

Fisher, Margery, *Intent Upon Reading* (1964) London: Hodder

Forest, Antonia, *Autumn Term* (1948, re-issued 2000) London: Faber & Faber

Forest, Antonia, *End of Term* (1959) London: Faber & Faber

Forest, Antonia, *Falconer's Lure* (1957) London: Faber & Faber

Forest, Antonia, *Peter's Room* (1961) London: Faber & Faber

Forest, Antonia, *Run Away Home* (1982) London: Faber & Faber

Forest, Antonia, *The Attic Term* (1976) London: Faber & Faber

Forest, Antonia, *The Cricket Term* (1974) London: Faber & Faber

Forest, Antonia, *The Marlows and the Traitor* (1953) London: Faber & Faber

Forest, Antonia, *The Ready-Made Family* (1967) London: Faber & Faber

Forest, Antonia, *The Thuggery Affair* (1965) London: Faber & Faber

Fox, Geoff et al. (eds.), *Writers, Critics, and Children* (1976) London: Heinemann Educational Books

Gardam, Jane, *A Long Way From Verona* (1971) London: Hamish Hamilton

Garner, Alan, *Red Shift* (1966) Glasgow: William Collins Sons & Co. Ltd.

Garner, Alan, *The Owl Service* (1967) Glasgow: William Collins Sons & Co. Ltd.

Godden, Rumer, *The Greengage Summer* (1958) London: Macmillan & Co.

Hardy, Thomas, *Jude the Obscure* (1896) London: Osgood, McIvaine

Hodgson Burnett, Frances, *A Little Princess* (1905) London: Frederick Warne & Co., Ltd.

Hollindale, Peter, *Ideology and the Children's Book* (1998) Stroud: Thimble Press

Hollindale, Peter, *Signs of Childness in Children's Books* (1997) Stroud: Thimble Press

Hughes, Shirley, *A Life Drawing* (2002) London: The Bodley Head

Hunt, Peter (ed.), *The International Encyclopedia of Children's Literature* (1996), London: Routledge

Hunt, Peter, *Criticism, Theory, and Children's Literature* (1991) Oxford: Blackwell

Kermode, Frank, *The Genesis of Secrecy; on the Interpretation of Narrative*, (1979) Cambridge MA, Harvard University Press

Lewis, Hilda, *The Ship That Flew* (1939) Oxford: Oxford University Press

Lewis, Naomi, Preface to *Twentieth Century Children's Writers* (1978), Tracy Chevalier (ed.), London: St James Press

Lodge, David, *After Bakhtin: Essays on Fiction and Criticism* (1990) London: Routledge

Mark, Jan (ed.), *The Oxford Book of Children's Stories* (1993) Oxford: Oxford University Press

Mark, Jan, *Aquarius* (1982) London: Viking

Mark, Jan, *A Can of Worms* (1990) London: The Bodley Head

Mark, Jan, *Carrot Tops and Cotton Tails* (1993), ill. Tony Ross, London: Andersen Press

Mark, Jan, *Dream House* (1987) London: Kestrel

Mark, Jan, *Feet* (1983), ill. Mary Rayner, London: Kestrel Books

Mark, Jan, *Finders Losers* (1990) London: Orchard Books

Mark, Jan, *Frankie's Hat* (1986), ill. Quentin Blake, London: Viking Books

Mark, Jan, *Fun with Mrs Thumb* (1993), ill. Nicola Bayley, London: Walker Books

Mark, Jan, *Fur* (1986), ill. Charlotte Voake, London: Walker Books

Mark, Jan, *God's Story* (1997), ill. David Perkins, London: Walker Books

Mark, Jan, *Haddock* (1994), ill. Fiona Moodie, Hemel Hempstead: Simon & Schuster

Mark, Jan, *Hairs in the Palm of the Hand* (1981) London: Viking Children's Books

Mark, Jan, *Handles* (1983) London: Kestrel.

Mark, Jan, *Heathrow Nights* (2002) London: Heinemann.

Mark, Jan, *Lady Long-Legs* (1999), ill. Paul Howard, London: Walker Books

Mark, Jan, *Long Lost* (2002), ill. David Roberts, London: Macmillan

Mark, Jan, *Nothing to Be Afraid Of* (1980) London: Kestrel Books

Mark, Jan, *Strat and Chatto* (1990), ill. David Hughes, London: Walker Books

Mark, Jan, *Taking the Cat's Way Home* (1994), ill. Paul Howard, London: Walker Books

Mark, Jan, *The Dead Letter Box* (1982), ill. Mary Rayner, London: Hamish Hamilton

Mark, Jan, *The Eclipse of the Century* (1999) London: Scholastic

Mark, Jan, *The Hillingdon Fox* (1991) Stroud: Turton & Chambers

Mark, Jan, *The Midas Touch* (1999), ill. Juan Wijngaard, London: Walker Books

Mark, Jan, *The Snow Maze* (1992), ill. Jan Ormerod, London: Walker Books

Mark, Jan, *The Tale of Tobias* (1995), ill. Rachel Merriman, London: Walker Books

Mark, Jan, *The Twig Thing* (1998), ill. Sally Holmes, London: Viking Children's Books

Mark, Jan, *They Do Things Differently There* (1994) London: The Bodley Head

Mark, Jan, *Thunder and Lightnings* (1976), ill. Jim Russell, London: Kestrel Books

Mark, Jan, *Trouble Half-Way* (1985) London: Kestrel Books

Mark, Jan, *Two Stories* (1984) Oxford: Inky Parrot Press

Mark, Jan, *Under the Autumn Garden* (1977), ill. Colin Twinn, London: Kestrel Books

Mark, Jan, *Worry Guts* (1998) London: Longman

Meek, Margaret; Aidan Warlow; Griselda Barton (eds.), *The Cool Web: The Pattern of Children's Reading* (1977) London: The Bodley Head

Meek, Margaret, *How Texts Teach What Readers Learn* (1988) Stroud: Thimble Press

Montgomery, L.M., *Anne of Green Gables* (1908) Boston: Page

Montgomery, L.M., *Anne of the Island* (1915) Boston: Page

Montgomery, L.M., *Anne's House of Dreams* (1917) Toronto: McClelland, Goodchild & Stewart

Montgomery, L.M., *Rilla of Ingleside* (1921) Toronto: McClelland, Goodchild & Stewart

Montogomery, L.M., *Emily of New Moon* (1923) Toronto: McClelland and Stewart

Nesbit, Edith, *The Railway Children* (1906) London: Wells Gardner, Darton & Co.

Pearce, Philippa, *A Dog So Small* (1962), ill. Audrey Maitland, London: Constable

Pearce, Philippa, *Minnow on the Say* (1955), ill. Edward Ardizzone, Oxford: Oxford University Press. (in USA, *Minnow Leads to Treasure*) (1955) Cleveland & New York: World Publishing Company

Pearce, Philippa, *The Battle of Bubble and Squeak* (1978), ill. Alan Baker, London: Andre Deutsch

Pearce, Philippa, *The Children of Charlecote* (1989) Oxford: Oxford University Press

Pearce, Philippa, *The Children of the House* (1968) London: Gollancz

Pearce, Philippa, *The Rope and other stories* (2000), ill. Annabel Large, London: Puffin Books

Pearce, Philippa, *The Shadow-Cage and other Tales of the Supernatural* (1977), ill. Chris Molan, London: Kestrel Books

Pearce, Philippa, *The Way to Sattin Shore* (1983) London: Kestrel Books

Pearce, Philippa, *Tom's Midnight Garden* (1958), ill. Susan Einzig, Oxford: Oxford University Press

Pearce, Philippa, *What the Neighbours Did and other stories* (1972), ill. Faith Jacques, London: Kestrel Books

Rose, Jacqueline, *The Case of Peter Pan, or the Impossibility of Children's Fiction* (1984) London: Macmillan

Rustin, Margaret & Michael, *Narratives of Love and Loss: Studies in Modern Children's Fiction* (revised edition, 2001) London: Karnac Books

Salinger, J. D., *The Catcher in the Rye* (1951) Boston: Little, Brown & Co.

Smith, Dodie, *I Capture the Castle* (1949) London: Heinemann

Smith, Emma, *No Way of Telling* (1972) London: The Bodley Head

Stevenson, Robert Louis, *Treasure Island* (1883) London: Cassell & Co.

Styles, Morag and Arizpe, Evelyn, *Children Reading Pictures: Interpreting Visual Texts* (2002) London: Routledge

Townsend, John Rowe, *A Sense of Story* (1971) London: Longman

Twain, Mark, *The Adventures of Huckleberry Finn* (1885) New York: Charles L. Webster

Voigt, Cynthia, *A Solitary Blue* (1983) New York: Atheneum

Voigt, Cynthia, *Come A Stranger* (1987) New York: Atheneum

Voigt, Cynthia, *Dicey's Song* (1982) New York: Atheneum

Voigt, Cynthia, *Homecoming* (1981) New York: Atheneum

Voigt, Cynthia, *Seventeen Against the Dealer* (1989) New York: Atheneum

Voigt, Cynthia, *Sons From Afar* (1987) New York: Atheneum

Voigt, Cynthia, The *Runner* (1985) New York: Atheneum

Watson, Victor (ed.), *The Cambridge Guide to Children's Books in English*, (2001) Cambridge: Cambridge University Press

Watson, Victor, *Reading Series Fiction* (2000) London: Routledge-Falmer

Wiggin, Kate Douglas, *More About Rebecca* (1907) London: A & C Black

Wiggin, Kate Douglas, *Rebecca of Sunnybrook Farm* (1903) London: A & C Black

Zindel, Paul, *A Begonia for Miss Applebaum* (1989) New York: Harper & Row

Zindel, Paul, *The Pigman* (1968) New York: Harper & Row

Index